James F. White

CHRISTIAN WORSHIP
in North America

A Retrospective: 1955–1995

A PUEBLO BOOK

The Liturgical Press   Collegeville, Minnesota

A Pueblo Book published by The Liturgical Press

Design by Frank Kacmarcik, Obl.S.B.

Library of Congress Cataloging-in-Publication Data

White, James F.
   Christian worship in North America : a retrospective, 1955–1995 /
James F. White.
     p. cm.
   "A Pueblo book."
   Includes bibliographical references.
   ISBN 0-8146-6156-4 (alk. paper)
   1. Public worship—History—20th century. 2. Liturgics—North
America—History—20th century. 3. North America—Church history—
20th century. I. Title.
BV8.W45   1996
264'.0097'09045—dc20   96-29446
                                                      CIP

For my grandchildren:

Jenna
Kasey
Thomas
Riley
Holly
and those yet to be

That they may discover what they
cannot remember

Contents

Preface

The decades from 1955 to 1995 have seen an avalanche of change in the worship life of most North American churches unprecedented in breadth and depth. Few churches with set liturgical forms have not seen major revisions of liturgical texts. And those without such texts have seen many changes in the forms of their worship as well as in its musical and architectural components. Furthermore, the period has seen the emergence of major new styles of worship that never existed before: feminist worship, mega-church seeker services, charismatic worship in mainline churches, to name but a few.

I have been fortunate to be able to observe these changes and to contribute to some of them. My work has been both that of a liturgical scholar trying to observe and analyze what was transpiring and that of a liturgical activist attempting to push or pull new ways into being. Thus I have been both a teacher of liturgical history and, in some small ways, a maker of liturgical history.

My first published article was in 1955 and my most recent ones, at this time, were written in 1995. In what follows I have chosen articles that both record liturgical history and have helped to shape it. Some, I hope, have value as historical studies in their own right. Others I have included because they give the feel of the period in which they were written. If they have value it is in showing what fires we were endeavoring to put out at what particular moment. Thus the date is especially important. What may appear true and obvious at one time may not be so at another. Marshall McLuhan is virtually forgotten today; in the 1960s liturgical scholars took him very seriously, at least the few of us who were around at that time! Discussions of inclusive language have gone far beyond where we were in the 1970s but I include an early discussion to show how the terrain appeared in that era.

Many of the things North Americans were experiencing in these four decades were common to much of western Christianity. Some of these experiences, so recent for us, still lie ahead for churches in other parts of the world. I am always delighted when I see practices and textual passages that they have inherited from us. It is a joy to see phrases that we use to voice our prayer now functioning in a similar fashion for others as in the liturgy of the Uniting Church in Australia. Just as North America has inherited so much in Christian worship from Europe, so now we are transmitting some of our treasures to churches in other parts of the world.

Only one of the articles included herein has not been published previously. All of them have been rewritten to update them or to remove duplications. My ideas have been fairly consistent so I have tried to remove some items that are repetitious even though I doubt many will read every article. I have added sequels to some in order to bring them down to 1995. In others I have simply inserted items that appeared since the article was initially published.

Choosing the articles has been frustrating since I can only include about one out of seven published items. I spent a summer of penance, rereading everything I had published in article form. Sometimes it was pleasant, sometimes painful. Some things I no longer recognized as my own. But I have tried to choose those things of most general interest to others. I hope I have succeeded and maybe, in the words of Robert Frost, "lodged a few pebbles."

Soon after I started seminary teaching in 1960 I was told I was far too narrow since I taught only Christian worship. Now I only teach graduate students the history of Christian worship in the West since 1500. The history of Christian worship is my central interest and it should surprise no one that most of the articles herein are historical.

I have, however, felt a particularly North American concern for worship and social justice. Here the influence of my teachers, Reinhold Niebuhr and H. Shelton Smith, has been deep. If there is a special North American flavor to liturgical scholarship it might well be the concern for linking worship and justice. I realize that the English could claim George Fox in the seventeenth century, F. D. Maurice in the nineteenth, and Percy Dearmer in the twentieth for a similar passion. But far more seems to have been written in North America than elsewhere about the alliance of worship and justice and I have included several of my own contributions.

I had the good fortune to be trained in architectural history at Harvard and at Cambridge University. The ways in which space shapes our expression and experience of worship has continued to fascinate me ever since I constructed a model of a Ralph Adams Cram chapel for Professor Kenneth Conant at Harvard in the early 1950s. Some of these essays are more than thirty years old but no one that I know of has picked up on the subjects. So I present them again in hope that others will pick them up and carry them further.

My love for both Church and academy are shown in a few selections on pastoral and pedagogic topics. Many more could have been included especially from United Methodist clergy publications. But those were written for a more limited audience than this book presumes.

Finally, I wish to thank those who have made this volume possible. As always, Cheryl Reed and Sherry Reichold have proven their great competence, ranging from deciphering my scribbling to the use of high technology. I wish to thank Walter Ray for great assistance in locating sources and in proofreading. It is my hope that my grandchildren will someday find these matters of history before their times interesting as a reminder of how deeply we are shaped by those who preceded us.

James F. White
University of Notre Dame
December 3, 1995

I. History

1. Roman Catholic and Protestant Worship in Relationship

Though last written (1995), this most appropriately comes first because of its synthesizing nature. It appeared in *Studia Liturgica* 26 (1996), and is used by permission.

I attend a United Methodist Church in South Bend, Indiana, where every Sunday service for the last twenty years or more has been the Eucharist. I am fond of saying that the only difference between our worship according to the official United Methodist "Service of Word and Table" and the Roman Catholic Mass is that they use real wine and we use real bread. So similar have the revised rites become in recent decades that an analysis of the texts would not yield any really significant theological differences and not many in structure. We have all borrowed from the *Apostolic Tradition*, other ancient texts, and the Eastern churches. Our hymn singing tends to be more fervent and the sermon more substantial than in many Roman Catholic parishes, but then there are plenty of exceptions to that generalization. And, of course, we were blessed with a very capable woman pastor for five years, something that has yet to happen officially among Roman Catholics.

But at a deeper level, beneath the obvious convergence of much Roman Catholic and Protestant worship in recent times, may still lurk a profound gulf. If I can express it in non-technical terms, it may lie in the expectations Catholics and Protestants bring to their worship. This is not something that would ever show up in liturgical texts and is sure to elude the probing of sociological questionnaires. In simplest terms I think Protestants approach worship with hopes that it will be edifying, Catholics with the desire that it be sanctifying. I grant that edification and sanctification, even in their Latin and Greek antecedents, are far from distinct categories. But I think that there is a general expectation among Protestants that worship will provide new insights or emotions that will build one up in living a Christ-like life. For Catholics, the expectation seems to be that of somehow being infused with Christ-likeness. Much of this is due, no doubt, to long centuries of respective concentration either on word or sacrament as alternative forms of Christ's presence. But even today when Catholics have recovered the word and Protestants the sacrament, centuries of expectations have not changed all that much. I suspect that despite all the recent changes most Protestants still approach the Eucharist as producing edification and most Catholics as infusing sanctification. Thus the exact same event may be approached with quite different expectations.

One evidence of this is the way hymn singing seems to function. For Protestants a service without hymnody is an anomaly for it denies the chief opportunity to sing what one believes and to believe what one sings. Hymns may be the most important way for Protestants to express religious feeling. Usually hymns provide the transitions in the service. These are not "soft spots" but quite the opposite, affirmations, corporate "amens" to what has preceded. In Catholic Masses, despite decades now of practice, hymns never seem to be an integral part of the Mass and many of the faithful are tight-lipped when a hymn is sung. Any sense that one's faith is built up through singing seems absent. The holiness that is imparted comes through quite different means. The best index to much Protestant piety is the hymns sung most frequently. Yet the hymns sung (or endured) at Mass would tell us little or nothing about Catholic piety.

Thus beneath the surface in the obvious ecumenical convergence in worship lies a deep geological fault, the spiritual equipment we bring to worship. Identical services are still approached in quite different fashions. And this is much more difficult to discern than comparative texts would disclose.

Four Centuries of Antagonism

Behind this disparity lie nearly five centuries of liturgical history that have shaped present realities. My purpose in this present short essay is to outline in brief fashion the relationships of Roman Catholic worship and Protestant worship over the trajectory of five centuries. During this time the relationship has changed from one of ferocious antagonism to one of considerable mutual borrowing and major rapprochement.

Both Catholicism and Protestantism are joint heirs of the worship practices of the late medieval Church in the West. But each appropriated different aspects of that inheritance, and then both moved on in different directions. Catholic worship experienced two major readjustments, the baroque era and the second liturgical movement.[1] Protestantism added to the reforms of the primary traditions—Lutheran, Reformed, Anabaptist, and Anglican—those of secondary traditions—Puritan, Methodist—and tertiary traditions—Quaker, Frontier, and Pentecostal.[2]

Catholicism essentially sought to maintain continuity with the medieval past except for those things suggesting "avarice, irreverence, and superstition." But the means found to accomplish this continuity brought a major discontinuity by establishing centralized control over every aspect of worship. The powers of liturgical revision Trent yielded to the papacy plus the establishment of the Congregation of Sacred Rites in 1588 were major changes after a millennium and a half of decentralized liturgical control. Even so, it took several centuries before Roman control was complete in France. Yet the new centralization effectively strangled the China mission by mid-seventeenth century.

Protestantism was no less stubborn in maintaining much of the late medieval past. The astonishing thing is not how radical, but essentially how conservative, several traditions were, especially Lutheran and Anglican. The *devotio moderna* in Germanic lands for two centuries had been placing its emphasis on the inward and spiritual and this was paralleled in Protestant worship, at least until the nineteenth century. Medieval piety had focused heavily on human unworthiness, reflected in the apologies added as the chief medieval contribution to the Mass. Much of Protestantism to this very day has continued a penitential Eucharist more attuned to Good Friday than to Easter. The liturgical diversity of the late Middle Ages seemed only natural to most Lutherans, Reformed, and Anabaptists. A variety of local Lutheran church orders abounded, enough from the sixteenth century alone to fill fifteen volumes.

[1]For more detail, see my *Roman Catholic Worship: Trent to Today* (New York: Paulist Press, 1995).

[2]These terms are developed in my *Protestant Worship: Traditions in Transition* (Louisville: Westminster/John Knox Press, 1989).

Yet, while conserving so much of the recent past, much of Protestantism appealed to an even earlier past, a past that today we can only speculate about, but one they felt they could match. Calvin's service book is entitled *According to the Custom of the Ancient Church*, meaning those first few centuries we find so elusive. Major changes were made in this direction, especially in making worship accessible. This was done chiefly by the use of the vernacular and simplification of rites and ceremonies. Calvin and Cranmer did succeed in making worship genuinely common. The result was to replace congregations actively involved in devotions with communities engaged in active participation in the liturgy. Devotions were pushed out of the public assembly into the bounds of the family where they survived, at least until recently.

Catholicism chose to emphasize the outward splendor of much late medieval worship and this led to the glitter and glamour of the baroque. Everything pointed to triumphalism with innovative efforts to intrigue and fascinate the eye even though the Mass remained nearly inaudible. Roodscreens and divisions in space disappeared, yet the result was not to unite priest and people in the liturgy but only to encourage more fervent devotions. Even during Mass, the host could be adored. The Mass was an occasion for devotions, not liturgical sharing. Communion remained for the most part as infrequent as it had been in the Middle Ages. Even Trent, while encouraging frequent communion, assumes yearly as the norm.

Because both sides were dividing up many areas of the late medieval landscape in worship, their conflicts were often extremely bitter. Most of the anathemas hurled by the Council of Trent dealt with matters of worship. Protestants were no less vehement in denouncing Rome. There were isolated attempts at being irenic: the *Augsburg Confession* complained "we [Lutherans] are unjustly accused of having abolished the Mass" and Bishop Stephen Gardiner could claim the 1549 *Book of Common Prayer* Eucharist was "not distant from the Catholic faith." Rumors of Rome's allowance of the *Book of Common Prayer* at the price of papal supremacy surfaced only to be ended with the excommunication of Elizabeth I in 1570.

From that time on, Protestant and Catholic worship existed in virtually airtight isolation until after World War II. The surest way to discourage any change was to call it "Catholic" or "Protestant," as the case might be. Up until fifty years ago such distrust has plagued liturgical reformers on either side of the great divide. Much of the Puritan agenda was abolishing those "nocent ceremonies" that had remained in the prayer book so that papists "were not a little confirmed in their superstition and idolatry." Catholics feared that conceding any Protestant reforms would involve loss of face. Trent would not even condone the chalice for laity although the emperor and several popes were quite willing to oblige.

The result was nearly four centuries of mutual hostility. This had the effect of stifling many possible reforms on either side. Well into the twentieth century the vernacular was considered a Protestant gimmick and hence taboo for Catholics; some traditionalists still feel this way. Elaborate ceremonial was considered a Catholic snare and delusion and Protestants were taught to beware of it. Patriotism came to play an insidious role in many of these defenses. Both Catholic and Protestant worship went on evolving but there were limits in directions they could shift, always bounded by the other.

Ironically, the musicians seemed able to leapfrog over these barriers. Handel, so quintessentially Protestant in many ways, spent some very productive months in Rome in 1717, writing such masterpieces as *Dixit Dominus*. Catholic musicians such as Beethoven were among Bach's greatest admirers. It seems that musicians could learn from and imitate whatever they considered valuable, transcending all the barriers of confession. Quality alone mattered. Indeed, there are instances of musicians being more utilized by the opposing camp than by their own allies.

The Enlightenment eroded contact between Catholics and Protestants in worship even further. Much of the sacral universe that had survived the sixteenth century languished in the eighteenth. We now know that in parts of Saxony many people came to daily prayer and thousands communicated each Sunday in Lutheran churches. But by 1790 that was no longer the case. Catholicism reacted to the Enlightenment with fresh devotions, especially visits to the Blessed Sacrament.

Catholicism's fortress mentality resisted any efforts at reform whether in Josephism, Febronianism, or Gallicanism. Many of the efforts of the Council of Pistoia (1786) have a curiously Protestant (and contemporary) ring but they were suppressed vehemently. The Constitution *Auctorem fidei* is one of the longest and most fervent in all of Denzinger. In the nineteenth century the efforts of Ignaz von Wessenberg to include vernacular singing and encourage preaching in the large diocese of Constance were undermined and brought to nothing. Who could doubt that what Rome really feared was too much accommodation to Protestant worship practices in Germany?

These competitive tendencies reached a climax of sorts in the 1830s. This well may be called the "liturgical decade" because there were liturgical movements in so many parts of the world: Kentucky, England, Denmark, France, and Germany. Yet they were all isolated. The recovery of frequent communion on the American frontier hardly affected other parts of Christendom.

The Catholic Revival in the Church of England was plagued by those who saw it all as a popish plot, probably a Jesuit trick. Newman's defection only encouraged these views. The battles that were fought over eucharistic piety and ceremonial, baptismal regeneration, and priestly confession all met the same objection: these were Catholic tendencies, hence unthinkable in the Church of England. Much of the literature of this period now reads like something from the communist hunters of the 1950s who were afraid that communist sympathizers might get a toehold in Texas. The same paranoia was apparent in riots in London over a cross on a bookmark in a pulpit Bible or Anglican bishops who smashed images and windows lest popery infiltrate.

Lutheran reformers such as N. F. S. Grundtvig in Denmark and Wilhelm Loehe in Bavaria faced the same problem. Their recourse was to cite practices that survived in Martin Luther. A similar tactic appeared in John Nevin's work within the Reformed tradition. Nevin appealed to Calvin for a fixed liturgy and a high eucharistic doctrine. But such tactics did not always work. Nineteenth-century Methodists gave up much that was distinctly Wesleyan for fear of being compromised by an Anglicanism that seemed to be lurching toward Rome.

On the Catholic side the paranoia was equally stark. Dom Prosper Guéranger referred to Protestantism as the "anti-liturgical heresy." He worked long and hard to extinguish the last remnants of neo-Gallican rites within France. The chief offense seems to have been that they tended to prefer biblical passages for some of the traditional proper prayers in the Missal and breviary. He endeavored to show that they had lessened devotion to Mary, Peter, and canonized popes. Recourse to the vernacular was equally suspect. Guéranger's solution was complete conformity to the Roman rite of the post-Tridentine books. And he was successful in stamping out anything that might seem Protestant. A French archbishop lamented in 1860 "in the matter of liturgy a bishop has no rights." Everything was to be safely controlled from Rome where no compromise need be feared.

Meanwhile the nineteenth century was proving an important nursery for adding to the rich variety of liturgical possibilities within American Protestantism. The American frontier saw the gaining of such important reforms as weekly communion, the evolution of liturgical democracy with lay-clerical distinctions largely obliterated, and a beginning of an end to the marginalization of women in worship. Most of these occurred in the contexts of the Frontier Tradition in worship. Frontier social conditions defied the rigid social stratification by class and gender of the East Coast and led to women praying in public in midweek prayer services. A major event was the "Declaration of Sentiments" framed at the Womens' Rights National Congress in Seneca Falls, New York, in 1848 in a Wesleyan Methodist chapel. Five years later, in nearby South Butler, New York, Antoinette Louisa Brown Blackwell was ordained as the first woman clergyperson of a major denomination (Congregationalist).

Encountering many of the same social conditions, Roman Catholic clergy, especially Passionists, Redemptorists, Jesuits, and Franciscans borrowed many of the techniques of Protestant revivalists. One priest told Charles G. Finney, the greatest American liturgical reformer of the nineteenth century, that he was deliberately using the same techniques that had worked for Protestants in Christianizing a continent. Protracted meetings or preaching missions seemed to work as well with Catholics in urban areas as they had worked on the frontier. But the social consequences, i.e., liturgical democracy and emancipation of women, were tightly checked.

The mutual paranoia continued well into the twentieth century. The growth of Anglo-Catholicism especially in the "Biretta Belt" of Wisconsin, Illinois, and Indiana continued but was also stubbornly resisted by Anglicans who worried about surrendering to Rome. Ralph Adams Cram, the architect, advocated returning to the sixteenth century and picking up the development of gothic church architecture where it ended. The eventual acceptance of many of his ideas by the Interdenominational Bureau of Architecture under Elbert M. Conover showed that many antipathies to the medieval past had mellowed.

Some mellowing on the Catholic side was evidenced by an increasing number of Georgian churches such as Corpus Christi in the shadow of New York's Riverside Church of Baptist gothic. The success of Father Stedman's *My Sunday Missal* (1932) was an important step in weaning Catholic laity away from total preoccupation with devotions at Mass. But by and large the old animosities continued right up to World War II. To label something Catholic was to make it suspect for Protestants; to call something Protestant made it taboo for Catholics. The biggest burden the liturgical pioneers of either side had to bear was the accusation of being too Protestant or too Catholic. Thus William Palmer Ladd, the pioneer of the liturgical movement in the Episcopal Church, went out of his way in his monthly columns to put down Catholic practices as absurd and to appeal to early Christianity. And such bugaboos plagued Catholics when they were accused of sounding too Protestant.

Five Decades of Rapprochement

A major transformation occurred in the years after World War II. Essentially what happened, in the words of my late colleague Mark Searle, is that Catholics found that it was all right to be Protestant when it came to worship, and many mainline Protestants found Post-Vatican II Catholic reforms quite appealing, especially those dealing with the lectionary, multiple options in texts, and contemporary liturgical language.

Behind such a major transformation lie many causes. Not least, and worthy of mention since they are rapidly disappearing from the scene, were the military chaplains of World War II. Having to minister to men and women of "all sorts and conditions" brought a great deal of mutual respect and accommodation. Witness the number of Protestant clergy who continued to wear clerical garb when they reentered civilian life even though they had never done so previously. And priests found, in the years after 1950, that they could lead services of singing and prayer from the *Armed Services Hymnal.*

Certainly the atmosphere changed in the years after the war. *Mediator Dei* of 1947, with its extreme clericalism, probably represents the end of an era rather than the beginning of a new one. And the death of Odo Casel the following year may mark the end of the first liturgical movement. It could be called the monastic liturgical movement or the restorationist. Casel, it will be recalled, opposed the use of the vernacular and was concerned with understanding the liturgy, not reshaping it. The American Virgil Michel (d. 1938) wanted to change people, not the liturgy.

All this happened in an astoundingly short time in the late 1940s. What became the Vernacular Society was founded in 1945. In boldest terms, what occurred was that Catholic liturgists adopted essentially a Protestant agenda for worship. People were to participate in the liturgy, not in devotions, and the chief means to that was the vernacular. The Bible and preaching were to play a much more prominent role in all of worship, and hymnody was to give people a larger role in participation. Luther was never mentioned but his reforms were always present.

It is no accident that the Catholic liturgical movement occurred almost entirely in countries with a Protestant majority (Germany and the United States) or strong minority (France). In the U.S. it was largely a midwestern phenomenon (with a few exceptions around Boston), right in the Protestant heartland. St. John's, Collegeville, is near the epicenter of Lake Wobegon country. Despite occasional efforts to prevent them, Protestants and Catholics mingled freely at relatives' weddings and funerals. The most influential liturgical pioneer in the U.S., H. A. Reinhold, had been taken to Protestant services weekly as a child in his native Hamburg. Lambert Beauduin had spent time in England during World War I and kept in close contact with Anglican leaders. Efforts have been made to show that the Anglican liturgical movement was essentially homegrown, but A. G. Hebert and others were in contact with Belgian Catholics. Obviously walls were crumbling and like the Berlin Wall they came down with a suddenness no one anticipated.

Increasingly the vernacular came to be the chief focus for reform and the chief source of resistance for those who saw it as capitulation to Protestantism. The archbishop of Pittsburgh flew off to Vatican II saying that never in a thousand years would the vernacular be allowed. And some American bishops argued (in very poor Latin) for the retention of Latin. One senses that far more was at stake than language; the Catholic minority that had defined itself in America largely by being different was feeling its identity threatened. The comfortable "club ecclesiology" was being questioned.

Needless to say, the conservatives' fears were all justified. The vernacular became completely dominant in a way the *Constitution on the Sacred Liturgy* had never hinted. A richer diet of scripture became imperative along with preaching (which Trent had demanded with less success). And church music at Mass was opened to the masses. Catholic traditionalists still feel the store was sold or rather given away. It is still common to hear them lament the "protestantizing" of worship.

The biggest change, of course, was that for the people the liturgy itself rather than devotions became dominant . Indeed, some worry that devotions have disappeared altogether. Many lay people saw the Mass as a quiet time to be alone with God while the priest did his stuff at the altar. Now the Mass has become a demanding intrusion in which they are expected to take part.

The other side of the coin is that mainline Protestants found so many of the Roman Catholic reforms after Vatican II the best options available that they adopted them or modeled their own reforms on them. The post-Vatican II Catholic reformed rites sparked a process of liturgical revision among Protestants or redirected efforts under-way. The Episcopal Church had begun prayer book revision in 1950 but it really took off in 1966. No one thought of liturgical revision without checking out what the Romans were up to or had already accomplished.

This worked, too, in the discovering of contemporary liturgical lan-guage. Some English Catholic bishops were anxious to have the re-vised books sound like the *Book of Common Prayer*, the only real model of liturgical prose in English. Fortunately the International Commission on English in the Liturgy pioneered a cautiously contemporary style and this became *de rigueur* for Protestants except for Episcopalians who had it both ways in the daily office, Eucharist, and funeral rite.

If imitation is the most sincere form of flattery, the three-year Sunday Mass lectionary has been highly praised. Almost instantly, in 1970, the Presbyterians, Episcopalians, and Lutherans produced their own versions and the Consultation on Church Union did a consensus lectionary in 1974. More recently the *Common Lectionary*, 1983, and then the *Revised Common Lectionary*, 1992, have become the most widely used lectionaries among English-speaking Protestants world-wide. Here is a good example of taking the best lectionary yet de-vised in two thousand years and then making major improvements (Old Testament narratives, feminist insights).

The amazing thing about use of the lectionary is how far it has spread across American Protestantism. It is not just the mainline churches but Brethren, Nazarene, and Mennonites who have latched on to it. And once they have bought it they soon realize they have purchased a much more extensive liturgical year as well. Now clergy groups in many American towns do their exegesis together, whether Catholic or Protestant, since they preach on the same texts.

Imitation has happened in the architectural setting of worship. Catholic plain style has become as aniconic as much of Protestant architecture. Far more important than the iconoclasm has been identification of and concentration on the essentials: altar-table, pulpit, font or pool, and presider's chair. There are about a hundred thousand churches in the U.S. with facilities for the immersion of adults. Until recently none were in Catholic churches; now each year sees more Catholic baptistries that would make a Baptist rejoice.

In all candor we should point out that there is a sizable element in American Protestantism that has not seen fit to use elements developed in post-Vatican II Catholicism. These include many congregations in the Frontier and Pentecostal traditions and especially those involved in the Church growth movement. This movement has taken inculturation to the extreme and speaks openly of "market-driven worship" and "entertainment evangelism." Questions as to the limits of inculturation are provoked by their popularity.

Many of the post-Vatican II changes, both Protestant and Catholic, have been motivated by the experiences of the Orthodox and Oriental churches. We have all recovered a distinct epiclesis, some even two. A variety of eucharistic prayers is now common. Some have experimented with the unification of initiation rites and others long for it. Creation and eschatology have regained a place for all in the West as has a strong pneumatology. Everyone, too, has borrowed from Justin Martyr and the *Apostolic Tradition*, perhaps too trustingly. Dix and Jungmann gave us all incentives for reform.

Some learning from the experiences of others has become explicit, as in the 1988 *Roman Missal for the Dioceses of Zaire*, which places the confessional act after the sermon as in the Episcopal and United Methodist rites.

Several other factors have brought Catholic and Protestant worship much closer in the U.S. than liturgical texts might indicate. One of these is the growing number of black Roman Catholics. We now know how much black culture contributed to the development of Protestant worship in the U.S., particularly in the Frontier and

Pentecostal traditions. Much of this was in musical idioms but also in a broader ethos of mutual sharing and dramatic excitement. Participatory preaching and a great tradition of pulpit eloquence have been carried with them by black Catholics.

At the same time there are now more than five million Hispanic Protestants in the U.S. These people are represented in the newest hymnals by hymns in Spanish and in the most recent service books by special festivals and practices, especially regarding the Christmas cycle. The blessings in the *United Methodist Book of Worship* now include one for a *quinceañera* (girl celebrating her fifteenth birthday). Churches with service books are busy publishing Spanish versions.

Television knows no boundaries and it is reported that thirty per cent of those sharing in televised worship (or evangelism) are Catholics. That is about the same per cent of Catholic visitors to Church growth congregations.

Another important confluence is among Pentecostalists or charismatics. The official myth is that Pentecostalism began on the first day of the twentieth century. Fire descended upon the earth in the Azusa Street mission in April 1906, and thence spread to the ends of the earth. It spread to Roman Catholics in 1966 and flared up at the University of Notre Dame the next year. Since then the blaze has not gone out but reached millions of Roman Catholics worldwide. Charismatic styles of worship may be the most unitive to appear so far.

Cooperative efforts have been present in other areas. In the 1960s the Consultation on Church Union Commission on Worship usually had Roman Catholic observers at its meetings. The Consultation on Common Texts (CCT) began in the mid-sixties as an effort to produce common texts. This led to the International Consultation on English Texts, (ICET) 1965–1975, and eventually to the English Language Liturgical Consultation (ELLC) 1985–present. Significant achievements have been made. Out of CCT came the *Common Lectionary*, ICET produced the translations of ordinary parts of the Eucharist used by many churches, and CCT produced *A Christian Celebration of Marriage: An Ecumenical Liturgy* (1987). The Committee for a Common Eucharistic Prayer (CCEP) produced a eucharistic text in 1975 and CCT has undertaken similar work more recently.

A major ecumenical event was the publication of *Baptism, Eucharist, and Ministry* and the Lima Liturgy by the World Council of Churches in 1982. These showed how far consensus had been reached on matters of liturgical theology and how far it had yet to go. For professional liturgists the founding of the North American Academy of Liturgy in 1975 has given an academic forum for scholarly discussions. The membership has steadily grown and now is almost equally divided between Protestants and Catholics. Similar groups exist in other countries.

If many centuries of antagonism can give way to so much mutual sharing and cooperation it should be a sign of hope. That is not to say that uniformity should ever be a goal. Protestantism will continue in its historical role of pioneering new possibilities in worship. We have not too many traditions in worship but too few. How distressing it must be to live in rural parts of Sweden or Spain where only one liturgical tradition is available! The independent churches of Africa, the feminists, the syncretists, the Church growth people, and many others will continue to expand our horizons.

Liturgical scholars must be impartial. After all, there is no objective basis for saying any one tradition of worship is more pleasing to the Almighty than another. The good news is that we can explore new possibilities together.

And the sudden breakthrough in worship, coming after ages of isolation, might give us hope that that most stubborn ecumenical problem, ordination, might eventually yield. God has a way of surprising us.

2. Liturgical Traditions in the West Since 1500

This is a revised and updated version of an article from *The New Dictionary of Sacramental Worship*, edited by Peter E. Fink, S.J., and published by The Liturgical Press in 1990. Used by permission.

Since 1500, Western Christianity has seen the flourishing of no less than ten different liturgical traditions. But before we chronicle each of these we need to begin with some basic definitions. By "the West" we mean the Christianity of western Europe and the areas colonized by it including the Americas, Australia, New Zealand, and segments of Africa and Asia. "Traditions" are inherited liturgical practices and the understanding of those practices that are transmitted relatively intact from generation to generation. We shall explore roughly five centuries, beginning at the start of the Reformation in 1517.

The process of developing new Christian liturgical traditions is a natural process of inculturation as worship patterns are adjusted to reflect (and sometimes create) changes in peoples. Within specific traditions there normally are distinct cultural and ethnic styles: black Lutheran congregations, for example, where gospel song seems more natural than chorales but where the liturgical tradition is definitely Lutheran. Thus it is easier to define the center of a liturgical tradition than it is to be precise about its edges since many accommodate a wide variety of styles. In addition, no tradition is static; all change from generation to generation so that they must always be seen as in transition even when service books are frozen. The 1662 prayerbook of the Church of England has not changed for over three hundred years but everything else in Anglican worship has. We are not examining unchanging essences but living tissues.

All the ten traditions ultimately derive from the worship life of late medieval western Europe. This was loosely centralized in Rome but existed in many varieties according to diocesan uses and religious communities. Our method will be to treat the ten traditions emanating from this background in order of conservatism, i.e., the degree to which they continued to reflect late medieval practice. Some elements persisted longer among Protestants than Catholics, and some Catholic changes were more radical than some changes among Protestants, so we must deal with a mixed bag. But the relative degree of conservatism in relation to existing practice can give us an organizing principle. Everyone thought in the sixteenth century that they were restoring the worship life of the early Church even more than we fancy we are doing so today. The political metaphor of conservative, moderate, and radical in degree of change will serve us well. Thus we have three basically conservative traditions: Roman Catholic, Lutheran, and Anglican; two moderate ones: Reformed and Methodist; and five radical groups: Puritan, Anabaptist, Frontier, Pentecostal, and Quaker. Our sequence is from right to left.

Roman Catholic

The Council of Trent (1545–1563) sought to bring about a conservative reform by radical means. The Fathers of Trent were concerned to end avarice, corruption, and superstition in worship but their minds were directed to defending the status quo whenever possible. This is partly because the lack of liturgical scholarship allowed them to believe, for example, that St. Peter had composed the Roman canon and that to change existing practices was to abolish that which was apostolic. Furthermore, any change would be seen as conceding that the Protestant reformers were right after all.

The method of reform chosen was that of liturgical standardization, a possibility with the advent of the printed book. The revision of the liturgical books was entrusted to the curia and proceeded with the breviary (1568), the missal (1570), the martyrology (1584), the pontifical (1596), bishops' ceremonies (1600), and the ritual (1614). The enforcement of global uniformity was entrusted to the new Congregation of Rites, established in 1588. So began almost four centuries of liturgical uniformity reaching even to China (and thus devastating evangelization of that country). The "era of rubricism" that ensued found theological safety in rigid liturgical uniformity.

At the same time much of worship did change because books and bureaucrats could control only so much. A brilliant period of baroque architecture spread around the world, inspired by the work of Gian Lorenzo Bernini (1598–1680) and the example of the Jesuit church in Rome, Il Gésu. Joseph Jungmann speaks of the baroque spirit and the traditional liturgy as "two vastly different worlds." New devotions came to the forefront, especially benediction and exposition of the Blessed Sacrament; the cult of the saints came to focus largely on the Virgin Mary. Devotions to the Sacred Heart of Jesus and visits to the Blessed Sacrament became popular. In France the new standardized books were resisted for three centuries, coming into consistent use only in the late nineteenth century after experimentation with much local variety and vernacular uses.

The Enlightenment of the eighteenth century failed to make much of a mark despite the efforts of the Synod of Pistoia (1786) to make reforms that were two centuries too early. The nineteenth century saw the beginnings of the first liturgical movement, led by Prosper Guéranger (1805–1875) and a series of monastic leaders, notably Lambert Beauduin (1873–1960), Virgil Michel (1890–1938), and Odo Casel (1886–1948). This lasted until after World War II and was acknowledged in the conservative encyclical *Mediator Dei* (1947). A later liturgical movement began after the war, deriving its agenda largely from Protestant worship (vernacular, cultural pluralism, active participation, preaching at Mass, popular hymnody) and centered largely in countries with Protestant majorities.

More recently, Vatican II in its *Constitution on the Sacred Liturgy* (1963) moved Roman Catholicism to embrace these newer reforms. The result has been revision of the Tridentine liturgical books in less than twenty-five years and translation of them all. The introduction of the vernacular has been accompanied by much more flexibility and greater variety of options in the rites. While these reforms have been widely welcomed by the laity, Rome seems presently concerned with preventing adaptation or inculturation from going too far. Even so, the distance traveled since Trent has been enormous.

Lutheran

There are a number of reasons for considering the Lutheran tradition the most conservative of the Protestant traditions of worship. Martin Luther (1483–1546) had a high respect for the existing Christian cultus; his inclination was to purge those aspects that could not be reconciled to his theology and retain the rest. He could be quite radical on occasion (as with the canon of the Mass) but on the whole retained more than he rejected. He tended to move carefully; others anticipated him on vernacular liturgies.

After statements in *The Babylonian Captivity* (1520) that were to be determinative for almost all subsequent Protestant sacramental theology, Luther moved to liturgical reform with vernacular baptismal rites in 1523 and 1526. The same years also saw new eucharistic rites, the *Formula Missae* (in Latin) and *Deutsche Messe* (in German). Later years saw forms for marriage, ordination, and penance. In general, existing practices endured but rites were in the vernacular and popular participation was promoted whenever possible.

Three new emphases stand out: congregational song, preaching, and frequent communion in both kinds. Luther considered music one of God's greatest gifts and cultivated its use in worship through service music and hymnody. He led the way in writing hymns himself and vigorous hymn singing has always been a hallmark of this tradition. Luther's insistence that preaching be a part of all congregational worship contributed to a rebirth of preaching. He also encouraged all the laity who were properly prepared to receive the bread and wine at each Eucharist.

As for vestments, images, and much of the medieval cultus that was theologically neutral, Luther allowed their continuance; they came to be known as *"adiaphora"* or things indifferent. Thus much more survived in Lutheran countries, especially in Sweden and Finland where Lutheran worship remained its most conservative, than in other Protestant countries. Recent studies have shown just how much survived during the long period of Lutheran orthodoxy. In Bach's Leipzig there were daily public prayers, a weekly Eucharist with a great many communicants, and a rich observance of the Church year. Although the services were in German one gets the feeling that not all that much had changed from the Middle Ages in two hundred years of Lutheranism.

The real change came not with the Reformation but with the Enlightenment. Daily services in Leipzig ended in the 1790s and much of the continuing medieval cultus vanished in the face of rationalism, even in the Church of Sweden. Much of this has been blamed on the influence of the Reformed tradition but more is probably due to Enlightenment tendencies. The nineteenth century saw a gradual reaction to the Enlightenment with an attempt to recover much from early Lutheran worship. In Germany, Wilhelm Loehe (1810–1895), in Denmark, Nikolai Grundtvig (1783–1872), and various other leaders elsewhere sought a return to Lutheran orthodoxy and orthopraxis. The indication of their success is the successive revisions of various service books and hymns. More recent versions, especially the American *Lutheran Book of Worship* (1978) have moved into the ecumenical mainstream while retaining a distinctly Lutheran character, especially in the emphasis on music.

Anglican

The Anglican tradition is ambiguous: what started off as a fairly moderate reformation and remained so for three centuries reversed itself in the nineteenth century and moved to reappropriate a great deal of the medieval cultus. To modern observers, Anglican worship seems more conservative than Lutheran but the theological origins are far more liberal. Anglican liturgy began with Archbishop Thomas Cranmer's (1489–1556) two editions of the *Book of Common Prayer*, that of 1549 and the much more radical 1552 book. Using the latest technology, Cranmer sought to put all the services in the hands of everyone by translating, condensing, and revising the rites before publishing them in popular versions with a ceiling on price.

Cranmer succeeded in recovering daily services of public prayer which became a staple of Anglican worship. Many of the ceremonies associated with the sacraments and other rites disappeared from the 1552 edition and the theology became much more unambiguously Zwinglian. Martin Bucer (1491–1551) provided much of the structure for the ordination rite but Cranmer was not prepared to accept as high a view of the Eucharist as Bucer and Calvin. A great ornament of the book was Cranmer's linguistic ability to cast traditional Latin prayers in the language of his contemporaries.

After the brief regression of the Marian years, Anglican worship tended to stabilize during the long reign of Elizabeth I. As a political settlement, episcopal forms of church government were retained as well as something of the appearances of medieval public worship, although there had been much iconoclasm even before the rise of Puritanism. Weekly communion proved to be too radical a step for most people and canon law eventually settled for a minimum of three celebrations a year. For several centuries the normal Sunday service came to be morning prayer, litany, ante-communion, and sermon. Popular hymnody was lacking but magnificent choral daily services characterized worship in the cathedrals. The poet-priest George Herbert (1593–1633) offered an example of Anglican parish ministry at its best.

The Puritan takeover of the Church of England from 1644 to 1660 moved things leftward in a radical direction but only temporarily. The restoration period afterwards attempted to return to the status quo of 1604, as the prayer book of 1662 showed. Despite the survival of a high church tradition (without much ceremonial) most Anglicans were comfortable in a tradition that avoided the excesses of either Catholicism or Puritanism. In the eighteenth century this meant worship that was edifying and moralistic but with little concern for the sacraments or anything overtly supernatural.

In the nineteenth century reactions came in the form of the Catholic Revival with its recovery of patristic theology (the Oxford Movement, Tractarianism, Puseyism) and a full scale restoration of late medieval ceremonial and architecture (the Cambridge Movement, Ritualism). These brought back weekly celebrations of the Eucharist at the same time this was occurring among Disciples of Christ, Mormons, Plymouth Brethren, and the Catholic Apostolic Church. A new emphasis was placed on baptism, penance, and the revival of medieval architecture, liturgical arts, and choral music. Congregational hymnody also made its advent.

The twentieth century has seen an indigenous liturgical movement in the Church of England, manifesting itself as the parish communion movement in the 1930s. Recent years have seen wholesale revision of Anglican prayerbooks around the world, usually either following the patterns of Cranmer or trading in such late medieval forms for the presumed third century model of the *Apostolic Tradition*.

Reformed

We now move further left to the central or moderate traditions: Reformed and Methodist. The Reformed Tradition has several roots: Zurich, Basel, Strasbourg, and Geneva. In some ways it preserved more than its share of the penitential strain of late medieval piety. In other respects, however, it moved beyond the forms that Lutheranism and Anglicanism were content to continue. In time it was largely seduced by the Puritan tradition (in Great Britain) and the Frontier Tradition (in America).

Ulrich Zwingli (1484–1531) began his reformation of Zurich heavily influenced by humanistic studies and a thorough biblicism. He was anxious to return worship to its biblical roots and eager to make it more spiritual, reflecting the gap he saw between the physical and the spiritual. Although a fine musician, he rejected music in worship as distracting one from spiritual worship. Iconoclasm in Zurich purified or devastated the churches, according to one's viewpoint. Zwingli retained the four Sundays or festivals when his people were accustomed to receive communion or the Eucharist, a preaching service being held on the other Sundays. These four occasions saw a drastically simplified rite that focused on transubstantiation of the people, not the elements.

Martin Bucer in Strasbourg and John Oecolampadius (1482–1531) in Basel began experimenting with vernacular services. At Strasbourg this included daily prayer services and a Sunday service derived from the Mass. Bucer's influence was spread further by a visiting preacher out of a job, John Calvin (1509–1564). While temporarily serving a French-speaking congregation in Strasbourg, Calvin adapted the German rite Bucer was using. Calvin brought this rite to Geneva and from 1542 on it became the model for much of the Reformed tradition. Although deriving its structure from the Mass via Bucer, it highlighted the penitential aspects of worship and was highly didactic and moralistic. Relief from this somber mood was wrought by encouraging the congregation to sing metrical paraphrases of the psalms, which they did with fervor. Such devotion to psalmody (and the exclusion of hymnody) marked Reformed worship for several centuries and still does in some churches.

Calvin's low esteem for human nature was balanced by a high view of God's word and the sacraments. His doctrine of eucharistic feeding on Christ through the operation of the Holy Spirit, although certainly not without problems, was the most sophisticated Reformation eucharistic doctrine, but was largely lost by his heirs.

John Knox (ca. 1505–1572) transmitted this tradition to Scotland as others brought it to France, the Netherlands, Hungary, and Germanic countries. Knox's liturgy, renamed the *Book of Common Order*, flourished in Scotland for eighty years after 1564. Only then did the Scots yield to the Puritan effort to achieve national unity in worship through the *Westminster Directory* of 1645. This moved away from set forms to more permissive patterns. The *Directory* remained vaguely normative in later editions in America. On the American frontier the newly emerging frontier patterns of worship tended to engulf the Reformed tradition.

A pattern of recovery similar to that we have already seen eventuated slowly in America. Charles W. Baird (1828–1887) led the way in

1855 with a title many thought oxymoronic, *Presbyterian Liturgies*. German Reformed Christians experienced a recovery of both theology and liturgy in the so-called Mercersburg Movement. Eventually an American service book, the *Book of Common Worship*, followed in 1906 as did service books in the Kirk of Scotland. In recent years Presbyterians have followed closely in the same post-Vatican II ecumenical mainstream as other traditions of the right and center, signified by publication of the *Book of Common Worship* (1993).

Methodist

We move to a later period, the eighteenth century, to observe the origins of Methodism. Basically it can be seen as a countercultural movement in the midst of the Enlightenment. When the sacraments were on the margin of Church life, early Methodism put them at the center; when religious zeal was in disrepute, Methodism made enthusiasm essential; where religion was confined to the churches, Methodism took it to the fields and streets. John Wesley (1703–1791), the founder of Methodism, was a faithful son of the Church of England and never ceased in his love for its worship. The Methodists under Wesley functioned virtually as a religious order under a General Rule within the established Church.

Distinctive features of early Methodist worship were "constant communion," i.e., frequent Eucharist, fervent preaching for salvation, vigorous hymn singing (then a novelty), care of souls in small groups, and a mixture of extempore and fixed prayer. Charles Wesley (1707–1788) wrote hymns by the thousands; he and John created a great treasury of 166 eucharistic hymns. John Wesley practiced pragmatic traditionalism, preferring ancient forms for modern needs when possible: vigils became the Methodist watchnight, the agape surfaced as the love feast, and the covenant service was adapted from Presbyterians. In 1784, John Wesley published his service book for America, the *Sunday Service*, advocating, among other things, a weekly Eucharist.

Much of this did not survive the transit of the Atlantic and American Methodism soon discarded Wesley's service book but not his hymn book. Much of the sacramental life was dissipated although the texts for the rites remained largely intact. Instead, Methodism tended to adapt many of the techniques of the frontier. Camp-meetings abounded for a time and eventually resulted in a distinctive revival-type service. Fanny Crosby (1820–1915) wrote many hymns of personal devotion to the blessed Savior while Charles A. Tindley (1856–1933) was a prolific African-American hymn writer.

Despite the prevalence of revival style worship there persisted in America a number of areas where more formal worship was preferred, such as Birmingham and Nashville. Thomas O. Summers (1812–1882) was the leader of a nineteenth-century liturgical movement in the South that effected the reprinting of Wesley's service book and produced a standard order of worship. Wesley's prayer book long remained in use in England, and even the *Book of Common Prayer* was used. In general, Methodists in the mid-nineteenth century reacted against the new ritualism of the established Church in England only to adopt some aspects of it several generations later.

Revivalism gave way to a period of aestheticism with much discussion of "enriching worship." This, in turn, gave way to a neo-orthodox period of recovering historic liturgies, especially Wesley's. Recent decades have seen more attention to assimilating the post-Vatican II Roman Catholic reforms, especially the lectionary and a plurality of forms, e.g., twenty-four eucharistic prayers. The *United Methodist Hymnal* (1989) and *United Methodist Book of Worship* (1992) show how far this has gone. At the same time the lure of Church growth forms has been extensive.

Puritan

We move beyond the central traditions in our progression to the left to look at the five remaining traditions. It is not always easy to say which is the most radical but we shall place Puritanism closer to the center than the Anabaptists because the Puritans insisted on national reformation through a state Church and the Anabaptists did not. The exception to this rule is small groups of Separatists who believed in reformation without tarrying for anyone. They went ahead and did in private what the Puritans did openly when they controlled the national Church. Since some Separatists picked up antipedobaptist ideas in the Netherlands there are also close links between them and the Anabaptists.

Puritanism began in the ranks of Anglican exiles fleeing the persecutions of Queen Mary although Edwardian Bishop John Hooper (?–1555) was a proto-Puritan. Puritans could favor various forms of Church government—episcopal, presbyterian, and congregational—

as biblical but they had one common theme in worship: it must be according to God's word. Even the blessed John Calvin had been so blinded by the brightness of the new light that he had not gone far enough. Calvin had been content with general prescriptions for worship drawn from Scripture; the Puritans wanted specifics. If it was wicked to disobey God's ethical injunctions, liturgical disobedience was no less reprehensible. Papistical ceremonies that survived in Anglican worship such as the sign of the cross in baptism, the wedding ring, confirmation, and holy days were all of human invention and therefore unscriptural. In this sense no issue was minor, for all were clear questions of obedience.

The Puritans' opportunity came when they controlled Parliament in the 1640s and 1650s and were able to enact a series of reforms. The *Book of Common Prayer* was abrogated from 1645 to 1660 and the *Westminster Directory* substituted. In Scotland a *Directory for Family-Worship* was instituted in 1647 and became the basis for a long-continuing practice of daily prayers in families. But it was in America that the Puritans first were able to institute a state Church reformed according to God's word. In Salem (1629) and Boston (1630) the Reformation was finally completed according to their lights. Holy communion was celebrated monthly, worship was heavily dominated by preaching but the congregation could respond and question the minister's exegesis and application, and psalmody provided another form of participation.

In the eighteenth century much of this was superseded by the emotional fervor of the Great Awakening, which brought a variety of other churches to New England villages. In England and America a considerable segment, usually those preferring a more dignified style of worship, moved into Unitarianism. In contrast to other traditions, little effort was spent in recovering past patterns. Much of the Puritan tradition passed into liberal Congregationalism or Unitarianism without much concern for recovering a seventeenth-century golden era. Many were engulfed in Frontier Tradition worship.

In recent years much of the same post-Vatican II assimilation has occurred, especially in accepting the lectionary, Church year, and other common themes. The newest United Church of Christ service book, *Book of Worship* (1986), is the most liberal denominational service book, especially in inclusive language, and is probably not widely used except for special services.

Anabaptist

We must return to the sixteenth century to pick up our last tradition originating in that period of liturgical ferment. It is not easy to generalize about the Anabaptist elements of the Radical Reformation known largely today as Mennonites, Amish, and Hutterites, but we can trace some common features. Surprisingly, the more radical traditions tend also to be most conservative when it comes to stabilizing and continuing the same worship forms across the centuries.

The earliest Anabaptists, the Swiss Brethren, began in contact with Zwingli in Zurich, but they took his biblicism a step farther than he was willing to and argued vehemently against the baptism of any but believers. Their basic premise came to be the need for a pure Church of believers who led holy lives. This was impossible to reconcile with the magisterial reformation relying on state support. Both Protestants and Catholics vied with each other to persecute Anabaptists or rebaptizers, as they became known because of their refusal to accept their own baptisms as infants. Immersion was not an issue and most of these groups baptized by pouring or sprinkling.

A variety of leaders arose with small groups of followers. The typical congregation met in a secluded spot under a leader called and ordained by the congregation. Because persecution was so constant, martyrdom was frequent and a rich hymnody of martyrdom developed, some of it still in use. For the Church to be kept pure, not only must the entrance be narrow in the form of baptism for believers only, but members not living a holy life were expelled by the ban and shunned in accordance with biblical precept (1 Cor 5:13).

Despite their radical origins, several Anabaptist groups have kept faithful with genuine conservatism. The Old Order (Amish) worship in private homes much as their ancestors did, the Hutterite communities even retain the use of sixteenth-century sermons, and even the larger Mennonite groups resisted most nineteenth-century American influences by remaining relatively isolated communities. Although their numbers remain relatively small, the disciplined lifestyle of these people makes them much admired.

Frontier

We leap forward now to the very beginnings of the nineteenth century in America. A new social situation developed after the Revolution with the movement of widely scattered pioneers to the frontier. No traditional parish system was adequate and large numbers of the population were as unchurched as they were illiterate. A means of reaching them soon developed, strangely enough out of the sacramental seasons that Presbyterians of Scotch-Irish origins observed each year. These periods of intense preparation before celebration of the Eucharist soon evolved into the campmeeting in which thousands of people assembled from miles around for a period (usually lasting four days) of preaching, singing, spiritual direction, and baptism of converts, all culminating in the Lord's Supper. More than any other individual, Charles G. Finney (1792–1875) brought the frontier techniques or "new measures" back to the East Coast despite stubborn resistance from fellow Presbyterian ministers. Domesticated into East Coast gentility, the new measures included protracted meetings lasting over several days, the mourner's bench, prayer for individuals by name, and midweek prayer meetings at which even women were allowed to speak.

The great attraction of this new Frontier Tradition was that it worked. It had completely substituted pragmatism for traditionalism (unlike Wesley) and Finney had a great scorn for previous forms of worship. Frontier-style worship worked in the sense that it made converts, snatching them from darkness into the blinding light of conversion, and it could rekindle that fire again and again. The normal patterns of worship came to be tripartite: prayer and praise, preaching for salvation, and harvest of converts. Music played a great part in the first portion, often caricatured as "preliminaries." So attractive did this style of worship become that like a liturgical black hole it pulled many a Lutheran, Reformed, Methodist, Puritan, and even Quaker congregation into its orbit.

As such it is the dominant worship tradition in the United States. Great denominations such as the Southern Baptist, Disciples of Christ, and Churches of Christ feel at home within this tradition although the latter two insist on a weekly Eucharist led by lay people. In recent years this tradition has felt little temptation to borrow from the recent Roman Catholic reforms although the lectionary has made some inroads. As worship for the unchurched, this tradition is a natural for modern television evangelism. Millions participate in this kind of worship via television each Sunday. By its standards it still works and works very well.

The latest development, largely of the 1990s, has been fueled by a Church growth philosophy and named the mega-church style. It involves minimalizing cultural barriers in a seeker-service format that focuses heavily on contemporary music, dramatic skits, and fervent preaching for conversion. In the seeker services a high premium is placed on relevancy in order to reach the unchurched; little concern is shown for conventional forms of worship. Converts may participate in weekday services that are somewhat more conventional. Consistently the mega-church style focuses on a specific homogeneous social and cultural unit of people. Praise-worship services or convergence services (sometimes with a Pentecostal flavor) often employ seeker-service approaches.

Pentecostal

The advent of the twentieth century brought an even more radical tradition, the Pentecostal. Whereas all the traditions we have examined thus far proceeded on the basis of structured worship, usually led if not dominated by a single leader, the Pentecostals turned the doors wide open to the Spirit that might blow anywhere or use anyone in the congregation. Granted that conventions do emerge in time even among Pentecostals, structures or clergy are not primary but somewhat accidental. Here was a tradition in which blacks and women played major roles from the very beginning.

The beginnings were inauspicious: a broken-down faith healer, Charles Parham (1873–1929), playing John the Baptist to a one-eyed black holiness preacher, William J. Seymour (1870–1922). From Topeka to Houston the fire smoldered, and suddenly in 1906 it burst into flame at the Azusa Street Mission in Los Angeles. Crowds attended from America and the fire spread to Portland, Chicago, Norway, England, soon touched Chile and Brazil, and eventually reached Africa.

Pentecostal worship centered in the unexpected possibilities of the Holy Spirit reaching out by showering gifts on individuals for the benefit of all. Speaking in tongues came to be the best-known gift, revealing an individual's baptism of the Spirit. But it was by no means the only gift: healing, interpretation, and prophecy blossomed where least expected. It was a true liturgical democracy. Women leaders were prominent and often more colorful than the men. Every African American neighborhood has a Pentecostal chapel or two, yet in recent years highly affluent communities have also seen the advent of this worship tradition.

Beginning in 1960, Pentecostal or charismatic worship made its advent among Episcopalians and in 1966 among Roman Catholics. After initial resistance it has been welcomed in Roman Catholic and Protestant communities alike. Meanwhile, classical Pentecostalism has reached millions of people in Latin America and become one of the largest forces shaping Christianity in Africa. Sober historians have predicted that the majority of Christians one day will be in the Southern Hemisphere and that most of them will be Pentecostals.

Quaker

It is easy to identify the Quakers or Society of Friends as the most radical tradition of all in its break from late medieval forms of worship. All the groups we have mentioned thus far retained clergy, the preaching of sermons, and outward and visible sacraments. The classical forms of Quaker worship have none of the above although we may detect some indirect links with medieval mysticism. Paradoxically, most Quakers have tempered their radicalism by being the most conservative in fidelity to their original forms. Roman Catholic worship has changed far more than has Quaker worship in England or the East Coast of America.

The origins of Quaker worship lie in the soul-searching of George Fox (1624–1691) and his discovery of the inner light in every human. This brought one closer to God than Scripture or sacraments for it was direct access to the Spirit itself with no need for the mediation of clergy or set forms. Furthermore such direct access was available to all, male or female, slave or free. It was as radical as Paul's concept of baptism. Thus any study of liturgy and justice must begin with the Quakers for what they practiced in worship was what they felt compelled to practice in all of life. What F. D. Maurice (1805–1872) and Percy Dearmer (1867–1936) or Virgil Michel (1890–1938) and H. A. Reinhold (1897–1968) later advocated had been common practice among Quakers for several centuries. Since all were equal before the Spirit women had as much right to speak in worship as men and anyone who could see the Spirit in a black person had no right to keep him or her in slavery. No one was marginalized in worship; this also meant that no one should be honored by fancy clothing or titles in society. Decisions were to be made by the "sense of the meeting" since a vote always means defeat for a minority. Whatever else it is, the Spirit seems to be fair and consistent.

But though it could dispense with sermons and sacraments, the one thing Quaker worship could not surrender was the Christian community itself, the "meeting." Hence, as all Christians have discovered, the most important act in worship is coming together in Christ's name. Quaker worship is a form of corporate mysticism in which the Spirit uses individuals to speak to the group. Greatly to be feared is putting oneself forward by rushing into words. Only after a time of centering down can one feel ready to speak under the compulsion of the Spirit. It was felt that Christ had not intended outward baptism and communion to continue any more than footwashing, so these sacraments occur in inward and invisible ways only.

Quaker worship involves a great sense of personal restraint and even great Quaker saints such as John Woolman (1720–1772) worried after first-day (Sunday) meeting that they might have spoken from the self rather than the Spirit. A high degree of biblical literacy is also presupposed. The Spirit, after all, is the author of Scripture too, and will not contradict itself whether in the Bible or in reason.

On the American frontier some Quakers adopted frontier forms of worship as had so many other traditions, especially in Indiana. Thus evolved services with structured worship, paid clergy, and even outward sacraments. Sometimes unstructured or unprogrammed worship could be integrated into services that were basically structured, but many East Coast and English Quakers worship still in ways that would not astonish George Fox, so stable has Quaker worship been.

Worship forms have continued to develop as people have changed. The evolution of new traditions is as natural as changes in people. Modern attempts to conflate liturgical traditions, to obtain any form of consensus in the ways a variety of Christian peoples worship their God, are highly dubious efforts. Just as social changes sneak up on us when we least expect them, so new liturgical traditions will evolve in the West although unexpected. These new traditions may be feminist, or incorporate insights of Eastern cultures, or reflect the effects of new technologies on people (as book publishing did for earlier liturgies), but they most likely will occur in ways no one yet can anticipate. They may be already in our midst.

3. Liturgical Reformation: Sixteenth Century and Twentieth

Written for *Reformed Liturgy and Music* 18 (Spring 1984), this is a comparison of liturgical epochs. This revised version is used by permission.

The year 1983 saw Christians around the world observing two important anniversaries: the five hundredth anniversary of the birth of Martin Luther (November 10, 1483) and the twentieth anniversary of the promulgation of the *Constitution on the Sacred Liturgy* (December 4, 1963). These events commemorated beginnings of the two greatest eras of liturgical reform that western Christianity has known: that of the sixteenth century and that of the twentieth.

It is tempting to claim that the Roman Catholic liturgical reformation of the last twenty years has been simply a much-delayed catching up with what Protestants did in the sixteenth century, but that kind of Protestant triumphalism is only partially true and obscures the realization that Vatican II's *Constitution on the Sacred Liturgy* has also provided an agenda for Protestant liturgical reformation in our time. The constitution has called Protestants back to many of the reforms of the sixteenth century but has pushed us all beyond them, too. Today reform has become reciprocal. To regard the recent Roman Catholic reforms as carbon copies is to miss the fact that the liturgical reformation of our times is a Protestant event as well as a Roman Catholic one.

One could compare the reforms of the two eras—sixteenth century and twentieth—by simply cataloging them side by side, but that soon gets tedious. I have decided, rather, to describe three areas of the most significant changes in the sixteenth century and to note recent developments in those areas: sacramental life, word of God, and congregational participation.

Sacramental Life

Frequently the most important results of actions are not those intended at all. The marginalization of the sacraments was certainly the agenda of no one among the great Protestant reformers, yet events eventually pushed the sacraments far from the center of Protestant life. Despite the efforts of John Wesley, Alexander Campbell, and Edward Pusey to reverse this development, the sacraments became and remain marginal for much of Protestant worship, observed occasionally but not the basis of worship life. Ironically, the shortage of priests may have the same effect some day among Roman Catholics.

The Reformers inherited the finely-polished sacramental system of the late Middle Ages. Pastoral care was handled almost entirely through sacraments and they were the chief form of the worship life of lay people. For a hundred years following Peter Lombard's listing of the seven sacraments (about 1150) theologians had perfected their teachings about the operation of grace in the sacraments. The whole sacramental system became a marvelous product of human ingenuity. Something similar happened in this country in the perfecting of the revival system in the century from Jonathan Edwards's *A Faithful Narrative of the Surprising Work of God* (1737) to Charles G. Finney's *Lectures on Revivals of Religion* (1835). God's actions became safely domesticated in calm confidence that when the right grain was planted the wheat would appear.

Luther's *Babylonian Captivity* (1520) foreshadowed the Protestant destruction of the medieval sacramental system. This vehement treatise still stands as the foundation stone for Protestant sacraments. In the years to come Protestant reformers simply built on Luther's reduction of seven sacraments to two and his overturning of the system's whole rationalistic basis. Ironically, Luther was simply working out a thirteenth-century qualification of the sacraments, namely that they must be "instituted by Christ" himself. For twelve centuries no such qualification had been deemed necessary and Christians spoke freely about Christian burial or monastic profession as sacraments. But in the thirteenth century Thomas Aquinas had written that "God alone can institute a sacrament" (*Summa Theologiae* III, 64, 2) and Calvin echoed these words, testifying that "God alone can establish a sacrament" (*Institutes* IV, xix, 2). The Reformers were simply pushing to a logical conclusion the late medieval qualification by asking "where?" And even the Council of

Trent, while reiterating "not more or less than seven" could not specify where all could be found in Scripture.

In his work of demolition Luther swept away not only a whole theological system of fine ingenuity but also a whole structure for the pastoral care of Christians from font to tomb. Gone was the sacrament of penance but certainly not the human needs to which it ministered. The result was to turn the Eucharist even more in a penitential direction, a trend accentuated by Calvin in the fencing of the table. The scholastics had treated marriage gingerly, often listing it last, but the Reformers saw it as something not meant to "confirm a promise" of God but as one of the "lawful ordinances of God" like "farming, building, cobbling, and barbering" (*Institutes* IV, xix, 34).

Extreme unction disappeared as the Reformers saw to it that no longer do "these fellows smear with their grease not the sick but half-dead corpses" (*Institutes* IV, xix, 21). Confirmation survived only in the Anglican case but as more of a graduation exercise than an act of God. Calvin was at first tempted by ordination: "I would not go against calling the laying on of hands, by which ministers of the church are instituted into their office, a sacrament" (*Institutes* IV, xiv, 20) but ultimately he resisted since so few received it. Some of the five disappeared; others became occasional services; but all lost the character of a sacrament.

On the other hand it must be pointed out that the Reformers proclaimed a rich evangelical sense that the two remaining sacraments were based upon God's command and promise. Instead of the rationalistic distinctions of the effects of grace they preferred to speak of promises made and covenants sealed. Thus God's promise and the sign that accompanies it becomes a mystery to be received in joy and gratitude, not a work to be offered. As Luther argued of baptism and Eucharist, "only in these two do we find both the divinely instituted sign and the promise of forgiveness of sins." Luther, Calvin, and Cranmer saw these two as joyful witnesses to God's love.

Certainly it was not the intention of these Reformers that sacraments be pushed to the margin of Protestant worship. Most made it clear they expected a weekly Eucharist. The English prayerbook is designed for a weekly celebration of the Eucharist, and to give up a weekly Eucharist would have seemed absurd to Luther. But getting the laity to commune weekly proved a major obstacle where most were accustomed to receiving communion only once a year. Calvin, not without protest, conceded in Geneva to infrequent celebrations, a practice he considered defective.

The centrality of the Eucharist for most Protestants ebbed away during the sixteenth century largely due to the difficulties in accomplishing weekly communion. In Saxony a weekly Eucharist survived until late in the eighteenth century. The Enlightenment undercut what eucharistic piety and practice had survived in Protestantism. The traditional concept of sacraments as God's action seemed much too supernatural to the world of the Enlightenment. Enlightened Christians did not discard a biblical literalism which insisted that Christ commanded two sacraments and hence two such "ordinances" had to be retained rather legalistically. But they could transmute these two remaining sacraments into infrequent pious memory exercises that had a practical function in teaching people to "be good."

There is little reason in the Enlightenment theology still prevalent in American Protestantism for the sacraments to be anything else than marginal. The original theologies of the Reformed or Methodist traditions have been almost eradicated by the Enlightenment perspective that the sacraments (or ordinances) are purely contingent upon the action and feelings of the worshiper. The Reformation sense that God acts out divine promises through the use of covenant signs has vanished.

The Roman Catholic Reformation in our time comes to opposite conclusions. Ever since Pius X (1903–1914), there has been a concentrated effort to accomplish what Catholics and Protestants both failed at in the sixteenth century, the practice of frequent communion. The sacraments remain central in all the Vatican II reforms. Two-thirds of the *Constitution on the Sacred Liturgy* deals explicitly with sacramental worship. All of the developments since the Council stress the sacraments.

An important change in the recent Roman Catholic approach has been to stress the paschal nature of the sacraments. All are grounded in Christ and his work through the Church. Death and resurrection resound through the reformed rites as was never apparent in the medieval rites that the Reformers knew. Much of the late medieval penitential piety survives in Protestantism and when, in the Lord's Supper, it is overlaid with Enlightenment moralism, the sacrament often becomes a scolding exercise. ("If Christ did, why can't you?") When emphasis shifts to the paschal nature of Christ's self-giving to his people received through sacraments, the orientation of the sacraments changes from that of human action to divine. At this point the joyful command and promise that the Reformers saw in the sacraments may again surface. There are signs of a revival of sacramental life in many churches of the Reformation today, especially in revised rites and many frequent Eucharists.

The Word of God

The most positive accomplishment of the sixteenth-century Reformation was the orientation of worship, as well as the rest of life, to the word of God. The most obvious expression of this in worship was in the greatly expanded role of preaching. But that should not cause us to overlook the new emphasis on Scripture in worship in other ways. In the Reformed tradition *lectio continua* ("continuous reading") of Scripture was developed, leaving the Church year a casualty. Lutherans and Anglicans retained the weekly traditional epistles and gospels but without adding an Old Testament lection. Anglicans did, however, recover daily lections from both testaments plus psalms in morning and evening prayers. Psalmody came to the forefront in Reformed congregational song, and Luther's hymns were largely biblical paraphrases. Cranmer's prayers, too, were heaped up and pressed down with biblical imagery. Two thirds of the *Book of Common Prayer*, it is said, is from Scripture.

Some, of course, were not content. Some Anabaptists and many Puritans pressed even farther, for the dismissal from worship of anything for which explicit scriptural warrant was lacking. Such biblicism retarded for a century or more the development of English hymnody and postponed even longer the reintroduction of a modicum of ceremonial.

Preaching came to be one of the great strengths of the Reformation as it was realized how essential hearing the word of God was to the Christian. Not unrelated was the rise of literacy and printing, which made it possible for lay people to own and read Bibles and prayer books. The Reformers made it clear that preaching and prayer were essential portions of all worship services. Thus Sunday worship without the sacrament could be tolerated but Sunday worship without a sermon could not.

In modern times preaching all too often has moved in the direction of supposed relevancy and away from exegesis. Likewise the reading of Scripture declined. It is instructive to look at what happened to the admonition of the *Westminster Directory* that "ordinarily one Chapter of each Testament be read at every meeting; and sometimes more, where the Chapters be short, or the coherence of matter requireth it." Until recently many Protestant churches contented themselves with only the few verses needed to launch a sermon. Such verses, often chosen with the help of a concordance to match what the preacher wanted to say, were all the Scripture read in the service. It has been basically a "when convenient" approach to the Bible in worship, employed by both evangelicals and liberals.

One of the most conspicuous reforms in the twentieth-century reformation of worship has been the recovery of the Bible. For Protestants this has been by far the most successful of the reforms. It is indeed ironic that much of the impetus for this reform has come from Roman Catholics. The Liturgy Constitution set the stage for much of this recovery. The topic appears first in an important theological statement about the various ways Christ is present in the Eucharist. In addition to other modes of presence, Christ "is present in his word, since it is he himself who speaks when the holy Scriptures are read in the Church" (SC 7).

In a variety of ways the constitution highlights the importance of the reading of Scripture in worship and the need for preaching on it. "There is to be more reading from holy Scripture" and the sermon's "character should be that of a proclamation of God's wonderful works in the history of salvation, the mystery of Christ, ever made present and active within us" (SC 35). A classic phrase appears in paragraph 51: "The treasures of the Bible are to be opened up more lavishly, so that richer fare may be provided for the faithful at the table of God's word." Few mandates of the constitution have been fulfilled as faithfully as this one.

The result was the 1969 publication of the *Lectionary for Mass*. Never in the history of the Church has a lectionary been so carefully prepared, never has one been so widely used. Presbyterians, Lutherans, and Episcopalians adopted versions of it in 1970 as did COCU and the United Methodists in 1974. Although the use of the so-called "ecumenical lectionary" has been optional for those liturgically to the left of Lutherans and Episcopalians it has been widely adopted where no lectionary had been used previously. While I was leading a workshop in a rural Indiana county it became apparent to me that Church of the Brethren and Nazarene pastors were using the ecumenical lectionary along with churches liturgically central (Methodist, Presbyterian) and right-wing (Lutheran, Episcopal).

It is embarrassing that Roman Catholics have called many Protestants to recovering the centrality of Scripture in Sunday worship. At least one can claim the Liturgy Constitution was reflecting authentic sixteenth-century ideas in demanding more Scripture in worship. Perhaps the greatest gain for everyone has been in giving, at long last, due emphasis to the Old Testament in worship. For a thousand years the West lost the weekly recital of the old covenant. Urged in Presbyterian directories and Methodist disciplines in the past, the Old Testament reading had largely disappeared from worship in recent decades. The *Revised Common Lectionary* (1992) now enables an even better treatment of the Old Testament readings by moving away from many typological choices, especially on the Sundays after the Epiphany and Pentecost.

Protestants have rejoiced in the sudden appearance of exegetical preaching in Roman Catholic churches since Vatican II. For a period immediately after the Council, Protestant textbooks on homiletics sold briskly among Catholic seminarians. Commentaries based on the ecumenical lectionary continue to sell well regardless of denomination. Indeed, the lectionary is the most important ecumenical resource of our times. Pastors meet to do exegesis together because they are preaching from the same texts whether they be Catholic priests, Lutheran pastors, or Presbyterian ministers.

Perhaps this vigorous flowering of preaching in Roman Catholic circles in the context of sacramental worship can help Protestants regain the sacramental half of Christian worship. William Skudlarek, a Benedictine professor of homiletics, argues (in *The Word in Worship*) that the logical conclusion to the preaching of God's works is celebration of the Eucharist. One normally gives thanks for good news and Christians give thanks through the Eucharist. Far from being a threat to preaching, the Lord's Supper enhances good preaching. Thus Roman Catholics raise for Protestants the question: "Why cannot preaching flourish in a sacramental context?" Surely this is what the sixteenth-century Reformers envisioned.

Congregational Participation
A common theme of the sixteenth-century Reformation was constant effort to encourage and enable full congregational participation

in worship. In 1547 a Roman Catholic bishop noted with approval that "the people in the church took small heed what the priest and the clerks did in the chancel, but only to stand up at the Gospel and kneel at the Sacring [bell], or else every man was occupied himself severally [individually] in several prayer. And as for the priests' prayer, they could not all have heard and understood." Contrast that with the Liturgy Constitution's call for "full, conscious, and active participation in liturgical celebrations which is demanded by the very nature of the liturgy. Such participation by the Christian people . . . is their right and duty by reason of their baptism" (SC 14). The same paragraph goes on to say: "In the restoration and promotion of the sacred liturgy, this full and active participation by all the people is the aim to be considered before all else."

Martin Luther could hardly have been more forthright in drawing the connection between the priesthood of all believers and worship. Different means were found among the various Reformers to promote "full, conscious, and active participation" but it was a common goal among them. We shall look briefly at four reforms of this type in the sixteenth century and at twentieth century parallels.

The crucial reform to enable participation of the laity was the *introduction of the vernacular*. Even for Luther it took five years of hesitation before he produced this key reform in the Mass. Others preceded him but from 1525 on the verdict was unanimous: worship must be in such language "as they [the people] understande and have profite by." It was the basic reform and perhaps the only one never relinquished. But in the sixteenth century it was so successful that Rome could hardly afford to concede as much and so its liturgy was locked up in Latin for another four hundred years.

Perhaps this is why the *Constitution on the Sacred Liturgy* was still so cautious about translation. It conceded that since "the use of the mother tongue . . . frequently may be of great advantage to the people, the limits of its employment may be extended" (SC 36.2). Competent authority was "to decide whether, and to what extent, the vernacular language is to be used" (SC 36.3). A further paragraph permitted use of the mother tongue "in the first place [for] the readings and `the common prayer,' but also, as local conditions may warrant, [for] those parts which pertain to the people" (SC 54). Within five years all such restrictions disappeared and Latin had become as remote from Roman Catholic parishes as from Lutheran.

The move to the vernacular, and a twentieth-century vernacular at that, had repercussions for Protestants. The 1970 Presbyterian *Worshipbook* was one of the first full service books to reflect the linguistic changes Roman Catholics had brought about in worship. We all were forced to question our own worship language and found none of us could go home again to the safely familiar. Archaic English in worship was rejected by many denominations in the course of the 1970s.

But once this decision was behind us we found our perplexities had just begun. A living language does not stand still. No one meant to be exclusive in 1970, but the *Worshipbook* was branded "sexist" by 1980. On this issue conservatives see no need for change; moderates would amend language about "man" and remove pronouns for the deity; radicals would eliminate even "Father," "Lord," and "King." A living language leads to constant fluctuation.

Closely related to the question of language was the need to *make common prayer possible for all the people*. One method was to produce prayerbooks in the vernacular. The price of the first *Book of Common Prayer* was regulated so that people could afford copies. The more radical elements of the Reformation moved away from books altogether and encouraged the laity to present testimonies and prayers spontaneously. But for all the Reformers prayer meant the listening, if not reading, speaking, or singing, participation of the whole congregation. Unfortunately this sometimes gave an opportunity for ministers to make prayer didactic. The desire to make worship do something useful does not originate with revivalism (conversion) or the Enlightenment (moral instruction) or even the Reformation (theological catechesis, congregational discipline). But yielding to these last temptations has tended to make the Reformed tradition the most cerebral form of Christian worship. Worship always suffers when made "useful."

The Liturgy Constitution also mandated recovery of "the common prayer" or "prayer of the faithful" (SC 53) at Mass. The result has been a surprising combination of both spontaneous and set forms. Thus the insights of both Puritan and Anglican are often conjoined. Various efforts to recover corporate prayer are a crucial part of overcoming the spiritual starvation of much Protestant worship. It is frightening to visit a church that has introduced puppets but has overlooked corporate prayer. Such dereliction surpasses as an apostasy the abandoning of Scripture.

A third effort to achieve congregational participation in the sixteenth century involved the *simplification of services*. As Cranmer complained, often "there was more busines to fynd out what should be read, then to read it when it was founde out." If the clergy were confused, the people were more so. The complexity of rites was reduced drastically and much of the disagreement among the Reformers concerned what could safely be discarded. Pruning continued until the Quakers had abolished all structure and ceremonial. Purification and simplification mark every Reformation liturgy.

Vatican II recognized such a need: in order to encourage "active participation," "the rites are to be simplified, . . . elements which, with the passage of time, came to be duplicated, or were added with but little advantage, are now to be discarded" (SC 50). The last gospel at Mass was one of the first additions to disappear but other simplifications came in time. Decisions as to what was essential and what was superfluous could be made on the basis of carefully-thought-out theological, historical, and pastoral concerns. Protestants have not always had the opportunity to separate essentials from other matters. Liturgical surgery must excise with a skilled hand, not with impatience.

Finally, many of the Reformation's accomplishments with promoting full participation relied on changes made in *music and church architecture*. The chief thing the Reformers did with church music was to make it accessible to a much greater portion of the congregation. Hymnody in Lutheran and Anabaptist circles and psalmody among the Reformed, Anglicans, and Puritans brought congregational song into prominence. Congregations, long mute, could now voice their worship in song. A whole new dimension of participation had been added to worship.

No doubt the weakest portion of the *Constitution on the Sacred Liturgy* is that which deals with Church music (Chapter 6). A prolonged debate ensued after the Council among Catholic musicians about the nature of Church music. It seems to have been resolved largely in favor of congregational participation over professional performance. The publication of *Music in Catholic Worship* in 1972 has remedied some of the weaknesses of the constitution. An advantage of observing the debate has been to make Protestants think through the relative claims of congregational song and choral music. Probably choirs are underused, but too often they subvert full congregational participation rather than making it possible.

The Reformation also saw major adjustments in church architecture. Not many new churches were built before the seventeenth century, but thousands of medieval ones were redesigned to make Protestant worship feasible. The chief thrust was to make hearing possible for all. This implied moving services out of the chancel, adding balconies, moving to a more centralized plan, and adding a prominent pulpit.

The Liturgy Constitution is hardly helpful on church architecture, a defect remedied by the superb American publication, *Environment and Art in Catholic Worship* (1978). A wholesale remodeling of churches very similar to that of the sixteenth century has led to small freestanding altar-tables cleared of all accumulations. Pulpits have become more prominent and hearing has become a major concern. The ideal architectural setting for Catholic and Protestant worship has become virtually the same. More recent concerns have focused on the design and location of baptismal fonts or pools.

Conclusion

Liturgical reform is not something safely filed away in the Church history textbooks. It is an ever-present reality in which both the accomplishments and failures of the sixteenth century still shape much of how we think and act about worship. But the liturgical reformation of the twentieth century has just as much claim upon us. Roman Catholicism has accepted many of the claims of the Protestant Reformation and recalled Protestants to them. But Catholicism has also gone beyond much of the sixteenth century and in so doing has called Protestants to come along too. Liturgical reformation in the twentieth century does not accept the tight denominational compartmentalization of the sixteenth; it belongs to all regardless of respective labels. All can contribute; all can receive. And so all ought to rejoice.

4. A Good Word for William Dowsing

Some of the realities of the situation of this article have faded by now, but not all. Revised from the original in *Theology Today* 18 (July 1961) and used by permission.

Few ardent Christians have been so sincerely despised as William Dowsing, the Puritan iconoclast. Dowsing began his short but spectacular career in 1643 armed with a commission from the Earl of Manchester for the destruction of "all Crucifixes, Crosses & all Images of any one or more persons of the Trinity . . . & all other Images & pictures of Saints & superstitious inscriptions." He undertook his visitation of the churches of Cambridgeshire and Suffolk, and before the year 1644 had ended he had purged scores of churches and chapels, carefully recording his work of destructiveness in a journal. The entry for the Church of All Hallows, Sudbury, is typical: "We brake about 20 superstitious Pictures, and took up 30 brazen superstitious Inscriptions, *ora pro nobis*, and *pray for the soul & c.*" "Superstitious pictures" received most of Dowsing's attention, and dozens of pictures of "God the father siting in a Chayer," crucifixes, angels, bishops, saints, and many a "popish inscription" were demolished or obliterated. Dowsing did a thorough job of destruction and one can easily tell the churches and chapels in the two counties that escaped his depredations.

Dowsing as Reformer

For more than three centuries lovers of medieval art have called Dowsing a rascal and a philistine. Fortunately he probably was not above taking a bribe to spare a church, but he certainly wasn't insensible to beauty. In the church at Ufford, Suffolk, Dowsing noted: "There is a glorious Cover over the Font, like a Pope's Triple Crown." The same font cover still remains intact today, its beauty widely recognized. Baptism was not a theological issue in England at this time. Dowsing destroyed medieval art not because it was beautiful, but because it possessed such great power in communicating ideas. He actually gave evidence of a much higher respect for art than many modern art lovers reveal. Dowsing had a very high view of the potency—for good or for bad—of the medieval art in the churches and chapels of England. And Dowsing, Puritan that he was, considered much of this art and its ideas patently dangerous.

Because this art possessed such a potency, diverting people from the proper worship of Almighty God and interfering with the maintenance of true doctrine, it obviously had to go. Stained glass was smashed not because of its beauty, but because it was such a powerful exponent of the invocation of the saints. Medieval art was a valiant antagonist of those who worked to complete the Reformation. It was not a museum piece. Indeed, had museums existed the Puritans could have found no surer way of destroying the power of medieval art than by shipping it off to museums. Safely buried in galleries, divorced from the life of the parish, the art of the medieval Church truly would have been dead. Dowsing simply took the more direct method; he raised his ladder and went to work with his axe.

If Will Dowsing could return today, the actions of his religious descendants would puzzle him. Not only do twentieth-century Protestants have no fear of the potency of art, they seem completely unaware of it. Instead, they generally demand that their churches be filled with those "images & pictures" which Dowsing felt so ominous. Dozens of large firms specialize in providing stained glass, carved woodwork, and countless varieties of painting and sculpture for the adornment of Protestant churches. Whatever one thinks of the quality of much of this output there can be no question of the fact that the amount of it has become enormous.

But there is a great difference between this art and the art that troubled Dowsing. Art is used in the modern church because it is decorative. With very few exceptions the potency of art as a theological force has been completely ignored. Art in modern Protestantism is safe because it has become so thoroughly tamed and domesticated. Dowsing would be considered a fanatic now, for no one believes that these painted or carved symbols possess any real power. They are totally dissociated from the life of congregations except as ornamentation for the churches we build or remodel.

The Situation Today

Actually such a situation is quite new to most of American Protestantism outside of the Lutheran tradition. Firm resistance to all visual symbols characterized Protestants in the last century. It is hardly remembered now that Anglicans were shocked by the introduction of crosses in their churches a century ago and that in 1851 the Bishop of Manchester personally destroyed the stained glass and sculpture with which one of his congregations had indiscreetly decorated their church. The change began in England, largely due to the efforts of the Ecclesiological Society which flourished from 1839 until 1868. Two Americans loom large in overcoming the suspicions of twentieth-century Protestants about art. Ralph Adams Cram (1863–1942) was an architect, a writer, and a staunch Anglo-Catholic. A convinced gothicist, he sometimes lapsed into other styles for Protestant clients. He loved to boast that one great gothic edifice he built for Presbyterians could be readied for high Mass in a few minutes. Even more influential than Cram's buildings were the score of eloquent books in which he sang the praises of beautiful churches fully adorned by all the visual arts.

The other great twentieth-century apostle of art and religion, Von Ogden Vogt (1879–1964), was minister of the First Unitarian Church in Chicago for twenty years. Through his work as a minister, a seminary teacher, and a writer, Vogt's views on the unity of religion and art became very influential. Scores of other writers and teachers completed the task of impressing upon the Protestant mind the desirability of art in the place where they worshiped. Many of the great Protestant churches built during the 1920s and 1930s were lavishly decorated with carved, painted, or glazed visual symbols of every kind.

Present-day taste is perhaps more restrained, but few new churches are built without being embellished with stained glass, carved panels, or even some painting. Almost as soon as the building has been completed, the minister or building committee produces a pamphlet describing and explaining the symbols employed. So common has the practice become that we fail to realize how extraordinary an example it is of putting the cart before the horse. The symbols have to be explained to the congregation. The church is virtually a museum, handing out guides to new acquisitions. The very fact that the symbols have to be explained to the congregation is good evidence that they are meaningless to it. Had these visual images sprung out of the life of the Church, had they participated in the same reality as the Church itself, had they conveyed the presence of the supernatural, they would need no explanation. But such spontaneity has been lost. Most likely the symbols were culled from one of the spate of recent books on Christian symbolism. Or perhaps worse, they were simply ordered from a church goods catalogue.

Dowsing would find very little to do today. There is plenty of "religious art" in our churches, but it has become completely innocuous so that it is now quite safe. The visual symbols have little meaning or spontaneity. At one period in our national history, visual symbols had these qualities. After the Revolution, furniture, buildings, coins, and other articles were emblazoned with images of Liberty, eagles, the flag, and George Washington. These symbols represented an exciting reality to the Americans of 1790 just as the hosts of saints ready to intercede for them had to the worshipers of the Middle Ages. But the textbook symbols of the modern Church are quite different. They do not grow directly out of something experienced, but out of a second-hand reality. They tend to be esoteric or antiquarian. In short, they are almost meaningless.

These tired old symbols are well represented by two secular symbols that share the skyline of the small midwestern town where I once taught. Above the court house is the usual statue of blindfolded justice holding the balances. To most of our townspeople justice is a remote concept we take for granted but that has little concrete meaning in our daily lives. The statue, in short, means little to our average citizen. But above the county jail there is a symbol that has the greatest significance to its few inmates. This symbol is a giant key, symbolizing in a rather perverse way the freedom they are denied. It is a meaningful symbol to those affected by it. Justice does not convey such a crucial significance to the townspeople for whom it is merely a theory.

Art as Power

The question arises, "who killed Cock Robin?" Why is it that the symbols we have in such abundance, glazed in every church window, stitched on every altar hanging, and carved on many a pulpit have lost all potency? Largely this stems from the fact that when

Protestants did return to the use of visual symbols they were resuscitated from the dead. They were merely antiquarian specimens. Religious art and symbolism became largely the cult of the esoteric. Medieval religious art had been strong because it represented a faith directly experienced. For people who depended on the intercession of the saints for their daily survival, representations of the saints possessed great power. But for modern Protestants who consider the saints remote figures with interesting legends (not all true, of course) the presence of saints is purely decorative.

Will Dowsing would be bored today. The symbols in our churches possess no dangerous potency. There is no need to smash what is merely a matter of taste, and this is what religious art in the service of the Church has largely become. But perhaps we might learn something yet from Dowsing. After all, he took art seriously, much more seriously than as a mere matter of taste. He lived in a time when the old symbols had become inadequate. To Dowsing's mind the art of the medieval Church, peopled with intercessors between humans (elect or not) and God, with references to purgatory rather than to an eternal decree, made powerful statements, though faulty. And so in his own crude but effective way Dowsing was a theologian. His task, accomplished with hammer and hatchet, was a theological one—defending humanity's true knowledge of God as the Puritans knew it.

And the theological task continues. Fortunately in our day it has become largely a constructive one. Is it possible that once again art can express the vigor and vitality of the Christian message? The best of contemporary art has demonstrated an extraordinary evocative power, reflecting much of the potency that offended Dowsing in medieval art. Perhaps now the time has come for the Church to make a positive acceptance of the genuine art of the twentieth century.

The work of Dowsing was necessary in his time. Unfortunately his successors forgot this and tried to revive the old symbols and forms. Today we need new iconoclasts to rid us of art that is dead in order that we may attain a truly religious art. Far better to destroy art than merely to decorate with it. It is noteworthy that the new churches built with the most theological consideration (mostly Lutheran) have been very reticent in their use of any symbols. A few, very few, have cared to take the next step—to work toward a utilization of the potency of contemporary art in stating beliefs and in mediating the presence of the holy. Perhaps some day soon we will come to as high an esteem of the power of art as that which Dowsing had. And then we will really be able to use it in a constructive fashion.

5. Writing the History of English Worship

Written long ago for *Church History* 47 (1978), this has become freshly relevant with the reissue in 1996 by Eerdmans of all five volumes of Davies' *Worship and Theology in England* plus the addition of a sixth volume. Used by permission.

These are days of small books and single volumes. Multivolume sets are a rare and endangered species. The advent of the sixth volume of Horton Davies' *Worship and Theology In England* caps a major and unprecedented achievement by a scholar now (1995) in his eightieth year. Never before has the worship life of an entire people for four and one-third centuries received such a balanced and careful scrutiny. Five decades of research have borne plentiful and rich fruit. This work of the Emeritus Henry W. Putnam Professor of Religion at Princeton University marks an achievement in liturgical studies unequalled by living scholars in the English-speaking world.

Although the five volumes are sequential, Volume Three was the first to appear (in 1961). Subtitled *From Watts and Wesley to Maurice, 1690–1850*, it covered the most years yet in shortest space (355 pages). Its successor, Volume Four, *From Newman to Martineau, 1850–1900* appeared the following year. Third came Volume Five, in 1965, *The Ecumenical Century, 1900–1965*, too soon to catch the post-Vatican II excitement. The year 1970 saw the publication of Volume One, *From Cranmer to Hooker, 1534–1603*. And 1975 brought a return to first and last loves; Volume Two is entitled *From Andrews to Baxter and Fox, 1603–1690* and totals 592 pages. It picks up a theme Professor Davies treated so well in 1948 in *The Worship of the English Puritans*, certainly one of the most useful works on Christian worship in recent decades. Twenty years later, as one untimely born, comes Volume Six, bringing the story down to the present.

The pages of *Worship and Theology in England* comprise a magnificent *summa* of scholarly writing on English worship since the Reformation. One can only marvel at the vast amount of research, much original and much secondary, that Professor Davies has used. By comparison, writing the history of worship in this country has scarcely begun. A vast array of monographs and dissertations must appear prior to a comprehensive history of worship and theology in the United States. Such a synthetic work probably cannot be produced in this century although I would love to attempt it.

Although Professor Davies does not argue this case he goes a long way to prove how central the history of worship is to the history of Christianity. One is reminded of Beauduin's famous phrase that liturgy is "the theology of the people." Page after page contains evidence that the theology absorbed by the person in the pew (and at times it was a considerable amount) came largely through the medium of worship. Professor Davies provides constant documentation for the folk theology of generations of the English. Occasional vignettes of diverse individuals call attention to the varying spiritualities of time and denominations. Worship, he shows, was an important agent in forming different types of piety.

One could argue that the series might well be called "Worship and Culture in England." It emphasizes worship rather than academic theology. There are some strange omissions even of theological discussions that concerned worship; Bishop Hoadly is hardly mentioned, Daniel Waterland never. The Gorham Case and the Denison Case share a paragraph; the debate over auricular confession does not get that much. Volume Four contains a chapter on late Victorian theology and Volume Five has two chapters on twentieth-century English theology. Though these are helpful in providing background they almost seem intruders in the narrative. The real theology of the series is the lay theology composed of what lay people were hearing, saying, and doing week after week when they attended church. Some of this is as much social and political history as it is theological, reminiscent of Nikolaus Pevsner's delightful book, *The Englishness of English Art*. On many pages we hear the Englishness of English worship. Where else could the cry "No popery!" lead a witch-hunt within a national Church? Where else could two archbishops of the same Church be put to death, one protesting that he was a good Catholic (Cranmer), the other that he died a good Protestant (Laud)? Worship and culture are the real themes of the books.

High marks must go to the comprehensiveness with which Professor Davies describes all the major traditions in worship from

Roman Catholic to Quaker. One does feel a bit cheated that the Muggletonians and Fifth Monarchy Men do not receive attention but the lasting traditions come out well. Some highly original material emerges in the treatment of Unitarian worship. Each tradition is treated in an appreciative fashion. Usually the temptation to depreciate one and exalt another is successfully resisted. Especially valuable is the sensitive understanding of how groups react and relate to each other. Negative attitudes about each other gradually give way to mutual appreciation in the final volume.

The volumes written more recently move in a more synthetic direction, enabling the reader to make fascinating comparisons of the positions of people in different traditions on topics as diverse as the Christian year, Church music, or sacramental theology. In this sense Volume Two is probably the most successful volume and also contains the most detailed research, though the concluding summary is disappointing. Volume Five is probably second in value; it brings together in a comprehensive way the extraordinarily varied movements of the first two-thirds of the twentieth century. Somehow it manages to do this without being gossipy, the danger in writing recent liturgical history. An unsurpassed treatment of the respective values of fixed vs. free prayer occurs at 3.27–30.

Professor Davies' work is certainly ambitious in scope. We need to analyze his success in carrying out such a mission. Despite some caveats I find his account solid, competent, and thorough. There are some built-in problems in having to restrict his scope to England and consequently ignoring his native Wales or Scotland (where he studied Arts and Divinity). This cramps the story of the Westminster Assembly or the history of English Presbyterianism, to say nothing of the relation of the Roman Congregation of Sacred Rites to English Roman Catholic worship. But it also shows how insular English worship really is, and his primary objective, chronicling worship within a national setting, is extremely well done.

Indeed, the writing is fascinating. Professor Davies' vocabulary would make William F. Buckley proud (or rather, prouder). Sprinkled throughout are insightful *bons mots*: "It is a short step from the inner light to the outer darkness" (2.519). Delightful aphorisms abound in summary passages: (of preaching) "in Whitefield there was more heat than light; in Wesley more light than heat" (3.146). Repetition is a problem occasionally (3.119; 4.19), perhaps inevitably so, but the books read amazingly well for over two thousand pages.

One of the highest marks must go for the use of nonverbal documentation. Since worship demands the public use of spaces, sounds, and actions it is indeed perilous to limit the study of Christian worship to the history of rites. Professor Davies consistently uses church architecture, Church music, and accounts of ceremonial as basic documents. The English still use "ecclesiology" in its original sense as the science of church architecture. Each volume of this series shows what a valuable tool ecclesiology is in unraveling the meaning of worship in different times or places. It well may be that Sir Christopher Wren was the most significant theologian of seventeenth-century England. His organization of liturgical space is still determinative for the worship life of thousands of congregations. Photographs are valuable assets in each volume, but I wished for floor plans as well, since they are so useful in identifying alterations in liturgical arrangements. Volume Five discusses the cultic arts more fully than the others and includes a detailed and appreciative, though not uncritical, analysis of Coventry Cathedral.

Church music or its absence is carefully recorded, especially in the first and fifth volumes. The same care goes into chronicling changes in styles of preaching. Possibly the best chapter in the whole series is that in Volume Three on "The Methodist Revolution in Popular Preaching: The Techniques of Wesley and Whitefield." Each volume contains important chapters on preaching based on original research, but it is somewhat disappointing that at certain points the author speaks of preaching as opposed to worship or as a "supplement" rather than as an integral part and one of the modes of Christ's presence in worship.

For a work of such length, there is an astonishingly high level of accuracy. Only a few minor errors have crept in. In 3.33 one should read "Walter Farquhar Hook," not "Theodore Hooker." The 1614 *Rituale Romanum* did not intend to terminate baptism of infants by immersion (2.476). Early editions contain a second rubric telling how to do it but this is usually omitted in twentieth-century translations. Intinction and the mixed chalice are confused (4.125). More distinction ought to be made between the medieval ideals of the Cambridge Movement and the ideals of the Oxford Movement that reached, instead, to the early Church and the Caroline divines (3.277). The summary of Brilioth (5.36) omits the decisive stress on presence or mystery.

Each volume contains an excellent bibliography and very helpful indices which show that the author has consulted all the major authorities on each topic he addresses. Obviously the volumes published in 1961, 1962, and 1965 miss recent scholarship such as G. J. Cuming's *A History of The Anglican Liturgy* (1969) and many specialized scholarly works. But all the standard authorities have been used extensively. This is at once a source of greatest strength and yet the most critical thing one can say about the books. Much of the series reads with a sense of *déja vu* to anyone familiar with this literature. Rarely does Davies criticize others' conclusions; his evaluation of Tillotson (2.300) is an exception. When authorities differ he considers disagreements with sound judgment and good sense. Occasionally he reduces disputes to too-vivid contrasts (1.69) or too neat categorizations (1.80). The reader will look in vain for any startling new hypotheses or new theories. Much of this ground, particularly Anglicanism, has been plowed many times before and now could lie fallow. The books are tame and well cultivated, maybe the quintessence of "Englishism," but one could wish for more adventuresome new theories.

Perhaps the reader's discontent points to the question of whether liturgical scholars, especially in England, ask the right questions. There is a long and distinguished school in English liturgical studies dating back to John Mason Neale. Most of its scholarship dealt either with questions of ceremonial or the comparative details of rites. Rarely did it ask the broader questions of how these fitted into what the total Christian community was experiencing. Although most students have abandoned the temporarily popular approach of McLuhan they recognize that the invention of the mass-produced book changed worship irrevocably. The maximum price of the first *Book of Common Prayer* was fixed by law so that the common people could afford it. The very notion that "the whole realm shall have but one use" or the Roman Catholic standardizing of the Missal down to the last comma (probably resulting in the loss of the China mission) are consequences of technical discoveries as much as theological ones. I do not think that liturgical scholars can afford today to ignore the history of technology though they certainly must not accept popular theories uncritically.

We need to address the broader questions, then, as well as the details. The greatest mystery of the English Reformation in worship is why the Mass, the weekly worship of Christians for sixteen centuries, disappeared as the normal Sunday service. The substitution of non-sacramental worship for sacramental worship is surely the most important change in the English Reformation, far more significant than the change to the vernacular or even the change in the contents of the worship. It is all the more remarkable for being unintentional. The prayer books with their weekly collects, epistles, and gospels certainly suggest weekly Eucharists, not thrice-yearly celebrations.

At this point these volumes are disappointing. They fail to give us any clue as to why sixteen centuries of sacramental worship were exchanged for non-sacramental. Professor Davies does give convincing documentation that for two centuries many Puritans and Dissenters were accustomed to monthly Eucharists while most of the rest of the Established Church was content with communion three times a year. Surely this sacramental drought needs extensive explanation.

Similarly, Protestant scholars are apt to overlook the rest of the sacramental system. References are made occasionally to weddings, ordinations, and funerals throughout these volumes. But what did it mean to the average Christian to discover suddenly that the sacrament of penance no longer existed, that there was no way to be shriven of one's sins with the certainty of an *ego te absolvo* spoken by one's parish priest? What deep human need had the sacrament of penance filled that suddenly went unfilled? Such needs do not disappear; they are transferred. Is it any wonder that the Eucharist became a penitential service in Anglican, Reformed, and Free Church circles? A generation later the reasons for this transferral would be forgotten, but in the meantime had not the Eucharist been irretrievably bent in a direction that made it a somber time for introspection? Certainly other elements in late medieval piety had contributed to this somber individualistic approach to the Eucharist. I think one can make a strong case that the Eucharist has had to be two sacraments in Anglicanism and Protestantism ever since the sacrament of penance was ousted. And what did it mean to the dying person to know that there was no *viaticum*, no apostolic blessing on the way out? The sacraments are a connected system and we make mistakes in dealing only with two.

Much liturgical scholarship in recent years has turned to the pursuit of liturgical theology or, more correctly, a theology of the liturgy. Here pride of place belongs to the eucharistic prayer which is a crucial *locus theologicus*. Increasingly we realize that the Church has no older or more important form of doctrinal statement than the eucharistic prayer, which preceded written gospels or epistles. Inevitably, in a Jewish milieu, such prayer was proclamation of the *mirabilia Dei*. It was a sign that the Jewish roots had been forgotten when creeds were later introduced into the Mass, else they would have been immediately recognized as blatantly redundant. Now it is true that such awareness was not present in the Reformation or until recently. When one recognizes the eucharistic prayer as the Church's supreme proclamation of its faith, entrusted only to a representative bishop or presbyter, it becomes a very valuable tool for understanding the theology of those who wrote and used it, even though unaware of its full significance. (Unfortunately Professor Davies calls it by its 1662 misnomer, "The Prayer of Consecration.") But some exciting possibilities could have been developed by analyzing some of the key eucharistic prayers of this period: 1549, Baxter's liturgy, 1928, and others. That would have helped put the "theology" back in the title in the way it really belongs. Worship is the only time most Christians hear and make deliberate theological statements. The observer who wants to hear their theology as it is articulated and acted out must observe their worship, especially the eucharistic prayer.

It is a great problem for anyone involved in liturgical studies to decide whether the discipline is purely descriptive or also normative. Professor Davies clearly intends to be descriptive. He is rarely critical of groups although he makes scathing remarks about the "school of spontaneity" during his childhood (5.35off.). He occasionally does slip into normative statements such as the reference to restoring "the weekly celebration of the Sacrament to its rightful position" (4.164–165). And there are frequent references to the Scottish *Book of Common Order* of 1940 as a kind of high water mark of liturgical rectitude, (5.381). Is it possible to write liturgical history without slipping into normative statements? Probably not; ethicists often tip their hand by the very topics they choose.

When all is said and done, writing the history of worship is a most demanding task. One can narrate the verbal and visual artifacts with some dexterity. But there is always the haunting fear that one cannot depict that inward and spiritual grace with the same clarity as one can the outward and visible signs of it. Fundamentally we are addressing deep human needs and how they are realized and ministered to in a public way—in short, the intercourse between Christians and God. And that is not amenable to the way scholars normally proceed with their research. Indeed, liturgical studies may be the only truly blasphemous discipline. Rather than taking off our shoes, we are tempted to measure the distance to the burning bush. There are limitations of the discipline.

Within those limitations Professor Davies has operated extremely successfully to place us all enormously in his debt. These six volumes will remain as an important landmark of twentieth-century liturgical scholarship.

6. Worship and Culture: Mirror or Beacon?

This paper resulted from a conference in Scottsdale, Arizona in December 1973, at which the foundations for the North American Academy of Liturgy were laid. It was published in *Theological Studies* 35 (June 1974) and is used by permission with minor revisions.

In December 1973 a number of us had the good fortune to hear an address by Walter J. Burghardt, S.J., on the occasion of the tenth anniversary of Vatican II's *Constitution on the Sacred Liturgy*. His address was later published in *Theological Studies* 35 (June 1974), as "A Theologian's Challenge to Liturgy." In his address, Father Burghardt touched on some of the key issues of liturgical reform since Vatican II in a provocative and highly original fashion. I would like what follows to be considered as an extended footnote to his remarks, with the hope of documenting some of the problems and clarifying the nature of others.

Since Vatican II the word "indigenization" has been a popular term among those concerned about worship, yet the perspective of ten years has shown us how elusive a goal this is. I hope to use some historical examples to raise questions about indigenization. Basically the issues seem to be: "How far do you go in worship in reflecting a culture without simply being a mirror of it?" or "How much is it desirable to shed light on a culture by being a beacon shining from a distance?" Those of us who live in the South have frequent opportunity to observe just how much Southern folk religion reflects in its worship all the limitations and glories of local culture. It is sometimes difficult to tell a naturalization ceremony in the courthouse from a service at a Southern Baptist church. But for those who remember the Middle Ages in Catholic worship (before December 1963) worship disjoined from culture may not be a very happy memory.

One of the most helpful discussions of the relation between Christianity and culture appears in a series of lectures H. Richard

Niebuhr gave in 1949 and published two years later as *Christ and Culture*.[1] Defining culture as "the total process of human activity and the total result of such activity,"[2] Niebuhr goes on to distinguish and illustrate five typologies of the relation of Christ to culture: "Christ against culture," "the Christ of culture," "Christ above culture," "Christ and culture in paradox," and "Christ the transformer of culture." Most of my readers are familiar with his brilliant exposition of these concepts. I cannot possibly do justice to them here. But I would like to give a few examples of how some of these typologies might be applied to looking critically at the problem of indigenization in worship. Most of the application of Protestant theological thinking to the life of the Church in the twentieth century has gone into ethical studies rather than liturgical. So we might do well to appropriate some of the categories the ethicists have developed, especially since we both deal with activities of the Body of Christ. I shall take only two of Niebuhr's categories, "Christ against culture" and "the Christ of culture," and try to exemplify some of the merits and disadvantages of each. One soon realizes that nothing fits these very neatly, yet they do provide useful bins into which to toss our descriptions.

Christ Against Culture

A good example of the "Christ against culture" approach may be seen in an extraordinary chapter in Anglican worship during the nineteenth century in England when an effort was made to return as much as possible to the visible forms of medieval worship. The amazing thing is that it could happen in England and then be transported to America, where it ran against all the main cultural currents of the time. Yet such is the story of the Cambridge Movement of the 1840s.

In 1839 a small group of students at Cambridge University founded the Cambridge Camden Society (afterwards named the Ecclesiological Society) "to promote the study of Ecclesiastical Architecture and Antiquities and the restoration of mutilated Architectural remains."[3] This may have sounded innocent enough. The pursuit of their newly-discovered science of ecclesiology, which

[1]New York, 1951.
[2]Ibid., 32.
[3]*Report of the Cambridge Camden Society for MDCCCXLII* (Cambridge, 1842) 44.

the Cambridge men defined as the inductive study of church building and church arrangement, appeared to many to be only a pleasant pastime. But these followers were mistaken. Ecclesiology soon turned out to be an attempt to make a change in the whole ethos of Anglican worship, beginning with church architecture and ending with tremendous impact on church music, vestments, ceremonial, and the mentality underlying worship itself. The journal of the Society, the *Ecclesiologist*, soon decided it could deal with "the general science of Ecclesiology, under which they [the Society] consider that Ritualism is legitimately included."[4] The scope of the Cambridge Camden Society's activities is indicated in one of its publications, *Hierurgia Anglicana:* "Let us endeavour to restore everywhere amongst us Daily Prayers, and (at the least) weekly Communion; the proper Eucharistick vestments, lighted and vested altars, the ancient tones of Prayer and Praise, frequent Offertories, the meet celebration of Fasts and Festivals."[5]

This may sound presumptuous for a small body of undergraduates and their adherents, a group that never numbered more than nine hundred people. But modesty was never their shortcoming. They accomplished two extraordinary things: they changed the outward appearance of Anglican worship for a hundred years, and they did it in defiance of many of the strongest cultural trends of England and America. We need to reflect briefly on these accomplishments.

To turn Anglican worship around, to reverse its post-Reformation development by leapfrogging back into the medieval past, was a high order for anyone, but not for the zealous Cambridge men. It is rarely realized today how "low church" Anglican worship was in the 1830s. Since communion was infrequent the altar often served as a place for the clergy to put their hats; congregational hymnody was unknown; chancels were considered a useless expense in new church buildings and often boarded off in old ones; candles and crosses on the altar were regarded as dangerous badges of popery that could cause riots; and eucharistic vestments were unheard of. In 1874 the Public Worship Regulation Act was passed to end what Disraeli called "mass in masquerade" and under it four clergymen went to jail for such extravagances as the use of vestments and communion wafers.

[4]"Eighth Anniversary Meeting," *Ecclesiologist* 7 (1847) 234.
[5]*Hierurgia Anglicana* (London, 1848) v.

The Cambridge men, or Ecclesiologists as I prefer to call them, launched a fervent attack via dozens of pamphlets and books. They began by popularizing their "science" of ecclesiology. But it soon became apparent that they were not interested just in studying all old churches; Sir Christopher Wren's churches and their successors were not considered worthy of study. No, it was medieval churches alone that were worth consideration. Thousands of people were persuaded to fill out detailed church schemes based on observation of a medieval church building. To do so they were often induced to read *A Few Hints on the Practical Study of Ecclesiastical Antiquities*[6] or the *Hand-Book of English Ecclesiology*,[7] both publications of the Society. This we would today call a process of consciousness-raising. It is amazing how many were intrigued by such a pastime.

Various other publications followed but the most important was a translation of a thirteenth-century work published under the title *The Symbolism of Churches and Church Ornaments: A Translation of the First Book of the Rationale Divinorum Officiorum, Written by William Durandus, Sometime Bishop of Mende.*[8] This book materially changed the course of ecclesiology both by its contents and by the 121–page introductory essay, "Sacramentality: A Principle of Ecclesiastical Design." The translators of Durandus and authors of this essay were two of the key leaders of the Cambridge Movement, John Mason Neale and Benjamin Webb. They attempted to give a philosophical basis to the movement and, though they showed any critical reader that philosophy was not "their thing," they convinced many that churches ought to be cruciform, that church architects ought to be holy men, and that everything in a church reeked of symbolism. So to this day building committees still want three windows "for the Trinity."

The Ecclesiologists were convinced that only Gothic is true Christian architecture, but it was far from that simple: "The Decorated or Edwardian style, that employed, we mean, between the years 1260 and 1360, is that to which only, except for some very peculiar circumstances, we ought to return."[9] It was conceded that while

[6]Cambridge, 1839.
[7]London, 1848.
[8]Leeds, 1843.
[9]*A Few Words to Church Builders* (3d ed. Cambridge, 1844) 6.

"second-rate architects may, for a few years yet, employ Romanesque or revived Pagan, those who are at the head of their profession will be guilty of such serious errours no longer."[10] This was not merely a matter of aesthetics; the period, they felt, had been one of great piety. A decline in piety and the growth of Erastianism had led to less glorious church architecture.

Medieval churches, then, were to be the model for nineteenth-century Anglican worship, despite the evolution of distinctive building types for prayer-book worship during the intervening centuries. It was proclaimed that "ancient churches should . . . be exactly copied as models for new ones."[11] The highest praise the Ecclesiologists could accord a new church building was that it might be mistaken for an old one.

The most important single feature of these buildings was that they have a "distinct Chancel, *at least* one-third of the length of the Nave" and separated from it by a chancel arch, a screen, or raised floor. This led to a further and rather basic problem: what to do with such additional space as a chancel provided, space Anglicans had lived quite happily without for several centuries. Of course there were no communities of religious, no minor clerics, to fill up these vast chancels. But an answer was at hand, that of filling up the chancel with a choir of lay people, of dressing them in surplices, and treating them as pseudo-clerics. It was a curious case of function following form, of a form being imposed and then a purpose devised for it. And Anglican churches until very recently have reflected this same twofold space, a nave for people and a chancel for clergy and choir.

It was, in short, a reversal of just about everything worship in the post-Reformation Church of England meant. Clericalism was highlighted in separating the clergy from the laity by placing them in two separate and not very equal spaces. The common prayer was more and more performed by clergy and choir for the benefit of a reverent audience. Choral music was made a part of worship in even the smallest parish church, and all manner of carved, glazed, and painted art proliferated throughout the building.

Neale himself initiated a major change in Anglican worship, congregational hymn singing, despite the charge that it was

[10]Ibid., 5.
[11]"Ancient Models," *Ecclesiologist* 3 (1843) 134.

"Methodistical snuffling." A master of twenty languages, Neale translated scores of medieval hymns, many of which are still found in modern hymnals. Church choirs were welcomed, too, now that there was a need to fill the chancel, though Neale had once referred to them as "the pest of the parish." Neale, despite his brilliance, was far from judicious, and Webb's contribution of tolerant and moderate judgment was a necessary balance.

Eucharistic vestments were virtually unknown in Anglicanism at the time. Neale began wearing a chasuble in 1850 and because of this (and other such outrageous practices) his bishop refused to allow him to minister in the diocese. He was also in the forefront in founding religious orders, establishing the Sisters of St. Margaret in 1855. Such extremism led to riots and an attempt to burn the home for the aged where he ministered.

These changes were not accomplished without violent resistance. The chief charge, of course, was that medievalism was popery. While heresy does not particularly trouble the English, popery does. So the Ecclesiologists were fair game for anyone who wanted to decry popery, and many people did. A stone altar the Ecclesiologists had placed in a church in Cambridge became the focus of court suits until it was replaced by a wooden table. And a tract entitled *The Restoration of Churches Is the Restoration of Popery*,[12] a November 5 sermon by Francis Close, a minister in Cheltenham, caused great furor. In four editions Close rang the alarm against "incipient, insidious, but unquestionable Popery."

Eighteen forty-five, the year of Newman's exodus from Anglicanism, proved to be a climactic year for the Ecclesiologists. It peaked in May with a battle that culminated in the renaming of the Society and its removal from Cambridge to London, many of the leaders having already "gone down" from Cambridge. The leaders managed to secure a tighter grip on control of the organization as a result of this battle.

The mark of the Ecclesiologists' effectiveness soon became apparent as more and more churches were remodeled and new ones built. Unfortunately they were not above correcting medieval buildings when these structures did not live up to their ideal. They also "restored" many buildings only recently built by adding chancels and

[12] London, 1844.

even encouraged the "recasting" of Wren churches into Gothic forms. It would be interesting to know whether the Ecclesiologists stimulated as much destruction of medieval art and architecture as did their *bête noire* William Dowsing, the Puritan iconoclast.

Architects quailed at their power. One of the Ecclesiologists' least subtle devices was reviewing new churches in the *Ecclesiologist*. As could be expected, they had few kind words for those who built anything but correct early English or decorated Gothic buildings with long chancels. But such bullying paid off. Building committees are notoriously insecure; they like simple answers that have the ring of authority. Few questioned the authority of the Ecclesiologists. If such tactics were successful in England, they were even more successful abroad at a time when the British flag was something on which the sun never set. Whether it is on Via Nazionale in Rome, in Copenhagen, in India, or in Tasmania, one can still spot an English church of the period. Fastidiously correct in its early English arches, steep pitched roof, and broach spire, it tells the power of a small group of vehement believers far off in the English drizzle.

The question before us is: how could such a small group so successfully defy the culture of the time by fleeing to the outward apparel of another age? Victorian England was filled with robust self-confidence as prosperity and affluence shone on the upper classes. It was easy to believe in automatic and continual progress, a smugness that showed its worst side in social Darwinism. World trade and military exploitation brought the wealth of the world to England. Science and engineering provided marvels in health, transportation, and manufactured goods. Reforms in government progressively extended the franchise and terminated such age-old plagues as slavery. There was good reason for self-confidence and trust in progress.

Yet the Ecclesiologists distrusted all this and chose as ideal an age when piety abounded. It was easy, as Chesterton remarked, to see the Middle Ages "by moonlight." But to propose seriously to reject the culture of one's time and to prefer that of another age demanded a real negativism about one's own time, a deep distrust of the very air one breathed. This was what the Ecclesiologists did, though, and their success affected Anglican worship for a hundred years. Not until the building of St. Clement's Church, Alexandria, Virginia in 1949 was their iron sway successfully defied and, in the last quarter century, finally overthrown.

It is all the more remarkable to note the effect the same movement had on nineteenth-century America. It should be remembered that during the nineteenth century the Episcopal Church moved from being the dominant Church in colonial America to a relatively small enclave. In many ways it became a counterculture Church in itself. This was accentuated by the gradual inroads of ecclesiology in the Protestant Episcopal Church, first under the auspices of the first bishop of Vermont, John Henry Hopkins, then under the New York Ecclesiological Society (1846–1858). What could have been more contrary to Jacksonian democracy than a return to thirteenth-century medievalism? What could be more out of keeping with the spirit of the age of the common man than neo-medievalism? Yet the Episcopal Church gradually moved in this direction and accentuated further its differences from other American denominations.

The Christ of Culture

If mid-nineteenth-century Anglican worship adopted a "Christ against culture" attitude it is time now to look at the opposite: worship in the mainstream Protestant churches in America. Here the picture we get is not that of opposing culture but of accommodating to it. Here we see not "Christ against culture" but "the Christ of culture." What we find is a series of shifts in the form and understanding of worship as shifts occurred in the culture.

We shall be discussing the worship of central Protestantism, by which I mean Methodists, Congregationalists, Presbyterians, and Disciples of Christ primarily. These are sometimes referred to as the liberal-dominated churches. We cannot trace the trend here, but it is interesting to note that the more conservative churches such as the Southern Baptists or the Churches of Christ have also tended to mimic the culture of conservative regions and segments of American culture. So Americanism and Christian worship sometimes become hard to distinguish, especially when both involve flag processions and patriotic songs. The more liberal churches seem equally sensitive to local culture and all too readily become mirrors of the culture they reflect. Thus both theological and political liberals and conservatives often seem to be prone to mirror culture rather than to shed light on it from a distance.

I would like to illustrate this with a quick survey of worship and culture in the central Protestant churches during the past hundred years. I am convinced that four quite distinct cultural eras are re-flected by four distinct eras in worship.

For the first half of the past century, the period from 1870 to 1920, the dominant pattern in worship in central Protestantism showed the strong impact of revivalism. Worship tended to become a means to an end, the making of converts and the nourishing of those already converted. With such a purpose in mind it became possible to shape worship to a practical and purposeful end, i.e., it worked. Whatever criticisms we may have of the effects of nineteenth-century revival-ism upon worship, we cannot overlook its pragmatic character. A century earlier Jonathan Edwards had written his *Faithful Narrative of the Surprising Work of God* (1737). Almost exactly a hundred years later appeared Charles G. Finney's *Lectures on Revivals of Religion* (1835). Edwards chronicles with amazement; Finney's book is a how-to-do-it manual, with the results almost guaranteed if one fol-lows the proper techniques. Plant the proper grain and the wheat will appear.

Finney's book could well stand as the prime example of this period in worship. Bold, brusque, and vigorous, he traces changes in wor-ship, only to show that nothing has abided long and therefore the preacher is free to ignore history and to introduce "new measures" that will be effective. Behind all this is the pragmatic optimism of the time. America had been liberated from the dead hand of the past and the future was dazzling. Call it manifest destiny, the age of reform, the frontier spirit, Horatio Alger, it had one thrust: use the right tech-niques and there was no limit to what could be accomplished.

Let us not be negative about the degree to which it worked. It Christianized a nation whose founding fathers had hardly been godly, righteous, or sober, despite myths to the contrary. And it gave vigor to dozens of reform movements including abolition. But it did have its faults, though today, after reacting against revivalism for half a century, we can see some of its virtues as well.

Its chief fault was that it was weak theologically. Dividing human-ity into the saved and the lost does simplify things considerably. But there are contradictions in the phrase "bringing souls to Christ." And trying to snatch them from outer darkness into the bright radiance of salvation by an instantaneous occurrence caused problems. It was easy to neglect children until they were ripe for conversion, and the passion for recruiting the outsider tended to overwhelm the care and discipline of those within the fold. The traditional means of grace were too easily replaced by more sensational new measures.

But theologically weak as it was, revivalism had some elements of keen psychological insight that we have had to relearn in the last five years. For one thing, revivalism knew that in order to move people spiritually you have to move them physically. We have seen a spate of books recently such as *The Body at Liturgy*.[13] The Church music we told people for years was not good for them (and they still requested) was based on the realization that music is a body art. Even more important was the element of spontaneity, the unexpected possibility in worship. When the 1905 *Methodist Hymnal* included an "Order of Worship," there was an outcry against such unfamiliar formality. Is it any wonder that older people in our churches have a curious nostalgia after the worship of this period, no matter how hard seminary-trained clergy discourage such hankering after the fleshpots of Egypt? Revivalism may have been theologically weak but it understood people and did a fine job of reflecting many of the dominant currents of nineteenth-century American culture.

But cultural currents were changing and the 1920s saw a new era emerging in worship, too. I would call this the era of respectability and would divide it into two periods: one a period of aestheticism, the other a period of historicism. The era of respectability in Protestant worship was the half century beginning in the early 1920s. It represents the assertion of sobriety over the ecstatic, of refinement over the primitive, of restraint over the boisterous. It was a reflection of the increased sophistication of Americans as education became available to most. There was a neat correlation between the changes in the educational level of the average Methodist and what was happening to his or her worship life. The displays of emotion, the freedom and spontaneity, the general folksiness of revivalism were all pushed aside or left behind for those who had not yet ascended the social and educational scale.

The first half of our period of respectability, roughly 1920 to 1945, saw a substitution for worship as a conversion experience (or renewal of such an experience) of worship as an aesthetic experience. The slogan, despite its inherent contradiction, was "enriching our worship." America is dotted with churches, usually Gothic where the

[13]Joe Wise (Cincinnati, 1972).

budget would allow, that reflect both the wealth and the sophistication of the period. These are examples of the second Gothic revival, not the robust and original Gothic of the 1840s and 1850s but the academically correct Gothic of the 1920s. The buildings contain accurate copies of medieval elements, correct, timid, and in good taste. For good taste had invaded the sanctuary and replaced the pragmatic, functional, though hopelessly unsophisticated Akron plan. Good taste had reached the choir loft and exchanged the folksy quartet or octet for a full-fledged choir singing "good" music by composers all safely a century dead. Good taste had created a formal order of worship, so that Methodists by 1932 had several orders of worship to choose from and by 1944 a whole *Book of Worship*. And with the mimeograph no one had to worry about saying the right thing. No chances to take, no risks, just read your lines. One could be secure in confidence that nothing unexpected or chancy would happen in worship. It was all very respectable.

I believe that during the first half of this period worship came to be understood as largely an aesthetic experience by many ministers and lay people. Probably the most representative book was Von Ogden Vogt's *Art & Religion*, published in 1921 and subsequently in 1929, 1948, and 1960.[14] The title itself is indicative. Pastor of a Unitarian Church in Chicago for two decades, Vogt was vigorously opposed to creedalism and dogmatism of any kind and could anticipate many of our contemporaries in defining "worship as the celebration of life" by advocating a "substitute Scripture reading taken from modern sources," and the use of a variety of art forms. The experience of beauty and the experience of religion seemed remarkably similar to him. The arts served to help the worshiper "to be reverent and to display to him the larger cause of religion."[15] Vogt advised ministers to select "from the materials of the past those treasures which are least burdened with abandoned concepts."[16]

For many, public worship became an art form itself. Tremendous efforts were made in raising the "quality" of Church music. A growing concern about church architecture was reflected in the creation of denominational building agencies. The use of classical prayers instead

[14]New Haven, 1921 and 1929; Boston, 1948 and 1960.
[15]Rev. ed. Boston, 1948, 53.
[16]*Modern Worship* (New Haven, 1927) 39.

of spontaneous ones increased considerably. Books were written on "the art" of public worship.[17]

The warm glow of the conversion experience (or its memory) had been replaced for many by the more refined thrill of aesthetic experience. Here there was no risk of spontaneous emotion, no danger of exposing oneself by outward commitment. It was worship in good form, in which nothing overmuch prevailed. It was, in short, middle class America with its primary values of security and comfort. Worship could continue to be a meaningful though highly subjective experience without the risks of self-disclosure that revivalism demanded. If you could no longer tap your feet to the music, you could no longer do a lot of things in the big city that you did back in small-town America. Once again the worship tended to mirror the values of the prevailing culture.

But the culture did not stand still and neither did the forms of our worship. The years after World War II saw a quite different interest in worship in which the dominant phrase was "recovering our heritage," a phrase not without its own self-contradictions. I remember how much this era troubled Vogt, how much he regarded it as regression to a dark age of creedalism and dogmatism. The times demanded still a period of respectability both in worship and in American culture in general. But the thrust in worship was quite different and aestheticism came to be looked at with real suspicion.

It must be remembered that the late forties and fifties were a period of great growth in the American churches, a tendency that lost momentum in the 1960s. Attempts were frequently made, and with some justice, to connect this growth in Church membership with the age of anxiety. Americans were learning to live at the center of the stage of world politics; we were managing to live with the atomic bomb; we had to live with Sputnik. In theology, neo-orthodoxy emphasized human sinfulness and offered us in turn a high christology.

It is not surprising that aestheticism hardly seemed sufficient to those distraught by postwar anxieties. All around there was a search for more secure foundations. The "recovering of our heritage" that flourished for a quarter century in worship now seems to have been a necessary and vital stage, though, I believe, one we have now gone

[17] Albert Palmer, *The Art of Conducting Public Worship* (New York, 1939), and Percy Dearmer, *The Art of Public Worship* (London, 1919).

beyond. We should not be surprised that two of the elements in worship that tended to be stressed were confession and creed. The fascination with confession was no accident; no one who lived through World War II could have much doubt about human sin. Professor Perry Miller once said he was an Emerson man till he led the tank corps that liberated the Buchenwald concentration camp; from then on he was a Jonathan Edwards man. Certainly we went to some excesses in stressing confession during this period, just as our predecessors had neglected it. And the creeds gave us something firm to stand on, a need we felt greatly.

We turned to the historians for more foundations. Bard Thompson's *Liturgies of the Western Church*[18] may well stand as the representative book of this period. It should be noticed that while he did pay homage to the ancient and medieval Church the great bulk of the book is devoted to Reformation liturgies and no space is given to the Eastern liturgies. This was characteristic of our interests at that time. We were rediscovering Bucer then, not Hippolytus. Presbyterians were re-examining Calvin and Knox, Methodists were beginning to recognize Wesley, and Lutherans were taking a new look at the early Lutheran agenda. Names such as W. D. Maxwell, J. E. Rattenbury, Luther Reed, and others stood out. Dix's *The Shape of the Liturgy*[19] was recognized in some of its aspects while others had to await a subsequent period. The Reformers were rediscovered with a bit of shock due to the belated realization of how much the nineteenth century had separated us from them.

One could argue that the rediscovery of confession with its emphasis on humanity's weakness and the indulgence in creeds with their threat of dogmatism signaled the end of the Enlightenment in worship as much as the age of anxiety did for culture in general. The comfortable pew still remained, but something was rattling the clouds overhead and we had to find a substance in our worship that we had previously neglected.

Something happened in the late 1960s and early 1970s to American culture and we are just beginning to see what it implies for our worship. It may be premature to recognize the significance of these changes, but I think of them as the splintering of society. Whereas a

[18]Cleveland, 1961.
[19]Westminster, 1945.

decade ago we had a well-agreed image of what the good life in America consisted of, it would be hard to find any unanimity on that today. The conformity of the past with regard to lifestyles, morality, proper dress, hair styles, almost anything you can name, was shattered in the 1960s. We have moved into a period of diversity, pluralism, three consciousnesses, or whatever label you use. This has not been without shock and conflicts as the old conformities came toppling down.

The cultural changes have been reflected in worship by the move to a pluralistic approach. I would attribute most of the recent changes in worship to the attempt to find forms that fit the perceptual and expressive patterns natural to a wide variety of people. We have recognized, belatedly perhaps, that those forms that appeal to a middle class group in their mid-forties may strike their children as unrelieved dullness. Even devout teenagers tell us that our worship is boring because nothing happens at church. We are realizing that we have, in effect, told children that they must behave as adults in order to worship. It is acceptable to be a child 167 hours a week but never on Sunday at eleven o'clock. That is the time to sit still and listen to someone talking literally and figuratively over one's head. I hope we are now beginning to hear what Dix meant when he said worship is far more than words.

In this pluralistic approach to worship we have rediscovered some of the things that revivalism knew. We need to know and understand people in order to plan Christian worship. We need to take seriously the importance of the whole body and all the senses in worship and to recognize that music is a body art. We need to sense the importance of spontaneity and its advantages over a professionally conducted and controlled service as smooth as butter. It is no wonder that so-called contemporary worship services seem to appeal especially to the long-haired crowd and the grey-haired crowd.

Our society is mixed. In almost every congregation there are folks who want to sing the "old" hymns (i.e., those of revivalism), people who want to sing the "good" hymns (i.e., those that are in good taste), and persons who want to sing "something that moves" (i.e., those songs that have a "beat"). I would submit that none of these is more Christian or more adequate than any of the others. We must learn to think of our Church music in terms of being "good for" whom, not in abstract terms of quality. When I fretted at my small-town congregation for not singing Ralph Vaughn Williams' "*Sine nomine*" I forgot that what was "good for" a seminarian might not be "good for" California ranchers.

The "in" word in worship these days is indigenization. Vatican II's *Constitution on the Sacred Liturgy* underscored the need to make "legitimate variations and adaptations to different groups, regions, and peoples, especially in mission lands" (no. 38). But suddenly we have found that the real problem of indigenization is right here at home. How do we devise forms of worship in which children can take "that full, conscious, and active participation in liturgical celebrations *which is demanded by the very nature of the liturgy*"?[20] Or how can youth fulfill their priesthood best? Or what of us middle-aged folks who want nothing that involves much risk but would like some real substance?

I would say that we see basically three models developing in an effort to work out worship forms natural to the way a variety of people perceive and express what is ultimately real for them. The first of these models I call "eclectic." It is the type of service that is carefully planned to reflect a cross section of the congregation. In the prayers appear the anxieties of both liberals and conservatives, the music varies from gospel song to Bach to folk song or farther, and the language ranges from Cranmer to Malcolm Boyd. Purists decry this type of polyglot service but it has advantages. It certainly demands that the pastor and worship committee know the people to whom they are ministering.

The second emerging pattern is the occasional service in which on certain Sundays the whole service is in a style congenial to a particular segment of the congregation. This may mean a youth Sunday once a month. This has some advantage to the purist and also is easier to plan and staff. But it is also easier to disregard if one feels one is not in the group primarily involved—unless, of course, the style of each service is not announced in advance. These first two patterns are possible in churches of any size.

A third pattern seems to be current in many large congregations. This is the multiple-service route. Several different styles and occasions of worship are offered. Frequently they occur in different

---

[20]*Constitution on the Sacred Liturgy* (Collegeville, Minn., 1963) no. 14. Italics supplied.

spaces and at different hours. One goes where one feels most natural. Such a system is rather difficult to staff and populate except in large congregations but it has received favorable responses in a number of these. In effect it means the development of communities within a larger congregation. I have been part of one such group for over three years now.

Not all attempts at these three models have been successful by any means, but they do seem to be an indication of what is happening in worship in 1974, just as hair styles and parallel moralities are symptoms of the same pluralism in our culture. The fact that the new Lutheran communion service first appeared with four musical settings as distinct as chant and folk song is a sign of the times. The pluralistic approach comes not without difficulties but there is good precedent for being all things to all people in order to serve them well. The slogan of this period may well turn out to be "serving everyone." This reflects, I hope, a broader tolerance, a more open society, a culture that has moved a bit closer to mutual respect.

What can we conclude from this quick survey? Is Christ best served by abandoning the spirit and style of our culture? Or is he better served by mirroring the *Geist* of an age? Is our worship best seen as a mirror reflecting the bright light of its surroundings or as a beacon shining in darkness? Obviously we cannot give a clear "yes" to either alternative. With one we get a sentimental baptizing of the values of small-town America, with the other we have the dark obscurantism of Catholic worship after Trent.

I would like to conclude by suggesting that there is a persistent tension between worship and culture in which worship both affirms and criticizes the culture with which it must live. I am convinced that Christian worship has functions and forms that are distinct from any given culture yet adaptable to all. If it could survive nearly twenty centuries and exist in nearly all countries of the world, surely it can adapt to many, if not all, cultures yet be identified with none. There is, then, a constancy in Christian worship that is not culturally contingent, and yet a dependency upon culture in order to minister to people. We do have to speak a language, but what we say with it is for us to determine.

7. Sources for the Study of Protestant Worship in America

Much has happened since this essay appeared in Worship 61 (November 1987) so I have updated it considerably. This interval of eight years makes one realize how rapid has been the pace of liturgical revision.

I like to think the day is past when Christian liturgical scholars can ignore the worship life of Christian communions other than their own. Unfortunately the day has not yet come when most library collections have caught up with this scholarly reality. All too often the tradition that supports a library is well represented in that library's liturgical holdings and other traditions are not. I remember my shock when I taught one summer at a Roman Catholic college and discovered that the library contained no copy of the *Book of Common Prayer* only subsequently to realize my own seminary library lacked a copy of the *Code of Canon Law*. Such oversights are not entirely things of the past. Librarians are not usually to blame. Liturgical scholars have often been too busy to keep current with traditions other than their own and rarely have had the time to delve into the history of others. Obviously, the way to remedy such gaps is by looking at the basic sources for other traditions. But how is one to know which are missing from the collection or which of those present are most significant? And how is one to go about building a complete or representative collection?

The present article is an attempt to identify some of the chief sources necessary for the study of Protestant worship in America. It is, of necessity, a limited effort because of space requirements. Even so, some explanations of the limits I have imposed on this study are necessary.

My present concern is to trace the chief sources for the study of developments in some major American churches representing right-wing and central traditions. It is impossible to deal here with all denominations within each tradition; I shall treat those churches of these traditions representing the largest number of people in this country. Perhaps others may write on some of the smaller churches, ecumenical rites, the Canadian churches, and the churches of the British Isles.

I shall limit myself to official service books and hymnals together with commentaries, companions, and manuals devoted to these service books. Again qualification is necessary. In various traditions the meaning of what is "official" varies. In general, the more one moves to the left the greater the degree of discretion increases. A title page that says "For Voluntary and Optional Use" does not suggest the same force as one that announces itself as "According to the use of" a specific Church. Yet both may be approved by the highest authority of respective churches and are equally "official" if not equally enforced. The centralization of liturgical authority among Roman Catholics does not translate into similar authority for other Western traditions. One would not think of dictating to Anglican priests when or even whether to incense.

Service books and hymnals are certainly not the only sources for the study of Protestant worship but they may be the most accessible. I shall limit myself in this article to such sources, ignoring most historical and theological studies when available and all homiletical, musical, architectural, or liturgical art sources.

My procedure will be to work backward from those books currently in force as of 1995. By moving backward in time one can see the various tributaries flowing into the mainstream as one proceeds farther upstream. I shall try to be as complete as possible in listing sources but would appreciate being apprised of any I have missed or misidentified. It is my hope that this essay will be helpful for those approaching these materials for the first time. I also hope this will prompt librarians to acquire materials they lack. I know of no single library that presently has all the books I shall cite. This is especially true when one moves to books of the ethnic and smaller churches. For example very few libraries, if any, have complete collections of the *Disciplines* of the three major black Methodist churches.

Books of the Episcopal Church

I shall begin with the right-wing traditions, first of all with the Episcopal Church. One can argue that theologically the Lutheran liturgies of the sixteenth century were farther to the right than the Anglican formularies. As late as 1800 it would have seemed wild speculation to imagine that Anglican worship would ever focus primarily on the sacraments but the Catholic revival of the nineteenth century changed that. The exact title of the Church we shall examine was from 1789 to 1967 The Protestant Episcopal Church in the United States of America. Since 1967 it is also known simply as The Episcopal Church and is so styled in recent liturgical publications.

It is essential to realize that Episcopalians (a noun, not an adjective) do things in three-year cycles, corresponding to the triennial meetings of General Convention (most recently held in 1994). Furthermore, according to the "Constitution" adopted in 1789 and amended occasionally since, changes in the prayer book must be ratified by one session of the General Convention "and be adopted by the General Convention at its next succeeding regular meeting." Thus changes take a triennium with the exception of "the Table of Lessons and all Tables and Rubrics relating to the Psalms" plus material proposed purely for trial use.

The book of paramount importance in present use is *The Book of Common Prayer and Administration of the Sacraments and Other Rites and Ceremonies of the Church Together with the Psalter or Psalms of David* (New York: Church Hymnal Corporation [hereafter CHC] and Seabury Press, 1977). Copies published between 1976 and 1979 contain the word "Proposed" in the title and the report submitted in 1976 carries the words "Draft Proposed." The 1979 *Book of Common Prayer* (BCP) is the official service book and will be found in use in virtually every Episcopal congregation. There is a French edition, *Le Livre de la Prière Commune* (CHC, 1983) and one in Spanish, *El Libro de Oración Común* (CHC, 1982). All American editions are certified by the "Custodian of the Standard Book of Common Prayer," usually on the copyright page.

Volumes before the present prayer book are *Authorized Services 1973* (CHC, 1973), published both in a "Pew Edition" and an "Expanded Edition" and containing services authorized for parishes in the triennium following the 1973 General Convention. Prior to that, *Services for Trial Use* (CHC, 1971) provided the alternatives authorized by the 1970 General Convention, essentially the texts from *Prayer Book Studies* volumes 18 through 24. Both volumes are essential for tracing the development of the rites finally appearing in the 1979 BCP.

Several important functions were performed by the various volumes of the *Prayer Book Studies*, now numbering thirty actual books (though some are bound together and there are supplements). They fall into two groups: those published before the end of Vatican II, numbers 1 to 16 (New York: Church Pension Fund [hereafter CPF] 1950–1963) and those published after the Council, volumes 17 to 18 (CPF, 1966–1970) through 30 (CHC, 1970–1989).[1] A significant change occurs in PBS 26, reflecting changes imposed at the 1973 General Convention. The report submitted was entitled "Holy Baptism together with a Form for the Affirmation of Baptismal Vows with the Laying-On of Hands by the Bishops also Called Confirmation." The version authorized by that Convention was renamed "Holy Baptism together with a Form of Confirmation or the Laying-On of Hands by the Bishop with the Affirmation of Baptismal Vows," a token of a battle fought and lost. The author in all instances is the Standing Liturgical Commission, except the "Supplement to PBS 26" which carries the name of Daniel B. Stevick, and 29 and 29 Revised, by Charles P. Price.

Besides these published volumes a stack of mimeographed reports was sent out at random intervals to members of the Commission and various consultants. As part of the process but not numbered as a PBS was *The Prayer Book Psalter Revised*, published in 1973 for trial use during the following triennium (CHC). Individual services were

[1] The series (some bound together) are: 1. "Baptism and Confirmation"; 2. "The Liturgical Lectionary"; 3. "The Order for the Ministration to the Sick"; 4. "The Eucharistic Liturgy"; 5. "The Litany"; 6. "Morning and Evening Prayer"; 7. "The Penitential Office"; 8. "The Ordinal"; 9. "The Calendar"; 10. "The Solemnization of Matrimony"; 11. "A Thanksgiving for the Birth of a Child"; 12. "The Propers for the Minor Holy Days"; "The Collects, Epistles, and Gospels for the Lesser Feasts and Fasts: A Supplement to Prayer Book Studies XII"; 13. "The Order for the Burial of the Dead"; 14. "An Office of Institution of Rectors into Parishes"; 15. "The Problem and Method of Prayer Book Revision"; 16. "The Calendar and the Collects, Epistles, and Gospels for the Lesser Feasts and Fasts"; 17. "The Liturgy of the Lord's Supper"; 18. "Holy Baptism with the Laying-On-Of-Hands"; 19. "The Church Year"; 20. "The Ordination of Bishops, Priests, and Deacons"; 21. "The Holy Eucharist"; 22. "The Daily Office"; 23. "The Psalter Part I"; 24. "Pastoral Offices"; 25. "Prayers, Thanksgivings, Litanies"; 26. "Holy Baptism" (two versions); "Supplement to 26 Holy Baptism"; 27. "The Daily Office Revised"; 28. "Dedication and Consecration of a Church and Celebration of a New Ministry"; 29. "Introducing the Draft Proposed Book"; 29. Revised, "Introducing the Proposed Book"; and 30. "Supplemental Liturgical Texts."

published separately for trial use: "The Liturgy of the Lord's Supper" (1967); "A Catechism" (1973); "An Order of Worship for the Evening" (1973); "The Celebration and Blessing of a Marriage" (1975 and 1977); "The Burial of the Dead: Rite One" (1977); "The Sunday Eucharist: Rite Two Advent and Christmas" (1976); "The Sunday Eucharist: Rite Two Epiphany Season" (1977); and "Holy Baptism: A Form for Confirmation" (1975). PBS 30 appeared in 1989 as "Supplemental Liturgical Texts" (CHC) and in 1991 came "Supplemental Liturgical Materials" (CHC) (not numbered). PBS has been superseded by the *Liturgical Studies* series of which two volumes have appeared by 1995 (CHC) and *The Occasional Papers of the Standing Liturgical Commission*, vol. 1 (CHC, 1987).

Several other contemporary books deserve special mention. *The Book of Occasional Services* (CHC), editions of 1979 and 1991, is entirely optional but provides additional seasonal materials, pastoral offices (including an Anglican version of R.C.I.A.) and some episcopal rites. *The Proper for the Lesser Feasts and Fasts*, editions of 1980 and 1991 (CHC) has been approved "for optional use," replacing earlier editions of 1963 and 1973. Another genre is represented in Marion J. Hatchett's important *Commentary on the American Prayer Book* (Seabury, 1981) and Leonel L. Mitchell's *Praying Shapes Believing* (Minneapolis: Winston, 1985), a theological commentary on the BCP. Mention should also be made of the various publications of the unofficial organization Associated Parishes, Inc., founded in 1946, especially its *Holy Week Offices* (Greenwich: Seabury, 1958) edited by Massey H. Shepherd Jr. Associated Parishes is the subject of a dissertation by Michael Moriarty to be published as *The Liturgical Revolution* (CHC).

The previous prayerbook was the *Book of Common Prayer of 1928* (various publishers and dates). This was supplemented by *The Book of Offices*, published in three editions (1940, 1949, and 1960 CPF). *A Proposed Book of Offices* had been published in 1910 "for tentative use until 1913" preceded by an unofficial *A Book of Offices and Prayers* (New York, 1898). There is an excellent commentary on the 1928 BCP, *The Oxford American Prayer Book Commentary* by Massey H. Shepherd Jr. (New York: Oxford University Press, 1950). An earlier work of the same genre is *The American Prayer Book* by E. L. Parsons and B. H. Jones (New York: Scribners, 1937). The next prior stage was the *Book of Common Prayer of 1892* (various publishers). This is the subject of a dissertation by Leslie A. Northrop. It reflects the tumults of the nineteenth century as the Catholic revival within Anglicanism grew in strength but not without controversy. The most extreme reaction was the schism of The Reformed Episcopal Church in 1874. In that year it adopted the *Proposed Prayer Book* of 1785 as its official book, claiming it to be "the second Evangelical revision" (1552 being the first). Subsequent editions of the Reformed Episcopal Church's *Book of Common Prayer* are dated 1882, 1894, 1896, and the current Revised Fifth Edition of 1963 (Philadelphia: The Reformed Episcopal Publication Society, Limited, latest printing 1980).

The convulsions of the nineteenth century belie the long use of the first officially approved American BCP of 1789 (reprinted by various publishers for a century). It is the subject of a careful study by Marion J. Hatchett, *The Making of the First American Book of Common Prayer* (New York: Seabury, 1982). Previously the English prayer books of 1662, 1604, and 1559 had been used in the colonies.

We can trace briefly the official musical books. The current volume is *The Hymnal 1982* (CHC, 1985) and *The Hymnal 1982 Accompaniment Edition*, 2 vols. (CHC, 1985). As with the prayer book, *The Hymnal 1982* is the result and source of a plethora of publications. Chief among these are the *Church Hymnal Series* volumes 1 through 6 published by CPF or CHC (1. *Five Settings*, 1976; 2. *Canticles*, 1979; 3. *Hymns III*, 1979; 4. *Songs for Celebration*, 1980; 5. *Congregational Music for Eucharist*, 1980; 6. *Gradual Psalms* in five volumes: *Years A, B, and C, Holy Days, Lesser Feasts*, 1981–1986). These succeeded *Hymnal Supplements I and II* (CPF, 1961 and 1976) and *Music for Ministers and Congregation* (CHC, 1978). Ethnic concerns were reflected in *El Himnario Provisional* (CHC, 1980) and the African American collection, *Lift Every Voice and Sing* (CHC, 1981). Explication of musical concerns is covered by the *Hymnal Studies* series with eight volumes projected (CHC, 1981–1987). Recently published are *A New Metrical Psalter* (CHC, 1986) and *The Anglican Chant Psalter* (CHC, 1986). *The Hymnal (1982) Companion* is in process currently.

The new hymnal replaces the highly revered *The Hymnal 1940* (CPF, 1943). *The Hymnal 1940 Companion* (CPF, editions 1940, 1951, 1956) is the commentary on tunes and texts. *The Hymnal 1940*, in turn, replaced *The New Hymnal* of 1916 (CPF, 1918), notable as the first in which both tunes and texts were officially approved. This succeeded *The Hymnal* of 1892 for which there were "at least six musical editions"[2] by different publishers. The 1892 volume was successor to *The Hymnal* approved in 1871 and revised and enlarged in 1874 which appeared in five different musical editions by various publishers. This was the first separate hymn book.

The earlier period used a combined prayer book, hymnal, and psalter, not unlike the current *Lutheran Book of Worship*. The *Proposed Book of Common Prayer* of 1785 contained 84 psalms and 51 hymn texts but the book accepted in 1789 contained the entire metrical psalter but only 27 hymn texts. The number of hymn texts grew in subsequent printings, reaching a total of 212 by 1826. The presence of hymns in the earliest American prayer book is significant given their late acceptance in the Church of England.

The other source for the study of official Episcopal liturgical documents is canonical: *Constitutions & Canons* published every three years and containing the "Constitution" first adopted in 1789 and amended since. Much of this material deals with processes of liturgical revision and authorization. A somewhat dated manual is *Canon Law, A Handbook* by Daniel B. Stevick (New York: Seabury, 1965).

Lutheran Books

The Lutheran sources make the study of Episcopal liturgy seem like simplicity itself. An unpublished Th.M. dissertation written by W.D. Steakelberg for Vancouver School of Theology requires 463 pages to catalog over two hundred service books: "Lutheran Rites in North America: An Annotated Bibliography" [1989]. Indeed it may be sheer madness to attempt a comprehensive survey of resources for the study of Lutheran worship in America, but at least we can indicate some of the main sources for the major bodies without tracing all the Slovak, Icelandic, and other smaller groups. Fortunately most of these national groups have now united in two main bodies, the Evangelical Lutheran Church in America and the Lutheran Church–Missouri Synod. In one aspect our work is made simpler by the Lutheran propensity to publish service books and hymnals together so that liturgical texts and music are rarely separated.

We start with the current book for the largest number of Lutherans, *The Lutheran Book of Worship* (LBW) of 1978 (Minneapolis: Augsburg

[2]Cf. "Four Centuries of Anglican Hymnody in America" by Mason Martens, *Hymnal Studies One* (CHC, 1981) 21.

Publishing House [hereafter APH] and Philadelphia: Board of
Publication, Lutheran Church in America [hereafter BP]). There are
several editions; the Pew Edition, the Ministers' Desk Edition (with
the services plus additional eucharistic prayers and Holy Week rites),
the Ministers' Edition (for use at the altar), The Organist Edition:
Hymns, and The Accompaniment Edition: Liturgy. The LBW contains
hymns, service music, and basic services. It is the product of a dozen
years of work of the Inter-Lutheran Commission on Worship whose
labors between 1966 and 1978 are represented in ten volumes of the
Contemporary Worship series, published between 1969 and 1976 jointly
by APH, Concordia and BP.[3] Three unnumbered pamphlets also
appeared in 1977 from the same publishers: "Commissioning Service
for Lay Ministries," "The Rite for Installation of a Pastor," and "The
Rite for Ordination." One of the most interesting products was published by ILCW itself (New York, 1975), *The Great Thanksgiving*, a collection of eight eucharistic prayers, each with interpretation. Most
seemed too radical at the time to be approved.

The LBW is supported by various other volumes, most notably
Occasional Services (APH and BP, 1982) produced by the Task Force on
Occasional Services. It includes a variety of occasional services such
as the ordination rite.[4] This volume is the subject of *Commentary on
the Occasional Services* by Philip H. Pfatteicher (Philadelphia: Fortress,
1983). The services in the LBW are the subject of *Manual on the
Liturgy: LBW* by Philip H. Pfatteicher and Carlos R. Messerli (APH,
1979). Pfatteicher wrote *Commentary on the LBW* (Augsburg Fortress,
1990). *Hymnal Companion to the LBW* by Marilyn Kay Stulken
(Fortress, 1981) treats the hymns. Pfatteicher also wrote *Festivals and
Commemorations* (APH, 1980) to interpret seasonal materials. *Psalm
Antiphons for the Church Year* by Roger T. Petrich (Fortress, 1979)
should be mentioned. A subsequent addition is the Lutheran–Roman
Catholic *Service of the Word*, pew and leader editions (APH and U.S.
Catholic Conference, 1986). Most recently, *Hymnal Supplement 1991*

[3]They include: 1. "Hymns" 1969; 2. "Services: The Holy Communion" 1970; 3.
"The Marriage Service" 1972; 4. "Hymns for Baptism and Holy Communion"
1972; 5. "Services of the Word" 1972; 6. "The Church Year" 1973; 7. "Holy
Baptism" 1974; 8. "Affirmation of the Baptismal Covenant" 1975; 9. "Daily Prayer
of the Church" 1976; and 10. "Burial of the Dead" 1976.

[4]Note the unpublished University of Notre Dame Ph.D. dissertation, "Lutheran
Ordination in North America: The 1982 Rite," by Paul R. Nelson, 1987.

(Chicago: GIA Publications) and *With One Voice: A Lutheran Resource for Worship* (Minneapolis: Augsburg Fortress, 1995) in pew and leader editions have updated resources.

Although it helped to produce the LBW, at the last moment the Lutheran Church Missouri Synod rejected it, although LBW has found use in a number of Missouri Synod churches. That Church published in 1982 its own version, *Lutheran Worship* (St. Louis: Concordia, 1982). Forces underway in the 1960s had led Missouri and smaller bodies to publish their own *Worship Supplement* in 1969 (Concordia) with an interesting variety of services and hymns, including what may be the last version of Prime. The 1969 Missouri *Supplement* was an attempt to bring up to date *The Lutheran Hymnal* (Concordia, 1941), for over forty years the standard hymnal and service book for Missouri and other groups comprising the Evangelical Lutheran Synodical Conference of North America. The newest commentary is *Lutheran Worship: History and Practice* edited by Fred L. Precht (Concordia, 1993). It replaces *The Handbook to the Lutheran Hymnal* by W. G. Polack (Concordia, 1942). Missouri's earlier stages were the *Evangelical Lutheran Hymn-Book* of 1927 and an earlier edition by the same title in 1912 (both Concordia). The Germanic era is reached in Missouri's *Kirchen-Gesangbuch* (St. Louis: Verlag der ev.-Luth. Synode von Missouri, Ohio u.a. St., 1878).

The much smaller Wisconsin Evangelical Lutheran Synod published *The Pastor's Agenda* (Milwaukee: Northwestern Publishing House, 1978) and *Christian Worship: A Lutheran Hymnal* (Northwestern, 1993).

If we seek to go back behind the LBW (other than Missouri), the next stage for eight Lutheran churches whose successors cooperated in the LBW is the *Service Book and Hymnal* (SBH) of 1958 (APH and BP). It broke Lutheran tradition in introducing a full eucharistic prayer as an alternative to the words of institution only. It was accompanied by *The Occasional Services* (APH and BP, 1962) incorporating materials agreed on jointly in 1950 and many additional offices, particularly blessings.

Before 1940 nothing is simple. Various mergers produced churches with confusingly similar (or identical) names; different national groups used books in Scandinavian and Germanic languages; and even common languages were not sufficiently unifying for two Danish, six Norwegian, and three Finnish Lutheran churches. A key book was the *Common Service Book of the Lutheran Church* published by the United Lutheran Church in America (BP, 1918), representing largely eastern Lutherans of Germanic origins. Mention should be made of Luther D. Reed (1873–1972) who lived long enough to be a major factor in both this book and the 1958 SHB. His *The Lutheran Liturgy* (revised edition; Fortress, 1960) provides a guide to SBH, the *Common Service Book*, and some of their predecessors among mainly east-coast Lutherans.[5]

Among the more significant of twentieth-century Lutheran hymnals and service books may be cited *The Concordia Hymnal* (APH, 1932), *The American Lutheran Hymnal* (Columbus: Wartburg, 1930) representing the work of eight synods; *The Lutheran Hymnary* (APH, 1935) and an earlier edition representing the hymnody and rites of three Norwegian Lutheran churches (Decorah, Iowa: Lutheran Publishing House, 1913). We note A *Hymnal for Church and Home* (Blair, Neb.: Danish Lutheran Publishing House) published in 1927 by a Danish group, *Hymnal and Order of Service* by the Evangelical Lutheran Augustana synod (Swedish) group (Rock Island: Augustana Book Concern, 1925), and the *Wartburg Hymnal* in 1918 by the Iowa Synod. Earlier books include *Evangelical Lutheran Hymnal* published by the Ohio and other Synods (Columbus: Lutheran Book Concern, 1908), and the *Book of Worship with Hymns* of the General Synod (Philadelphia: Lutheran Publication Society, 1899).

The most important development of the nineteenth century was the "Common Service" of 1888. This found its way into the service books of several eastern varieties of Lutherans such as *The Common Service With Music* (Philadelphia: Lutheran Publication Society, 1888) or the *Church Book for the Use of Evangelical Lutheran Congregations* (Philadelphia: General Council Publication Board, 1893). Other key events of this century were the General Council's *Church Book of 1868* and the *Agende* of Wilhelm Loehe of Neuendettelsau sent to America in 1844 and widely used in Michigan and Iowa. The genesis of Lutheran rites originating in America is a handwritten liturgy by the American Lutheran patriarch, Henry Melchior Muhlenberg, produced in 1748 and circulated in manuscript. Portions and additions finally were printed as *Kirchen-Agende der evangelisch-lutherischen vere-*

---

[5]I have also relied on an unpublished paper by George Muenich, "The Victory of Restorationism: The Common Service 1888–1958." Note also *Liturgical Reconnaissance*, edited by Edgar S. Brown Jr. (Philadelphia: Fortress, 1968).

inigten Gemeinden in Nord-America in 1786. Muhlenberg's dream of a single liturgy for American Lutherans has come close to being fulfilled in the 1978 LBW.

Methodist Books

When we move to the liturgical center we enter a different world. Service books may have the approval of the highest ecclesiastical authority but their use is not enforced with the same vigor and members find their unity expressed in other ways than the liturgy. We shall begin by looking at the United Methodist Church. With eleven million baptized members it is the largest American Protestant Church with official service books.

Two things must be kept in mind when looking at Methodist liturgies: United Methodists do things in four-year intervals so that liturgical decisions (not necessarily publication dates) occur in the same years (coincidentally) that American presidents are elected. Thus it is common to date liturgical materials from the quadrennium in which materials are approved, for example, *Book of Worship of 1964* (actually published in 1965). The other thing is the use of the term "Ritual" which since 1848 (1870 in the Methodist Episcopal Church, South) has been used to include all officially approved services although they would once have been parts of the Missal, Ritual, and Pontifical. The term through 1844 was "Sacramental Services, &c."

At present, two books have top priority in United Methodist worship: *The United Methodist Book of Worship* (Nashville: United Methodist Publishing House, 1992) has all the official liturgical texts; *The United Methodist Hymnal* (UMPH, 1989) contains the most common services, the hymns, and the psalter. Carlton Young has written a massive *Companion to the United Methodist Hymnal* (Nashville: Abingdon, 1993). Manuals were edited by Hoyt Hickman, *The Worship Resources of the United Methodist Hymnal* (Abingdon, 1989) and by Diana Sanchez, *The Hymns of the United Methodist Hymnal* (Abingdon, 1989).

The previous *Book of Worship*, which contained all official services, was approved in 1964 (Nashville: Methodist Publishing House, 1965) replacing the first (1944) *Book of Worship* (MPH, 1945). The 1964 *Methodist Hymnal* (MPH, 1966) was subsequently renamed *The Book of Hymns*. In 1968, the Evangelical United Brethren Church joined with the Methodist Church to form the United Methodist Church. The last

EUB books were *The Book of Ritual* (Harrisburg and Dayton: Board of Publication, 1959) and *The Hymnal* (Dayton: Board of Publication, 1957).

The process of liturgical revision behind the present books has been lengthy and thorough. *The Hymnal* and *Book of Worship* approved in 1964 reflected a tendency to look to the Reformation and eighteenth century, not the concerns of the post-Vatican II era. They were followed by *Companion to the Book of Worship* edited by William F. Dunkle Jr. and Joseph D. Quillian Jr. (Abingdon, 1970) and *Companion to the Hymnal* by Fred D. Gealy, Austin C. Lovelace, and Carlton R. Young (Abingdon, 1970). But by the time these companions appeared it was already obvious that a new era had begun.

The new era was recognized at a special session of the General Conference in 1970 that authorized development of new worship materials. This eventuated in a seventeen-volume series, the *Supplemental Worship Resources*—hereafter SWR (all UMPH or Abingdon, 1972–1988). The first to appear was *The Sacrament of the Lord's Supper* (SWR 1) published in 1972 and revised somewhat in 1980 and 1984. It was followed in 1976 by *A Service of Baptism, Confirmation, and Renewal* (SWR 2), revised in 1980 and 1984. Of special importance are SWR 8, *From Ashes to Fire* (services for Lent and Easter), SWR 9, *At the Lord's Table* (twenty-two eucharistic prayers), and SWR 10, *We Gather Together* (representing the second generation of the five basic services). The final volume, SWR 17, *Commentary on the Book of Services*, appeared in 1988.[6] Individual services were also published in leaflet form. *The Book of Services* (UMPH, 1985) represents third generation revisions of the five basic services. Several services have also been published in Spanish and Japanese. *Handbook of the Christian Year* (Abingdon, 1986 and 1992) represents second generation versions of seasonal materials found in SWR volumes 3, 6,

[6]The complete series includes: 1. "The Sacrament of the Lord's Supper"; 2. "A Service of Baptism, Confirmation, and Renewal"; 3. "Word and Table"; 4. "Ritual in a New Day"; 5. "A Service of Christian Marriage"; 6. "Seasons of the Gospel"; 7. "A Service of Death and Resurrection"; 8. "From Ashes to Fire"; 9. "At the Lord's Table"; 10. "We Gather Together"; 11. "Supplement to the Book of Hymns"; 12. "Songs of Zion"; 13. "Hymns from the Four Winds"; 14. "Blessings and Consecrations"; 15. "From Hope to Joy"; 16. "Holy Communion"; and 17. "Commentary on the Book of Services." Volumes projected on healing and reconciliation services never appeared.

7, 9, 15, and 16. It contains much commentary, historical and practical, as well as the rites. *An Ordinal* was approved in 1980 as an official alternative (UMPH, 1979).

When we move back to an earlier period some things get more simple, others more complex. Until 1964 the important document is the "Ritual" which through that year always appeared in the *Discipline*. The correct title is *The Doctrine and Discipline of the Methodist Church* or its predecessors. A privately printed *Disciplinograph* by George A. Zimmermann (1994) is a valuable guide. Published at four-year intervals (and in 1939), the *Discipline* always contained the rites for baptism, Eucharist, weddings, funerals, ordination, and (from 1864 on) forms for reception of members, laying a cornerstone, and dedication of a church. *The Ritual* was occasionally published as a separate volume for the minister's use. Since it could be revised every four years minor emendations often occurred, especially in rubrics, probably reflecting the ways things were actually being done more than prescribing practice. There were occasional major changes, especially in 1792, 1864, 1916, and 1932. Through 1926 these can be charted in Nolan B. Harmon's *The Rites and Ritual of Episcopal Methodism* (Nashville: Publishing House of the M.E. Church, South, 1926), a Methodist parallel to F. E. Brightman's *The English Rite*.

The complex part is that until 1939 there were not one but three major Methodist churches for nearly a century, each publishing *Disciplines*. The Methodist Episcopal Church, South (MECS) published disciplines every four years from 1846 to 1938, from 1870 on in Nashville at the Publishing House of the Methodist Episcopal Church, South. Apparently none was produced in 1862. Copyright dates should be checked, since title pages often refer to reprintings during a quadrennium. The *Constitution and Discipline of the Methodist Protestant Church* (MPC) (a group without bishops) began in 1830 and ran (rather irregularly) through numerous editions until quadrennial revision commenced in 1880. Early editions were published by the Book Agent or Book Committee of the Methodist Protestant Church which became The Board of Publication of the M. P. Church, both located in Baltimore.

The parent body, The Methodist Episcopal Church (MEC), dates from 1784 and published *Disciplines* from the Conference of that year (actually published in 1785) through 1936. The early ones are yearly until 1792, then somewhat irregular but with each edition numbered until the twenty-fifth (1826). They begin to be of interest to liturgists with the eighth edition of 1792 when the "Sacramental Services &c." first appear although there are canons previously about receiving communion kneeling or demanding a communion token from communicants. The publishers are manifold, not settling down until 1912 with the Methodist Book Concern, New York and Cincinnati. Liturgical changes began on a quadrennial basis in 1816 although "editions" published between quadrennial years reflect the actions of the previous General Conference.[7]

The foundation is John Wesley's 1784 revision of the 1662 BCP, *The Sunday Service of the Methodists in North America with other Occasional Services* (London, 1784). A bicentennial edition of this is available, *John Wesley's Sunday Service* (UMPH, 1984). Several editions under various titles were published in England in 1786, 1788, 1790 and 1792 but the Americans tacitly dropped it in 1792, the year after Wesley's death.

Besides the *Disciplines*, two hymnals are noteworthy for liturgical reasons. In 1935, the three churches (MEC, MECS and MPC) on the verge of merger published *The Methodist Hymnal* (MPH). This was the standard pew book until replaced by the 1964 *Hymnal* and contained much worship material. It was the subject of a commentary, *Our Hymnody* by Robert G. McCutchan (New York: Methodist Book Concern, 1937). The previous hymnal was *The Methodist Hymnal* of 1905, published jointly by MEC and MECS. This was a landmark book since it was the first to contain orders of worship although a single "Order of Public Worship" had appeared in some late printings of the 1878 *Hymnal of the Methodist Episcopal Church* (New York: Phillips & Hunt), the first one to include tunes. The commentary on the 1905 hymnal was *The Hymns and Hymn Writers of the Church* by C. S. Nutter and W. F. Tillet (Methodist Book Concern, 1911). A full chart of the nineteenth-century hymnals appears in *Companion to the Hymnal*, 52–53, but these books lack service materials. Ultimately the hymnals derive from the sixty-four hymn collections written or edited by John and Charles Wesley. These began with the first

---

[7]For a roadmap to some of this material, note the unpublished Ph.D. dissertation by William N. Wade, "A History of Public Worship in the Methodist Episcopal Church and the Methodist Episcopal Church, South from 1784 to 1905," University of Notre Dame, 1981.

American and first Anglican hymnal, John Wesley's *Collection of Psalms and Hymns* (Charleston, 1737).

Presbyterian Books

When we turn to the Reformed tradition we have to be selective and shall choose the largest single body, the Presbyterian Church (U.S.A.), formed by merger in 1983. There have been important recent works in other bodies with a Reformed heritage, specifically the *Book of Worship* of the United Church of Christ (New York: Pilgrim Press, 1986), *Rejoice in the Lord*, a hymnal edited by Erik Routley for the Reformed Church in America (Grand Rapids: Eerdmans, 1985), and the *Psalter Hymnal* published by the Christian Reformed Church (Grand Rapids: CRC Publications, 1988).

It should be remembered that the Presbyterian General Assembly meets yearly and can act yearly on liturgical matters. We need to look at three sources: service books, hymnals and psalters, and *Directories*.

By being the last in the post-Vatican II series of liturgical revisers, the Presbyterians have been able to profit from the mistakes of everyone and to utilize the best of others' efforts. There is especially a close relationship to the United Methodist process and products. The current state of the art in North American liturgical revision is the 1993 *Book of Common Worship* (Louisville: Westminster/John Knox, 1993). It follows closely on the heels of *The Presbyterian Hymnal* (Westminster/John Knox, 1990) which contains little liturgical material. LindaJo H. McKim produced *The Presbyterian Hymnal Companion* (Westminster/John Knox, 1993).

The 1993 *Book of Common Worship* was preceded by a seven-volume series of *Supplemental Liturgical Resources*.[8] One can trace current concerns in such areas as inclusive language, the initiation process, and the shape of the eucharistic prayer in these various volumes. The previous stage of Presbyterian liturgical revision was the *Worshipbook: Services* (1970) and the *Worshipbook: Services and Hymns* (1972), both published by Westminster. The timing was bad for producing these materials especially since the service materials were essentially

---

[8]All Westminster/John Knox Press: 1. "The Service for the Lord's Day," Complete Text and Pew editions, 1984; 2. "Holy Baptism and Services for the Renewal of Baptism," 1985; 3. "Christian Marriage," 1986; 4. "The Funeral," 1986; 5. "Daily Prayer," 1987; 6. "Services for Occasions of Pastoral Care," 1990; and 7. "Liturgical Year," 1992.

completed by 1968. But the Lord's Supper was presented as the norm for Sunday worship, contemporary language was used throughout, and the ecumenical lectionary appeared. Many of the lessons of Vatican II and its consequences had yet to be learned and such concerns as inclusive language had not yet arisen. An earlier version of some materials appeared as *The Book of Common Worship: Provisional Services* (Westminster, 1966) following *Service for the Lord's Day and Lectionary for the Christian Year* (Westminster, 1964) which had a two-year lectionary following the pattern of trinitarian seasons A. A. McArthur had advocated.

The remaining history of service books is brief although the details vary from the major Presbyterian bodies. Very gingerly, the northern Presbyterian Church in the U.S.A. had approved in 1906 its first *Book of Common Worship* (Philadelphia: Presbyterian Board of Publication, 1906), clearly labeled "For Voluntary Use." It was revised and approved in 1932 again "For Voluntary Use" (Philadelphia: Presbyterian Board of Christian Education). The third edition appeared in 1946, this time without any warning label (Board of Christian Education). The southern Presbyterian Church in the U.S. was more cautious and slower in its acceptance of these volumes, but did authorize the use of the 1932 BCW and the 1946 BCW when they appeared.

Behind this lies a period of unofficial individual productions, most noteworthy being Charles W. Baird's *Eutaxia, or the Presbyterian Liturgies* (New York, 1855) noteworthy for its cautious hope "to see the want of a formulary of Public Prayer and administration of ordinances supplied . . . while we have little expectation that such a formulary, however perfect, will ever be adopted as a standard of the Church." A reprint, *The Presbyterian Liturgies*, appeared in 1960 (Grand Rapids: Baker).

We do not pretend to be comprehensive on hymnals since there were (and still are) a variety of Presbyterian bodies prior to (and since) the 1983 merger. Still in use in many churches are *The Hymnbook*, a joint venture of 1955, or *The Hymnal* of the PCUSA (northern) dating from 1933 (Presbyterian Board of Christian Education), both with little worship material. The *Hymnal* of 1933 is the subject of *Handbook to the Hymnal* by W. C. Covert and C. W. Laufer (Presbyterian Board of Christian Education, 1935). An interesting sidelight is the recent *The Book of Psalms* of the Reformed

Presbyterian Church, a body that does not allow hymnody other than metrical psalms (Pittsburgh: Board of Education and Publication, 1973). It contains metrical versions for every verse of the psalter. The Presbyterian Church in the U.S.A. published *The Hymnal* in 1895, revised it in 1911, and added a supplement of three "Patriotic Hymns" in 1917 (Philadelphia: Presbyterian Board of Publication and Sabbath-School Work). *The Presbyterian Hymnal* of 1874 followed the *Hymnal of the Presbyterian Church* of 1866 (Philadelphia: Presbyterian Board of Publication). The southern Presbyterian Church in the U.S. published *The Presbyterian Hymnal* in 1927 (Richmond: John Knox).

As early as 1751 a challenge against the use of hymnody was denied by the Synod of New York, rejecting an absolute ban on uninspired texts. By 1843 the Old School wing of the Church had produced *Psalms and Hymns* and nine years later published tunes, a sign of break from reliance on a precentor. The early books lack service materials; before the *Worshipbook* the worship sections were largely collections of responsive readings of Scripture.

A distinctive Presbyterian feature is the *Directory for the Public Worship of God*, a form ultimately springing from the 1644 replacement of the *Book of Common Prayer*, the Westminster *Directory*. The most recent *Directory* is that of 1989. It represents the latest in a series of American *Directories* that, from 1787 on, replaced the Westminster *Directory*. The *Directories* are a series of theological and practical instructions about the ordering of worship, leaving much to local initiative within certain doctrinal confines. Some indicate topics for prayer but without providing texts. The focus is on normative structures and elements.

There seem to be ten *Directories* of prime importance for the study of Presbyterian worship in America without including the smaller Presbyterian bodies. Before the 1989 *Directory* was "The Directory for the Service of God" found in *The Book of Order* (Philadelphia: Office of General Assembly, 1986–1987). It replaced "The Directory for the Worship of God" of 1960 for UPCUSA and the 1963 "The Directory for the Worship and Work of the Church" of the southern PCUS when these bodies merged in 1983. The southern church had published "The Directory for the Worship of God" in 1929 and the same title in 1893 (Richmond: Presbyterian Committee of Publication). Previous versions for another body, the United Presbyterian Church of North America (1858–1958) appeared in "The Book of Government and Worship" of 1910 and the "Directory for Worship" (Pittsburgh: Presbyterian Board of Publication, 1873). The first American source is "The Directory for the Worship of God" of 1788 based on "A Draught of the Form of the Government and Discipline" (New York: S. and J. Loudon, 1787) of the previous year.[9]

[9]I am indebted to Stanley R. Hall for this information. His 1990 unpublished University of Notre Dame dissertation was "The American Presbyterian Directory for Worship: History of a Liturgical Strategy."

8. A Short History of American Methodist Service Books

The occasion for this address was the celebration at Drew University of the publication of the 1992 *United Methodist Book of Worship*. The address subsequently appeared in *Doxology* 10 (1993) and now, with expanded citations, is used by permission.

I want to begin with an anecdote from my first contact with the national Commission on Worship of the Methodist Church. The occasion was the spring meeting in 1965 in Champaign–Urbana for which the main event was the dedication service for the new 1965 *Book of Worship*. Two liturgical styles prevailed in that service. One of each came from two men who had spent the last eight years working on and arguing over the contents of the book. One wanted to add a note of levity to the occasion by clowning around in a warm and informal fashion. The other wanted to recognize the solemnity of the service by following the printed program and acting with due decorum. It seems to me that those two men epitomize the history of Methodist worship in this country: the folksy and informal versus the dignified and formal.

In what follows I am very much aware that I am treating solely the latter approach even though it has always been the minority position. But how does one document the folksy and informal even though it has always been more prevalent? It is usually too ephemeral to take written form. On the other hand the desire for forms and standards can easily be shown by the ongoing efforts to provide these items. So I shall chronicle these efforts only. And they do show an important element in Methodist worship, the persistence of a Methodist "high church" position throughout Methodist history. This has been an important undercurrent in Methodist worship and certainly is today. I frequently encounter United Methodist pastors who say "we must

cherish our Anglican inheritance" even though many of their colleagues see themselves basically as Baptists with bishops.

The history of Methodist service books in this country began with
John Wesley's 1784 *Sunday Service of the Methodists in North America
With Other Occasional Services*.[1] This was usually bound with Wesley's
letter advising a weekly Eucharist and daily prayer using the litany
on Wednesdays and Fridays and praying extemporaneously on other
weekdays. Psalter readings are provided for daily morning and
evening use. Editions appeared in 1786, 1788, 1790, and 1792 under
various titles. *The Sunday Service* was basically a rather conservative
revision of the 1662 *Book of Common Prayer*. But its fate was not what
Wesley anticipated. Hardly was he buried when the 1792 General
Conference whittled it down from 314 pages to thirty-seven pages of
"Sacramental Services, &c." plus the "Articles of Religion." Renamed
"The Ritual" in 1848 and 1870, the two baptismal rites, Lord's
Supper, wedding rite, funeral rite, and three ordination rites re-
mained in the *Discipline* until 1968 and formed the printed backbone
of Methodist worship for two centuries.

The Nineteenth Century

Looking back, Jesse Lee wrote in 1810 that most of his fellow ministers felt "they could pray better, and with more devotion while
their eyes were shut, than they could with their eyes open. After a
few years the prayer book [Wesley's] was laid aside, and has never
been used since in public worship."[2] Without questioning his statement we can show a desire on the part of some Methodists for more
fixed forms. This is evident as early as the 1820 *Discipline* which in
the section "On Public Worship" calls "for the establishment of uniformity in public worship amongst us, on the Lord's day." It then
gives minimal directions for the morning, afternoon, and evening
services. In 1864 the Methodist Episcopal Church expanded "The
Ritual" to include services for "Reception of Members," "Laying a
Corner-Stone," and "Dedication of a Church." As early as 1851
(MECS) and 1864 (MEC) *The Ritual* was published as a separate book.

---

[1](London, 1784). Facsimile edition: *John Wesley's Prayer Book* (Akron: OSL
Publications, 1991).

[2]*A Short History of the Methodists*, facsimile edition (Rutland, Vermont:
Academy Books, 1974) 107.

But as yet no worship materials appeared in the hymnals. Of course changes appeared in the ritual part of the *Discipline* from time to time. Usually these must be understood as more descriptive than prescriptive. They tell us what was becoming accepted practice. By the time something reached the *Discipline* it is usually safe to believe that it was being practiced widely.

But surprises begin. In 1867 the southern Church published a partial reprint of Wesley's *Sunday Service* as *The Sunday Service of the Methodist Episcopal Church, South.*[3] This was edited by Thomas O. Summers (1812–1882) who might be said to be the American Methodist Edward B. Pusey. In 1859 Summers had published *The Golden Censer*,[4] a privately-edited collection of prayers and the beginning of a series of private resources by various Methodists. Summers also published a *Commentary on the Ritual of the Methodist Episcopal Church South*[5] in 1873. As publisher of the southern Church, dean of Vanderbilt Divinity School, and secretary of the General Conference, he was an enormously energetic and influential person. He was doubtless a force behind the southern Church in publishing an outline order for morning, afternoon, and evening services in the *Discipline* of 1870.

The activity now shifts to the northern Church, which in 1891 published *Select Psalms . . . with Other Selections and the Order for the Sacraments and Occasional Services of the Church.*[6] Edited by Charles S. Harrower, the psalms are arranged (via Wesley) for daily reading, morning and evening, plus an additional collection of alternative texts. "The Ritual," the catechism, and parts of Wesley's *Sunday Service* complete what is intended to be "a useful Hand-book of Methodist Worship." In the "Episcopal Note," Bishop Edward G. Andrews tells us the northern Church in 1888 "established and enjoined a uniform order of public worship."[7] This appears as an outline in the 1888 *Discipline*, very similar to the southern order but with the addition of a "collection." Bishop Andrews notes that "recently a natural desire to dignify and enrich public worship has arisen in

[3](Nashville: Methodist Episcopal Church, South, 1867).
[4](Nashville: Methodist Episcopal Church, South, 1859).
[5](Nashville: Methodist Episcopal Church, South, 1873).
[6](New York: Eaton & Mains, 1891).
[7]Ibid., 3.

many quarters" and speaks of the need "for a harmonious, reasonable, and historic order." He ends by commending this volume "to all who prize order, dignity, and a not too inflexible uniformity in the service of the sanctuary." Two years later, in 1893, another version, *The Sunday Service Recommended to the Societies in America by the Rev. John Wesley . . . Including Select Psalms, with the Order for the Sacraments and Other Occasional Services according to the Use of the Methodist Episcopal Church*[8] was published and went through numerous printings. This was modeled on the prayer book of the Wesleyan Church in England.

The General Conference adopted an "Order of Public Worship" in May 1896, an order that was subsequently bound in copies of the 1878 *Hymnal of the Methodist Episcopal Church* printed after that date. The order appeared (slightly changed) in the jointly-published 1905 *Methodist Hymnal*. This seems harmless enough today, but it was a revolution in 1896 to include an order of worship in the *Hymnal* and brought protests of "formalism."

Twentieth Century Books

The genre of private books continued to grow. In 1903 Charles LeVerne Roberts of Chicago published *Divine Service: A Compilation of Collects and Psalms for Use in the Public Worship of God in the Methodist Episcopal Church.*[9] He tells his readers: "The cry in our Church, in the matter of the form in Public Worship, is `Back to Wesley.' This liturgical movement is felt in many Churches, and for several years has been gathering form and force."[10] This well may be the first Methodist use of the term "liturgical movement." Roberts tell us of the desire to make worshipers "participants" rather than "auditors," a familiar theme even today. His collection of collects and psalms is mostly from Wesley and there are orders of worship for morning, evening, communion, baptism, reception of members, matrimony, and burial of the dead.

Bishop Wilbur P. Thirkield of Connecticut made notable contributions with his 1918 collection, *Service and Prayers for Church and Home.*[11] It contains two hundred pages of prayers, the 1905 "Order of

8(New York: Eaton and Mains, 1893).
9(Cincinnati: Jennings and Pye, 1903).
10Ibid., 4.
11(New York: Methodist Book Concern, 1918).

Public Worship," portions of Wesley's *Sunday Service*, and the 1916 "Ritual." Somewhat later, Thirkield and Oliver Huckel (a Congregational minister from Greenwich, Connecticut) produced an entire service book entitled *Book of Common Worship* (1932, second edition 1936).[12] Some of the materials assembled here, especially affirmations of faith, continued to be used long after the book was forgotten, and the Korean Statement of Faith is still in the *Hymnal*, though altered.

The 1905 *Hymnal* had been a joint work of two churches but that of 1935 preceded union by three churches and bore contributions from each. There now appeared not one but four orders of worship, together with a collection of prayers, "The Ritual," and responsive readings. The latter seem first to have appeared among Methodists in a northern Church publication of 1932: *The Book of Service: Orders of Worship, The Ritual, and Responsive Readings*.[13] Responsive readings were a twentieth-century innovation that appeared in many churches during this period as a substitute for the traditional psalter. These collections of favorite verses arranged topically flourished for about forty years but have been replaced today in almost all churches by the psalter. (This process would make an interesting study.) "The Ritual" now included a much fuller eucharistic rite from the northern Church (with Methodist Protestant contributions) but with a memorialist rewriting of the prayer of consecration and the prayer of humble access. The southern Church's rite appears as "An Alternative Order" with these items unchanged but with no service of the word appended. This was the last time the phrase "most precious blood" appeared in Methodist worship after 150 years of use.

Almost immediately after reunion, the General Conference appointed a Commission on Ritual and Orders of Worship in 1940. Some significant names appear on this, some of whom might be called part of the high church mafia: Bishop Ivan Lee Holt (chair), Oscar T. Olson (secretary), Fred Winslow Adams, Clarence T. Craig, W. F. Dunkle, Nolan B. Harmon, and J. N. R. Score. Olson, pastor of Epworth–Euclid Church in Cleveland, had been on the Commission on the Revision of the Hymnal and Psalter in 1928 (MEC) and Dunkle was to be active on what became the Commission of Worship

[12](Both editions New York: E. P. Dutton).
[13](New York: Methodist Book Concern, 1932).

(UMC) until 1972. Adams had led the way with the Federal Council of Churches in producing *The Christian Year* (1937 and 1940) and promoting the season of kingdomtide.

In a rather amazingly short time these men produced the first *Book of Worship for Church and Home*,[14] approved in 1944 and published in 1945. A suggestion of possible resistance occurs in the title page warning: "For Voluntary and Optional Use." No such phrase appears in subsequent volumes. The 564-page book is a surprising production for a Church that had allotted less than 150 pages to worship materials and responsive readings in the previous *Hymnal*. There are now eleven orders of worship, possibly a consequence of revision by committee. There was a major growth under the category of "Festival Observances of the Christian Year." "The Ritual," "The Holy Rites and Offices of the Church," has been amplified by a large number of occasional offices for the life of local congregations.

The postwar years saw a great interest in neo-Reformation theology and the liturgical reflection of this was a rediscovery of Reformation and Wesleyan liturgies. In 1957 the National Methodist Student Movement published *The Wesley Orders of Common Prayer*.[15] It was edited by Edward C. Hobbs, then at Perkins School of Theology. The *Wesley Orders* had been preceded the year before by *The John Wesley Prayer Book*,[16] edited with commentary by W. Maynard French. Both volumes were signs of the times in the drift away from the liberal optimism of the pre-war years to a more realistic view of humanity with a need for confession and creeds. The dogmatism in Hobbs's "Introduction" ("There are other ways to worship—but not before this God") seems very out of date today. But it is significant that Wesley seemed to answer the needs of that time.

The process of liturgical revision began to accelerate. After only a dozen years the 1956 General Conference appointed a committee to begin further revision of the *Book of Worship* and *Hymnal*. An interim volume, the "Green Book" or *Proposed Revisions for the Book of Worship for Church and Home: For Trial Use 1960–1964*[17] was approved in 1960 for trial use. Some of the services went through considerable revision

---

[14](New York: Methodist Publishing House, 1945).
[15](Nashville: National Methodist Student Movement, 1957).
[16](Nashville: Parthenon Press, 1956).
[17](Nashville: Methodist Publishing House, 1960).

after that (eight versions of the Eucharist) before *The Book of Worship for Church and Home*[18] was approved in 1964 and published in 1965. It is now described as "according to the usages of The Methodist Church." Fred D. Gealy did much of the editorial work on it. The second *Book of Worship* begins with what are now called "The General Services of the Church" which include a long and short version of the Eucharist. A compromise on eucharistic theology had been reached in the ambiguity of "so to partake of this Sacrament." The term "confirmation" now entered Methodist vocabulary and since has proved impossible to eradicate. The Christian year looms large, begun with a one-year lectionary produced by William F. Dunkle, Jr. The psalter has returned along with "Canticles and Other Acts of Praise," and there is an abundance of "Occasional Offices of the Church." Three services from Wesley conclude the book. For the first time a woman's name appears on the Commission on Worship, Mrs. Floyd W. Rigg.

The Methodist Hymnal, approved by the 1964 General Conference and published in 1966, contained the newly-recovered psalter, other acts of praise, over a hundred pages of "aids for the ordering of worship" (many based on the Christian year), service music, and "the Ritual," all in the back of the book. Previous hymnals were accompanied by companion volumes (*The Hymns and Hymn Writers of the Church*[19] by Charles S. Nutter and Wilbur F. Tillett [for 1905] and *Our Hymnody*[20] by Robert Guy McCutchan [for 1935]). *Companion to the Hymnal*[21] by Fred D. Gealy, Austin Lovelace, and Carlton R. Young was devoted to the 1966 *Hymnal* and the 1989 *Hymnal* received a *Companion to the United Methodist Hymnal* by Carlton R. Young.[22] A new genre evolved in 1970 as the *Companion to the Book of Worship*, edited by William F. Dunkle, Jr. and Joseph D. Quillian, Jr.[23] Meanwhile, in 1968, the Evangelical United Brethren Church had joined with the Methodist Church to form the United Methodist Church. Since its union in 1947 the EUB had produced no less than three editions of the *Book of Ritual* (1952, 1955, and 1959).

[18](Nashville: Methodist Publishing House, 1965).
[19](New York: Methodist Book Concern, 1911).
[20](New York: Methodist Book Concern, 1937).
[21](Nashville: Abingdon Press, 1970).
[22](Nashville: Abingdon Press, 1993).
[23](Nashville: Abingdon Press, 1970).

By the time the *Companion to the Book of Worship* was published in 1970 it was clear to everyone that a revolution had occurred in worship and that the winds of liturgical change were blowing, and blowing hard, from a quite different direction. The most radical proposal for the 1964 Eucharist had been "a brisk version of 1549." But the storm let loose by Vatican II swept away both late medieval and Reformation possibilities alike. Ironically, the reports to general conference for the second *Book of Worship* and the *Hymnal* must have gone to the printer at just about the same time the *Constitution on the Sacred Liturgy* was promulgated in December 1963. No one knew then that we were publishing the last service books of the old order.

The new order for United Methodists began with a meeting of the Commission on Worship at United Theological Seminary in November of 1970. There some of us (then) young turks were able to convince the tired members of the Commission on Worship that it was imperative that we start all over again to do what some of them had only recently finished. Under the leadership of H. Grady Hardin of Perkins School of Theology, the Committee on Alternate Rituals began work and produced in leaflet form *The Sacrament of the Lord's Supper* in 1972. To our amazement this sold over two and a quarter million copies and encouraged work to proceed on *A Service of Baptism, Confirmation, and Renewal* that came out in 1976. *Ritual in a New Day* as well as *Word and Table* also appeared in 1976. In that year the series was named the *Supplemental Worship Resources*. Between 1972 and 1988 seventeen volumes were published in this series. *We Gather Together* (1980) was a second generation of the General Services (except ordination rites). The third generation appeared in *The Book of Services*[24] approved by the 1984 General Conference and published in 1985. Considerable fine tuning went on in the next quadrennium to produce the services as they finally appeared in *The United Methodist Hymnal*, approved in 1988 and published a year later. And the fifth generation may be said to be the additions that took place in the next quadrennium, were approved in 1992, and were published that same year as *The United Methodist Book of Worship*.[25]

---

[24](Nashville: United Methodist Publishing House, 1985).
[25](Nashville: United Methodist Publishing House, 1992).

Two enterprises during this period should be mentioned. The Committee to Study the Ordinal, consisting of representatives from the Section on Worship of the Board of Discipleship, the Board of Higher Education and Ministry, and the Council of Bishops, began work in 1978 on new ordination rites. The writer for this project was Dr. John D. Grabner who later produced a doctoral dissertation on Methodist ordination rites. The results of this committee's work was the publication in 1980 of *An Ordinal.*[26] This remained in optional use a dozen years until superseded by the rites in the *Book of Worship* that built upon it.

At the suggestion of the Publishing House, work was begun by what some called "the liturgical mafia" which led to the publication of *The Handbook of the Christian Year*[27] in 1986. This drew heavily on volumes in the *Supplemental Worship Resources* but was meant to appeal beyond the United Methodist Church. United Methodists were involved in producing the *Revised Common Lectionary*[28] and this led to the revision of the *Handbook* in 1992 as *The New Handbook of the Christian Year.*[29]

The publication in 1989 of the *United Methodist Hymnal* brought the *Supplemental Worship Resources* series to an end. This *Hymnal* marks a major event in Methodist liturgical history. Now the services for Sunday, with or without the Eucharist, and for baptism are up front, attractively printed with the rubrics in red and service music in several settings. Other services are in the back. Most amazing of all, there are a hundred psalms, each with the words and music of antiphons. No other Church had accomplished this in a hymnal. I still am astonished each Sunday by how much we got in the 1989 *Hymnal.* At last women came to play important roles in the process in the 1970s; Louise Shown chaired the Section on Worship for a number of years. Hoyt L. Hickman edited a most useful volume on *The Worship Resources of the United Methodist Hymnal*[30] and Diana Sanchez edited a similar volume on *The Hymns of the United Methodist Hymnal.*[31]

[26](Nashville: United Methodist Publishing House, 1979).
[27](Nashville: Abingdon Press, 1986).
[28](Nashville: Abingdon Press, 1992).
[29](Nashville: Abingdon Press, 1992).
[30](Nashville: Abingdon Press, 1989).
[31](Nashville: Abingdon Press, 1989).

The latest chapter, of course, is the 1992 *United Methodist Book of Worship*. It proclaims itself accurately as "the most comprehensive worship resource ever presented to our Church." If anything, that is an understatement. Just placing it alongside its two predecessors shows a startling increase in size. It now makes available to United Methodists all the liturgical resources that Roman Catholics, Episcopalians, or Lutherans enjoy with the exception of a detailed daily service, and it includes things they lack such as twenty-three eucharistic prayers (mostly seasonal) or some of the ethnic materials.

The third *Book of Worship* represents a liturgical maturity in American Methodism in which the resources are available and are second to none in quality. Part of this, no doubt, is because the North American churches have all borrowed so heavily from each other in their processes of liturgical revision. But American Methodists now have liturgical scholars of international reputation. It is not insignificant that the year the book appeared also marked the first time all thirteen United Methodist seminaries had a member of the North American Academy of Liturgy on their faculties.

And the real thrust now turns to teaching. The new services are not just a refurbishing of older materials in new language. They represent a radical shift in our thinking about the nature of the Church and what it does. At long last the recourse of reprinting Wesley, which helped us through a century (1867–1965), has been superseded although frequently with the intention of doing exactly what Wesley advocated.

I am still haunted by the question a member of my annual conference asked at a workshop: "Why haven't we heard about these things?" There is a tremendous amount of education and re-education that must go on before the worship resources we now have available can be understood and utilized to the best capacity. That is the challenge to us in the remaining years of this century: learn to use what we now have. We enjoy magnificent resources such as some of us and most of our predecessors never even dreamed would be possible. Our responsibility is to make good use of these resources through an educated ministry.

9. The Missing Jewel of the Evangelical Church

Given originally as a lecture to graduate students at Wheaton College in the mid 1980s, this eventually found its way into print in *Reformed Journal* 36 (June 1986). I would be more descriptive today and less sermonic.

When evangelical writers, concerned about the role of worship in the life of their churches, write on worship they often quote an important mid-century evangelical leader, A. W. Tozer (1897–1963) who declared in 1961 that "Worship is the missing jewel of the evangelical Church." In the years since then a revolution has transformed the worship of Roman Catholics and millions of Protestants in every part of the world. How has this revolution affected the worship life of evangelical churches? Is worship still "the missing jewel of the evangelical Church?" To find answers we need to explore the past sources of worship in the evangelical churches, to look critically at the present situation, and to examine factors currently operating to change evangelical practice.

Whence Evangelical Worship?

Evangelicals are found in considerable numbers in all nine worship traditions of American Protestantism: Lutheran, Reformed, Anabaptist, Anglican, Puritan, Quaker, Methodist, Frontier, and Pentecostal. But the overwhelming majority of American evangelicals (and the majority of American Protestants, for that matter) belong to a Church that worships in the Frontier Tradition. So pervasive is this tradition in America that the Reformed (Presbyterian) and Methodist traditions largely collapsed into it, leaving few distinctive Reformed and Methodist remnants in the worship of many of their congregations. Something over fifty million American Protestants worship in one style or another of the Frontier Tradition and a large portion of these millions are evangelicals. I shall direct most of my comments, then, to the Frontier or Revival Tradition of worship.

The concentration of American evangelicals in the Frontier Tradition of worship has sound historical roots. The Frontier Tradition traces its ancestry to both the English Puritans and the Methodists. The Puritans had insisted that Luther, Calvin, and Cranmer, revered though they were, had hesitated to go the full way in reforming worship completely according to God's word. The Puritan message was firm: no compromise with human traditions in worship. Completing the work of reformation meant that all of worship was to be shaped according to God's will as declared in Scripture. This did not necessarily mean the elimination of set liturgies but it did mean the end of much ceremonial for which biblical warrant was lacking. Methodism brought the development of new (or very ancient) forms for bringing worship to the unchurched. It introduced street preaching and hymnody.

In its origins, then, Frontier worship was essentially worship patterned on the Bible. But although traditions may preserve many original characteristics they do not remain static. The chief change in the last two centuries was movement not in a more scriptural direction but in a more practical one: worship was made useful. Time after time in the history of the Church Christians have tried to find a practical purpose for worship instead of worshiping for its own sake. Worship has been used to teach doctrine, improve morals, even entertain. In the nineteenth century worship in America was put to work, in this case the work of making converts. There was a great need in a largely unchurched nation to convert people to Christianity. Worship was used to do just that. Worship became a means rather than an end in itself. The net result was that revivalism reshaped Christian worship in a new Frontier Tradition. Charles G. Finney, the greatest of the revivalists, could promise that "the right use of means to raise grain" would produce "a crop of wheat." And worship came to be the prime means of planting the seed.

Thus freedom in worship became not so much freedom to follow God's word but freedom to do what worked. In short, much of American worship became highly practical. Do what works in worship—praying by name, the anxious bench, protracted meetings, and other new measures—and forget the customs of the past that no longer worked. One can ignore psalms if gospel songs work better;

one can eliminate common prayer if choral music is more productive. In other words, the Frontier Tradition forgot an essential aspect of worship, that worship has no purpose except the service of God.

Worship came to work wonderfully well in making converts for Methodists, Presbyterians, or Baptists. As a result, their worship became increasingly similar as Disciplines and Directories faded away in favor of the new techniques that worked so well. Although congregational autonomy in the ordering of worship was an earmark of much American worship, in practice there came to be little variety in worship among congregations or even denominations. (The Disciples of Christ and Churches of Christ stood out for their insistence on the weekly practice of the Lord's Supper as in the New Testament Church.) The result of the prevalence of Free Church worship was not immense variety as one might expect, but a very similar order of Sunday worship that varied little in structure whether in Methodist, Baptist, or independent congregations.

The usual order is a three-part structure: opening acts, a fervent sermon, and a harvest of those touched by the morning's sermon. The opening acts (significantly often called "preliminaries") usually include hymns, choral music, a pastoral prayer, a Scripture lesson, and an offering. The style of these varies according to the cultural milieu of the congregation, but the structure changes little. The sermon is often a call to decision for Christ. The harvest usually includes an invitation to join the Church or to be baptized. This often is followed by the singing of a hymn during which the candidates gather, then comes their reception, and, finally, the dismissal of everyone. There is nothing the least bit scriptural about the order; its only credential has been effectiveness in making converts.

The result of all this, no matter how sophisticated the music and preaching may get, is a worship tradition shaped more to producing converts or fresh adherents than to prayer and praise. This pattern is beautifully portrayed on television on several channels each Sunday. At worst the music is used as a softening-up technique, playing on sentiments and emotions; at best the music becomes a means of proclaiming God's word. In either case it is music geared to accomplishing a purpose rather than a spontaneous outpouring of praise. Unfortunately the essence of the historic roots of this tradition, namely to worship God as God prescribed, for which Puritans suffered imprisonment and death, has long ago been forsaken.

Given these historical developments, has evangelical worship today managed to outgrow its nineteenth-century utilitarianism? How successful have American evangelicals been in returning to scripturally-based practices in worship rather than functionally useful ones? We shall discuss four areas in which most evangelical worship, because of commitment to other priorities, still seems to ignore its scriptural foundations: the role of the community, the order of worship, the use of Scripture itself, and the sacraments.

One of the great losses of the nineteenth century was that of any strong sense of the Church as the community of "those who were being saved." The unity of the Church is everywhere an essential part of the biblical witness to New Testament worship. The oneness of the Body of Christ, about which Paul speaks so eloquently in 1 Corinthians 12 and Romans 12, was overlooked in favor of a fierce individualism. Revivalism sought to bring individuals to faith; it virtually ignored the Church as the community of faith where the Christian life is lived in the Body of Christ. The central concern of revivalism was with producing an individual relationship with God. The Church existed largely as a catalyst to make this reaction take place but it was not part of the new compound. The model of the Church was proclamation, not life together. Individuals heard the call to repentance and faith in the context of worship but the Church itself was not an intrinsic part of the message.

The picture of the individual alone with God is anything but the New Testament image of Christian worship. Paul's criterion for worship is clear: "All of these must aim at one thing: to build up the church" (1 Cor 14:26 NEB). For the New Testament Christian the assembled Church seems to be central in worship; to the modern evangelical it often seems simply an option. The gathered community can even be traded in for a television audience!

The New Testament speaks most emphatically about the Church when it mentions the sacraments. Paul's metaphor of the body is strong in many places when he speaks of baptism: "We were all brought into one body by baptism, in the one Spirit" (1 Cor 12:13). It is no less strong with regard to the Lord's Supper: "Because there is one loaf, we, many as we are, are one body; for it is one loaf of which we all partake" (1 Cor 10:17). Many other instances could be cited to show that for the New Testament Church the *koinonia* (community) in the Body of Christ is an essential dimension of worship. Far from being merely instrumental (in producing converts), the Church is essential as itself a foretaste of life in the kingdom of God.

Thus one of the greatest apostasies of evangelical worship today is the unscriptural notion of the Church that still lingers, that the Church is merely an instrument in gaining citizens for the future kingdom rather than involved as an essential part of life in the kingdom itself. Evangelicals need to recover the value that the New Testament itself attributes to life in the Body of Christ here and now. The Church as an optional collection of individuals is simply not faithful to the biblical witness.

A second area of unresolved difficulty is in the still-prevalent order of worship concocted by revivalism: preliminaries, a sermon, and harvest. The basic orientation of this order is, as we have said, worship as a means for changing humans rather than our offering of praise and glory to God. Worship directed to changing humans is hardly the offering of ourselves, "a living sacrifice, dedicated and fit for [God's] acceptance, the worship offered by mind and heart" (Rom 12:1). By focusing on the human object, much evangelical worship misses the center of biblical worship, the celebration of what God has done, is doing, and promises yet to do. The concentration on humans makes us overlook the real object of worship, God.

In the early Church, the Church of the martyrs, the unconverted were not even allowed to be present to pray with the congregation of the faithful. They were ushered out after hearing the preaching of the word so they would not contaminate the worship of "those baptized in the Lord's name" (*Didache* 9:5). Worship was primarily for faithful Christians to offer their worship "by mind and heart." This function has been largely relegated to the preliminaries, those parts of the service preceding the sermon. Yet the prayer and praise of Christian people is no preliminary. They are the basic reason the primitive Church assembled and an essential part of the breaking of bread together.

It is shocking to visit evangelical churches today where corporate prayer has almost completely disappeared except for a rapid recitation of the Lord's Prayer. The rest of prayer is relegated to the pastoral prayer which, all too often, turns out to be filled with preaching or announcements. The sense is largely absent that the community gathers together to join in the prayer of many voices. If the pastor has largely monopolized prayer, the choir has often done the same with the musical portions of the service. Frequently choral music simply replaces congregational song. Indeed, choral music has become to a large extent a reflection of upward social mobility in a congregation: the more sophisticated the people, the more singing tends to be delegated to trained singers.

When the sermon is placed close to the end of the service it becomes the chief focus. People come to worship to hear Pastor Smith rather than to offer prayer and praise together as in the biblical accounts. As worship becomes more professional, congregational participation declines. It is forgotten that in the Puritan meeting the congregation had the last word, for it could question the preacher's handling of Scripture.

The whole shape of the usual order of worship in evangelical churches deserves serious scrutiny in light of Paul's dictum that worship be a "living sacrifice" of ourselves. The "preliminaries" should be seen to be important acts of offering, the sermon ought to come near the center of the service, and the congregation must unite in response to the good news it has heard by joining in prayer of intercession and thanksgiving. Then worship would be more closely modeled on the biblical witness. A worship centering on our activities is not likely to produce martyrs; the worship of the New Testament Church with its focus on God's work produced many living sacrifices. Worship, after all, is largely a response to God's work. The community's response, its "so-what" to what it has heard about God's work, should be ringing from the rafters as the people depart.

A third area in which evangelical churches seem to be unscriptural is in the actual use of Scripture in worship itself. It is an amazing contrast to go from a Roman Catholic Sunday Mass with three full lessons from Scripture plus a psalm to a so-called "evangelical" service with only a few verses read as a sermon text. What is actually being said in these services? The Mass proclaims that Scripture is a basic part of the Christian life; the evangelical service indicates that Scripture is an option used as necessary. This "when convenient" use of Scripture in most evangelical services is hardly different from similar use of Scripture in many liberal Protestant churches.

Scripture is read in worship as God's word to God's people. Although the sermon is usually based on a biblical text, the sermon in no way replaces hearing God's word read for its own sake. Our earliest detailed description of Christian worship says "the memoirs of the apostles or the writings of the prophets are read as long as time permits" (Justin, *First Apology, 67*). If persecuted Christians would risk their very lives to hear God's word read, certainly such reading has value today. As the community listens to the readings it recovers its own corporate memories and receives its own identity. Each reading is an interpretation through which the voice and body of the reader give a here-and-now quality to timeless truth.

The most conspicuous change in worship in many Protestant churches during the last decade has been the widespread adoption of the ecumenical lectionary. This three-year cycle of three lessons (usually Old Testament, Epistle, and Gospel) for each Sunday and major festival has brought about significant restructurings of the order of worship and major changes in preaching. Nearly half the United Methodist and Presbyterian congregations in this country now structure their worship around the three lessons, whereas ten years ago few services had more than a single brief lesson. Psalms, hymns, or anthems link the passages with responses of praise or commentary. Preaching has moved much more in the direction of biblical interpretation rather than being topical or problem-centered. The sale of commentaries has soared. In the process, the Church year has been rediscovered as a means of putting worshipers in closer touch with the life of Christ.

A major question evangelical churches must face today is how much they wish their worship to reflect the centrality of Scripture in the Christian life. All revivalism needed was a verse or two to launch a sermon. But a community of faith needs a strong diet of God's word both read and preached. One can hardly blame many modern Christians for their biblical illiteracy when even at worship they hear only a few verses of Scripture read.

Preaching has gained much from the new use of the lectionary. Studies show that the average Presbyterian pastor preaches from no more than sixty-five biblical texts, for the most part those user-friendly texts with which he or she feels comfortable. The lectionary has forced the preacher to triple his or her repertoire and to study many unfamiliar texts. In that wrestling with difficult texts preaching has grown in depth as well as relevance.

Evangelicals should have much to rejoice in as they see lectionary reading and preaching spreading within Protestantism. It is the most encouraging sign we have of a new seriousness about the Bible in worship. When will evangelicals themselves join in this recovery of the use of the Bible in worship?

Finally, evangelicals have tended to prefer an approach to the sacraments more characteristic of the rationalism of the eighteenth-century Enlightenment than of the New Testament. The New Testament Church certainly considered the sacraments central in its life together, even to the point of daily breaking bread in the Jerusalem church (Acts 2:46). Baptism is prominent throughout Acts and the epistles.

If sacraments played a central role in the worship of the New Testament Church they certainly do not do so for most American Protestants other than the Disciples of Christ and Churches of Christ. The view of the sacraments as divinely appointed means of grace, so characteristic of Luther, Calvin, the Puritans, and Wesley, has little currency in most evangelical churches, even those where the Lord's Supper is celebrated weekly. The Enlightenment disbelief that anything physical can convey the spiritual, although at odds with Scripture, still dictates the approach of most evangelicals to the sacraments. In other areas they would repudiate Enlightenment rationalism as faithless and shallow, but such rationalism seems to be accepted uncritically with regard to the sacraments. The Enlightenment did not abolish sacraments, but it did relegate them to the margin of Church life by making them merely pious memory exercises and moralistic incentives rather than divine means of grace through which God works.

The traditional view that God works through the sacraments in gracious self giving is certainly closer to the feeding on the body and blood of Christ that Paul speaks of as the proclamation of the death of the Lord (1 Cor 11:26). The Enlightenment saw that moral values could be encouraged by the sacraments but the agency was entirely human: simply people reminding other people of what God had once done. This is quite different from discerning the body of the living Lord, failure to do which proved fatal to some Corinthian Christians (1 Cor. 11:30).

The legacy of the Enlightenment among American evangelicals led to infrequent celebration of the Lord's Supper and then in a most perfunctory fashion. Instead, preaching tended to make worship more cerebral as if there were no need for God's love to be made visible in sacraments. Indeed, the term "ordinance" was often substituted for "sacrament" and tended to foster a legalistic attitude. Christ commanded baptism (Matt 28:19) and said "do this" of the Lord's Supper (1 Cor 11:24-25). The legalistic term "ordinance" hardly touches the sense of mystery in God's self-giving that sacrament implies.

As yet the return to richer sacramental worship in many Protestant churches has not been reflected among evangelicals. It may well be that recovery of frequent celebration of the Lord's Supper on the New Testament pattern would help evangelicals recover the biblical sense of community, gain a more adequate order of worship, and bring the Scriptures to a greater centrality in worship. These four reforms are the wellspring of the worship revolution of our times. They ought to bring joy to the hearts of evangelicals, for they are rooted in Scripture.

Whither Evangelical Worship?

There has never been a period in Church history when worship remained absolutely unchanging. Even the Eastern Orthodox churches continue to adapt their worship to modern times and conditions, albeit without altering a single word. Like any other human activity, worship continues to change to this day. Not all such change is beneficial, as we have shown in surveying the deterioration of Puritan biblicism into American pragmatism. What factors are working today to move evangelical worship in more Scriptural directions? What more can be done to accelerate the process?

The Protestant Reformation of the sixteenth century was largely brought about by scholars, and most major reform movements since have been led by scholars. Competent scholarship is essential to insure that changes in worship are based on solid biblical, historical, theological, and pastoral principles. Otherwise worship change is all too subject to personal hobbies and notions and to factors irrelevant to the gospel.

Evangelicals have barely begun to invest the time and energy in liturgical studies that must undergird useful change. The Roman Catholic liturgical revolution, climaxing in 1963, represented sixty years of scholarly preparation. A symbol of the present state of evangelical liturgical studies was the recent republication by a major evangelical publishing house of a 1936 book on worship. Yet more has happened to change worship in the last fifty years than in the previous four hundred years. To trail half a century behind in the study of worship is not something to publicize!

There are a few bright moments to celebrate. A highly-respected New Testament scholar, Ralph P. Martin of Fuller Theological Seminary, has led the way with several significant books, including *Worship in the Early Church* (1964), *Carmen Christi* (1967), and *The Worship of God* (1982). He begins where all serious liturgical scholarship must start, with the worship of the first-century Church.

Another pioneer is Professor Robert E. Webber of Wheaton College. No one has done as much to acquaint evangelicals with the wider traditions. Full of energy, he has written, organized programs, and taught with zeal. Well versed in current liturgical scholarship, Webber has been a vigorous advocate of the idea that the maturity of American evangelicalism should be reflected in Church consciousness and worship renewal. His *Common Roots* (1978) and his textbook *Worship Old and New* (1982) are faithful to evangelical principles and based on solid scholarship. Most recently he has edited the seven volume *Complete Library of Christian Worship*. Professor Thomas Howard, formerly of Gordon College, has written apologetic works, especially *The Liturgy Explained* (1981) and *Evangelical Is Not Enough* (1984). A kindred spirit is Peter E. Gillquist, *The Physical Side of Being Spiritual* (1979). Most encouraging signs appear in two recent books: Marva Dawn's *Reaching Out without Dumbing Down* (1995) and C. Welton Gaddy, *The Gift of Worship* (1992).

These have been joined by less scholarly works in recent years, most notably Ronald Allen and Gordon Borror's *Worship: Rediscovering the Missing Jewel* (1982) and Robert G. Rayburn's *O Come, Let Us Worship* (1980). Others have contributed on the popular level: Anne Ortlund, *Up with Worship* (1975); Judson Cornwall, *Let Us Worship* (1983); Anne Murchison, *Praise and Worship* (1981); John MacArthur, Jr., *The Ultimate Priority* (1983); and Paul E. Engle, *Discovering the Fullness of Worship* (1981). Some of these writings, however, simply assume that worship scholarship either does not exist or is irrelevant.

Beyond the development of scholarship about worship is the need to make the study of worship a vital part of the seminary preparation of future ministers. The great evangelical seminaries have developed impressive faculties in recent years, yet not a single one has on its faculty a person who has completed Ph.D. studies in Christian worship. Until such scholars are trained, worship will either not be taught at all or will be taught by people who have not done advanced study of their subject. Seminaries would hardly tolerate such a situation in ethics, New Testament, or pastoral counseling. A genuine commitment of people and resources is necessary. I am happy to note that Dallas Theological Seminary now (1995) has a faculty member who has applied for membership in the North American Academy of Liturgy, the scholarly body in the field. Library materials must be built up in this area. (Some of the most valuable books in my personal library were discards from a leading evangelical seminary library.)

Programs in sacred music are no substitute for the serious study of worship. Quite frankly, a degree in sacred music without substantial study of worship may equip one to do the Church more harm than good. Music professionalism tends to stress quality of performance rather than congregational participation. If music is to be used for anything other than a softening-up technique or a flaunting of sophistication it must become an integral part of the order of worship and the Church year. The church musician must have pastoral and theological training as well as musical skills.

Beyond scholarship and seminary teaching are other necessities for constructive worship change among evangelicals. Many denominations have come to regard denominational staff in worship as essential. Yet where is the evangelical worship executive? Or better still, let us ask: "Where is the person trained to fill such a position were it open?" It is not a job for a benevolent amateur but for someone with the scholarly training and pastoral experience to answer questions, produce publications, and conduct workshops for clergy and laity.

Periodicals about worship are an ongoing means of educating ministers and laypeople. There are some long-established ecumenical publications. Evangelicals never seem to contribute to them and probably few subscribe. But so far no evangelical alternative has appeared.

Finally, evangelicals need workshops that can help remedy deficiencies in seminary training and keep ministers current. The Lutherans held 750 workshops to help introduce the 1978 *Lutheran Book of Worship*. That involved a great deal of work but was necessary for worship changes to be understood and well used. A beginning was made by a conference at Southwestern Baptist Theological Seminary in September 1995.

A revolution in worship has swept through much of Christianity in recent decades. In many ways it has brought the churches of the world closer to their origins in the worshiping Church of the New Testament. Evangelicals ought to rejoice in these changes but have, for the most part, been content to pass by on the other side. It is time for them to acknowledge that Church growth must be growth in depth as well as in numbers. Evangelicals must make a serious commitment to worship reform and not leave it to Roman Catholics and other Protestants. And there is no better way to begin than by making their worship more scriptural.

10. Protestant Public Worship in America: 1935–1995

First published as an essay in *Altered Landscapes, Christianity in America, 1935–1985: Essays in Honor of Robert T. Handy* (Grand Rapids: Eerdmans, 1989), this has been expanded by adding the past decade. Used by permission.

The past sixty years have seen momentous changes in the public worship of many of the Protestant churches of America. I shall pick up the account where Henry Sloane Coffin left it in 1935 in *The Church through Half a Century*[1] although it is a quite different kind of history that I must survey. This is especially true because of the difficulty of doing justice to the full spectrum of Protestant worship in America. One has nine major liturgical traditions plus many ethnic, racial, and cultural styles within each of those traditions. At best we can only hint at the diversity present in American Protestant worship, a diversity ranging from the right-wing liturgical traditions, Lutheran and Anglican, to the central traditions, Methodist and Reformed, to the left-wing traditions, Anabaptist, Puritan, Quaker, Frontier, and Pentecostal.

Clearly, in American Protestantism the majority tradition is the Frontier tradition. Unfortunately, little liturgical scholarship has been directed to the study of its development in America, particularly in its various sectarian expressions. This makes it a "soft" tradition when confronted with a tradition whose development has been carefully documented and articulated, a "hard" tradition. The soft traditions are often vulnerable to being shaped into conformity with traditions that have benefited from liturgical scholarship simply because there is no one to defend the values of an unstudied tradition. Such lacunae certainly make it difficult to write a comprehensive

[1](New York: Charles Scribner's Sons, 1936) 185–206.

history of worship in this period since some traditions are so much less accessible for historical documentation than others.

On the one hand there are the right-wing traditions in which service books such as the *Lutheran Book of Worship*[2] or the *Book of Common Prayer*[3] are mandatory and the degree of predictability for the words (rite) is high although actions (ceremonial) can vary widely. In the central traditions, except for the sacraments, which usually follow a service book, the usual Methodist or Presbyterian Sunday service has no uniform structure and the degree of predictability is much lower. For the left-wing majority, the only predictability comes in the use of a hymnal (which may or not be denominational) and the Bible. Obviously, the higher the degree of predictability, the easier it is to chronicle developments, but since the right-wing traditions are a minority such an account is always only partial.

I shall trace the scene in Protestant public worship in America chronologically from 1935 to 1995. This time span seems to divide into three parts: the period of aestheticism from 1935 to 1945, the period of historicism from 1945 to 1965, and the period of ecumenism from 1965 to 1995. Our only clue as to future developments is to note the likely continuance of present-day tendencies and some of their probable consequences.

Aestheticism (1935–1945)

Our first decade represents the growing sophistication of American society and the tendency to substitute the experience of the beautiful for emotional outbursts. My home congregation decided, when it built its new gothic church, to forbid shouts of "Amen" during services, much to the consternation of some. But the buttoned-down emotions found alternate forms of expression in printed services, the splendor of stained glass, and choral music. Vested choirs replaced the gospel octet; prayers of confession were printed for all to read in unison, and the altar was safely fixed to the wall, near to God and away from people. For all except Pentecostals and Quakers this period saw the triumph of that greatest liturgical innovator since Gutenberg, one A. B. Dick, a Chicago businessman whose stencil duplicator made every pastor an instant Cranmer when it came to preparing services.

[2](Minneapolis: Augsburg Publishing House, 1978).
[3](New York: Church Hymnal Corporation, 1979).

The two great leaders during this era for much of central and left-wing Protestantism were Von Ogden Vogt (1879–1964) and Elbert M. Conover (1885–1952). Vogt's four books, especially *Art and Religion*,[4] advocated borrowing "from the materials of the past those treasures which are least burdened with abandoned concepts" (*Modern Worship*, 39).[5] This encouraged an eclectic style of blending past treasures with present relevance, placing Darwin and Marx in stained glass for example. Conover's influence was in church architecture. As Director after 1934 of the Interdenominational Bureau of Architecture, Conover advocated building gothic churches with divided chancels. His books such as *Building the House of God*[6] and *The Church Builder*[7] were widely used. Conover's legacy was scattered all over the land as Methodists, Presbyterians, Congregationalists, and Baptists erected their own less expensive versions of the elegant gothic that Ralph Adams Cram (1863–1942) had popularized among Episcopalians.

Valiant efforts were made during this period to improve the quality of church music. Individuals such as Archibald T. Davison of Harvard (*Protestant Church Music in America*)[8] led the way. The anthem became a well-established part of mainline church music. In black congregations the gospel hymn was brought to new heights by Charles Tindley (1856–1933) and Thomas Dorsey (1899–1993).

Preaching tended to be topical with great concern for relevancy. William Stidger in Boston typified the concern for "preaching to real life situations." Issues of pacifism were raised as war loomed ahead and then preachers had to address the concerns of a nation at war.

There seems to have been little awareness either among Protestants or most Roman Catholics of the presence of a small group of liturgical pioneers whose work would help bring about a new reformation in worship, both Roman Catholic and Protestant. Roman Catholics, especially Virgil Michel (1890–1938), H. A. Reinhold (1897–1968), William Busch (1882–1971), Martin Hellriegel (1890–1981), Gerald Ellard (1894–1963), and Reynold Hillenbrand (1905–1979) were busy sowing the seeds on this side of the Atlantic for changes that would

[4](New Haven: Yale University Press, 1921).
[5](New Haven: Yale University Press, 1927).
[6](New York: Methodist Book Concern, 1928).
[7](New York: Interdenominational Bureau of Architecture, 1948).
[8](Boston: E. C. Schirmer Music Company, 1933).

sweep across the face of American Christian worship after Vatican II. William Palmer Ladd (1870–1941) was doing the same in the Episcopal Church.

For Methodists the era produced the first *Book of Worship*,[9] the first full service book since Wesley's in 1784. This 1945 volume, labeled "For Optional and Voluntary Use," gathered together a variety of orders of service plus materials for the Church year. Much was borrowed from Anglican sources but the use of the book was rather limited except for the official "Ritual." In similar fashion, the next year the Presbyterian Church in the United States of America published a new edition of the *Book of Common Worship*[10] garnished by widespread borrowings from Anglican and Reformed churches and with the addition of a lectionary. In a sense these volumes show the direction the central and left churches were leaning. Much of the borrowing from other traditions seems to have been motivated by fascination with the aesthetic quality of the materials borrowed.

Historicism (1945–1965)

The period after World War II saw major shifts in worship priorities among American Protestants. Somehow worship as a parallel to the experience of the good, true, and beautiful was simply not enough. Perry Miller once remarked that before the war he was an Emerson enthusiast; after leading the tank corps that liberated Buchenwald he became a Jonathan Edwards follower. The theological expression of this shift forced on a whole generation by world history was neo-orthodoxy. Once faith in humanity's innate goodness was shattered, something more sound had to replace it. This found expression in a period of historicism or neo-reformation focus in worship. For twenty years these trends tended to be dominant in what was written about worship and shaped what was practiced in thousands of congregations.

The usable past that best suited the needs of this era was the Reformation of the sixteenth century although Methodists got equal mileage out of the eighteenth. We now realize why the worship of this era had such appeal. The heavily penitential language of the Reformation liturgies spoke directly to and for those who were bent

[9](Nashville: The Methodist Publishing House, 1945).

[10](Philadelphia: Publication Division of the Board of Christian Education of the Presbyterian Church in the United States of America, 1946).

on recovering the great Christian doctrine of original sin. The most conspicuous part of Anglican morning prayer that Methodists incorporated in the second *Book of Worship*[11] was the penitential preface added by Cranmer in 1552. "Miserable offenders" may still have been a bit strong for Methodists but the penitential tone was certainly there. Indeed, it is nearly impossible to persuade ministers who received their theological training in the 1950s and early 1960s that they can dispense with a prayer of confession on any occasion, even weddings. Certainly the penitential aspect of worship received more than its due share of attention in this period.

This was also the period of Sputnik. Americans learned to feel the insecurity of trusting in military might alone. A much greater concern with the historic Christian faith became evident, especially as that faith was stated in the historic creeds. While the previous era delighted in impromptu affirmations of faith, frequently composed weekly, the period of historicism recovered the thrill of tradition. The Apostles' or Nicene Creeds once again became an important part of worship. Curiously, this concern with firm foundations did not yet translate into widespread use of a lectionary outside the right-wing traditions. Lutherans became embroiled in controversy over the addition of a eucharistic prayer in the 1958 *Service Book and Hymnal*.[12] A clear break with Lutheran tradition, it nevertheless meant the addition of that important creedal element to "The Communion."

Beyond these specific items the liturgies of the Reformation and Wesley eras had a great appeal. The most representative book of this period was Bard Thompson's *Liturgies of the Western Church*,[13] which provided ready access to the great Protestant liturgies from Luther to Wesley. Among the Reformed the Mercersburg School of the nineteenth century, which had recycled similar materials a hundred years earlier, was the subject of much scholarly attention. Presbyterians were busy rediscovering that Calvin and Knox had produced service books and Methodists found that much of Wesley's warm heart was

[11](Nashville: The Methodist Publishing House, 1965). Note that the 1945 edition said on the title page, "For Voluntary and Optional Use." This does not appear in the second (1965) edition. Instead, it claims "according to the usages of the Methodist Church."

[12](Minneapolis: Augsburg Publishing House, 1958).

[13](Cleveland: World Publishing Company, 1961). This book still remains in print (with various publishers).

fueled by the cold print of his *Sunday Service*.[14] In essence what was beginning to happen in the central churches and some on the left wing was that the dominant revivalistic order of worship with its invariable three parts—preliminaries, sermon, harvest—was beginning to be challenged by alternative possibilities. Services might still end with "An Invitation to Christian Discipleship" but there now was an alternate past to use other than that of nineteenth-century evangelism.

Some evidence of the amount of change in two decades is found in the next generation of Methodist and Presbyterian service books. The second *Book of Worship* (1965) shows Methodists looking to Wesley for guidance in terms of his Anglican heritage. One of the compilers claimed the 1965 revision of the Eucharist was meant to be "a brisk version of [Cranmer's] 1549." This return to the Reformation era was a major feature of the book, which also added a lectionary, recovered portions of the psalter, and incorporated resources for the Church's year. The language was still Elizabethan. The 1970 Presbyterian *Worshipbook*[15] was largely completed by 1968. It appeared late enough to adopt contemporary language but too early for inclusive language. Like the Methodist book it could not anticipate most of the revisions of the era after Vatican II although the brand new ecumenical lectionary was included. Essentially the *Worshipbook* is a neo-Reformation book, making a valiant effort to achieve the weekly Eucharist that Calvin had sought. The service also follows him in keeping the warrant detached from the eucharistic prayer. In both books the focus is much more on the sixteenth and eighteenth centuries than the third and fourth. The usable past was to change drastically in a few short years.

At the time important agents for the transformation of worship were still in embryonic form and scarcely recognized as consequential at the time. Associated Parishes, founded in 1947, became the spearhead for liturgical renewal among Episcopalians. Two years later, the 1949 General Convention authorized the beginning of the *Prayer Book Studies*[16] series that, beginning in 1950, began to publicize

[14]Cf. *John Wesley's Sunday Service of the Methodists in North America* (Nashville: United Methodist Publishing House, 1984).

[15](*Services* edition Philadelphia: Westminster Press, 1970; *Services and Hymns* edition, 1972).

[16](New York: Church Pension Fund or Church Hymnal Corporation, 1950–1989, volumes 1–30).

the case for revision of the 1928 prayer book. In 1946 William E. Slocum and Romey P. Marshall founded the Order of St. Luke among Methodists. We have already mentioned the Roman Catholic liturgical pioneers who had begun to plant for a great harvest that finally came in the 1970s.

Surely one of the most significant developments of this period was the growth of liturgical scholarship among American Protestants. This new phenomenon was reflected by such men as Cyril C. Richardson, Massey H. Shepherd, Jr., Luther D. Reed, Arthur Karl Piepkorn, and others. Liturgical scholars were gradually appointed to seminary faculties, particularly the Methodist seminaries. There they could help break the captivity to the familiar that so many seminarians brought with them. As early as 1955 the United Lutheran Church in America led the way in appointing the first full-time denominational worship executive, Edward Brown.

The 1950s and 1960s saw much attention given to congregational song (hymnody). Hymnbooks of this period tended to look back to the recovery of the best from the past. Instrumental and choral music were improved by nine schools of sacred music, including the Westminster Choir College (established in 1926) and Union's School of Sacred Music (1928).

The 1950s had seen an enormous amount of church building, which became a billion-dollar annual industry during this period. Many of these buildings were built on the twin assumptions that Christian worship was basically unchanging and that the Church occupied a dominant place in society. Both assumptions were to undergo serious questioning during the 1970s but the buildings of this period remain obstinate monuments to prior opinions.

Preaching during this period, in many cases, moved to more impassioned pleas for social reform as the civil rights movement (and opposition to it) engulfed the attention of many congregations. Lectionary preaching was still only a little cloud on the horizon although the denominations were now making lectionaries available. New exegetical tools, especially the *Interpreter's Bible*,[17] gave the preacher improved resources for biblical study.

---

[17](New York: Cokesbury–Abingon Press, 1951–1957), 12 volumes.

Ecumenism (1965–1995)

No one, least of all Roman Catholics, was prepared for the hurricane of liturgical change that came in the wake of Vatican II. The next two decades saw more liturgical change for western Christians than the past four centuries. For Roman Catholic worship the Middle Ages came to an abrupt end on December 4, 1963 with the promulgation of the *Constitution on the Sacred Liturgy*.[18] Few Protestants suspected then that Vatican II had also written much of the agenda for Protestant liturgical change. A period of glacial change was transformed overnight into one of hurricane velocity.

The Liturgy Constitution approved at Vatican II was the result of sixty years of scholarly and pastoral work. But the immediate response was anything but scholarly. The late sixties was a period of euphoria for ministers and priests, who acted like people released from long years of imprisonment. All manner of common assumptions about worship were questioned and found to be purely arbitrary. The organ was challenged by the guitar, stained glass by cloth banners, and the seated congregation by dancers.

From the perspective of thirty years much of this late 1960s response now seems inevitable. We have now accepted as dogma that worship can and should change. But this discovery in the late 1960s was an important moment of liberation. Much that now seems silly— the balloons and confetti, the wordy banners and placards—was a necessary part of experiencing liberation before the work of reconstruction could begin. Clearly much of the impetus for change among Protestants was the excitement of Roman Catholics when they first realized they could be folksy, too. Nothing was as well publicized as those so-called "underground" Masses. The new folksong music with a beat delighted many while textile art blossomed in churches. All these were contagious among Protestants. The spirit of the 1960s, exacerbated by an unpopular war, encouraged rebellion from set forms.

Something much more important was happening than was then apparent. We had moved into a new era in which it became impossible to view worship in terms of the old isolated traditions. The period 1965–1995 was, above all else, the ecumenical era in which worship led the way in breaking down many remaining juridical and theological barriers. Once freed from inhibitions everyone shame-

[18](Collegeville: The Liturgical Press, 1963).

lessly borrowed from everyone else. Denominational hymnals, for example, became something of an anomaly; the contents were becoming more and more similar with each revision. If one's only criterion was finding the best available, denominational labels were no longer important.

Much of the post-Vatican II hurricane came as the result of earlier and lesser storms of the Liturgical Movement. Whether one traces this movement back to Prosper Guéranger (1805–1875) in France, Lambert Beauduin (1873–1960) in Belgium, or the host of other liturgical pioneers, the Liturgical Movement set the stage for the post-Vatican II reforms, Protestant and Catholic. In this country one can trace shortly after World War II the growing urgency of the vernacular for Roman Catholic liturgical reformers. Certainly this issue became the linchpin for the new reforms although the Liturgy Constitution itself was remarkably reticent beyond allowing at Mass "a suitable place . . . [for] their mother tongue," particularly in the readings, common prayer, and responses. The complete abandonment of Latin was hardly envisioned.

Keys concepts in the Liturgy Constitution have governed the reforms of many churches, especially "full, conscious, and active participation," "a noble simplicity," a "richer fare" of Scripture, and indigenization. Whether any Church has achieved much of the last named is questionable although efforts have certainly been made. But participation, simplicity, and Scripture stand out as keynotes in all that liturgical reformers in the various western churches have attempted in recent years.

Vatican II mandated the revision of all the liturgical books, work that began in 1964 and was virtually complete with the publication of *De Benedictionibus*[19] in 1984 and *Caeremoniale Episcoporum*[20] the same year. By comparison, the Tridentine books took nearly fifty years (1568–1614). Unlike the Tridentine books, the new rites had great consequences for Protestants as well.

One of the most obvious changes was the adoption of a modern English vernacular when the stage of translation was reached. Until 1970 all Protestant service books were written in Elizabethan English. Long forgotten was that the Reformers had insisted on addressing

[19](Vatican City: Congregation for Divine Worship, 1984).
[20](Vatican City: Congregation for Divine Worship, 1984).

God with the familiar second person, "Du," "Thou" instead of more formal forms. In the four centuries since then the language of worship had again become sacralized, just the opposite of what the Reformers desired. The 1970s saw much controversy over this issue. Eventually Episcopalians were to compromise and publish rites 1 and 2 in Elizabethan and contemporary English with both traditional and contemporary collects. The Presbyterians led the way with a complete service book in contemporary language. Some of this material from the early 1970s now seems a bit flat but it was probably necessary to get the theology straight before moving on to more lyrical language.

One Reformation pattern that did surface in the local liturgies of the late 1960s was the tendency to didacticism. One can spot the services of this time because they put into the mouths of the people lengthy theological or ethical statements. The compulsion to make worship useful led to didacticism just as had John Knox's tendency to pray a commentary on the Lord's Prayer.

Folk music became a popular idiom as the pendulum swung farther to popular participation. Professionally trained church musicians felt shouldered aside by guitar-plucking teenagers. Often sung to rather simplistic lyrics, the music had a winsomeness to invite participation by anyone who could hum a simple tune. Various supplements were issued to augment denominational hymnals but they were often outsold by private collections in paperback.

Such custodians of good music as Erik Routley (1917–1982) sought to channel the best of the music and texts into new hymnals. Monuments of this period are *The Hymnal of the United Church of Christ*,[21] the *Lutheran Book of Worship* (1978), *The Hymnal 1982* (Episcopal),[22] and Routley's own product for the Reformed Church of America, *Rejoice in the Lord*[23] (1984). Later on came *The United Methodist Hymnal* (1989), *The Presbyterian Hymnal* (1990), and *New Century Hymnal* (United Church of Christ, 1995). Each of these has had to incorporate new musical idioms including folk song, ethnic materials, and the more conventional texts of such modern hymn writers as Brian Wren and F. Pratt Green. These hymnals are dis-

---

[21](Philadelphia: United Church Press, 1974).
[22](New York: Church Hymnal Corporation, 1985).
[23](Grand Rapids: Eerdmans, 1985).

tinctly political documents, trying to relate to a wider variety of constituents than ever contemplated in previous hymnals.

Enormous changes have had to come in the architectural setting of worship. It became hard for anyone to justify altar-tables fixed against the wall when Roman Catholics had made them all free-standing. Once one celebrated the Eucharist facing the people it was difficult to turn one's back on them again. There was a widespread move toward more centralized space with the people gathered as closely as possible about pulpit, altar-table, and font. Participation became the key word in architecture as well as in rites. A new concern developed late in this period with gathering space and its effect on the process of coming together to form a community. Increasing attention was shown to the design of baptismal fonts so that the baptism of babies (among pedobaptists) by immersion would be possible and immersion of adults feasible in all cases.

Clearly a very significant characteristic of this period was the revision of liturgical texts by many of the major denominations. In several ways this process was different from all previous revisions. Certainly much of the revision of Protestant liturgical books was sparked by the major revisions underway among Roman Catholics. The resources made available in Vatican City and the priority given this process by Paul VI had assured that the Roman Catholic revisions would be the most careful in history. No other church could match the full-time paid staff and 800 consultants used in developing the Roman Catholic Sunday Mass lectionary. In this case the lectionary was simply revised and adopted by Protestants.

Behind the reforms was a vast body of scholarship in which the work of non-Roman Catholic scholars such as Yngve Brilioth or Gregory Dix played important roles whether in shaping revisions by Presbyterians or Roman Catholics. More than any other document the third-century *Apostolic Tradition* ascribed to Hippolytus helped shape the course of liturgical revisions such as the Roman Catholic Eucharist or the 1980 United Methodist *An Ordinal*.[24] The same documents, the same scholarship were accessible to everyone; it is not strange that the revised liturgies looked alike. Ironically, the conservative Hippolytus sparked much liturgical change in the twentieth century by opposing it in the third.

[24](Nashville: United Methodist Publishing House, 1979).

Few churches participated in this process without constantly being aware of what other churches were doing. And there were few inhibitions about borrowing whatever was considered superior. Episcopalians took from Lutherans the observance of Transfiguration as the last Sunday after the Epiphany, a practice dating back to Johann Bugenhagen. United Methodists adopted the Reformed custom of a prayer of illumination as Calvin had practiced. All made their own versions of the Roman Catholic Sunday lectionary. Far more than that of any other period in history this was an ecumenical approach to worship reform.

Much depended on when one entered the process and when one went into print with hardbound books, effectively stopping the process. Numerous issues arose, so later entrants benefited from the solutions and mistakes of the earlier arrivals. By the time the decision to accept contemporary English became common to all, new concerns had already arisen over the use of inclusive language for humans and, eventually, for God. The process of initiation posed new issues. The books prepared by Methodists and Presbyterians in the 1960s had split the process and used the term "confirmation." In the 1970s, attempts were made to reunite the process and (unsuccessfully) to eliminate the term "confirmation" altogether.

All entered the process with a tradition of few or no options other than a standard form. Roman Catholics surprised everyone by authorizing in 1967 four, then eventually nine eucharistic prayers. Episcopalians produced six, Lutherans six (counting the *verba* alone), Presbyterians eight, and United Methodists a total of twenty-four. Such a variety of anaphoras had disappeared in the West for nearly a thousand years. In almost every new rite a variety of options and possible variances is provided. Flexibility and adaptability became favored terms in modern liturgical revision.

As the seventies progressed, new questions of justice became more and more acute as it was increasingly realized that worship had often been a source of injustice. The exclusion of language about women and children or the use as negative images of such terms as "black," "blind," "old," or "child" led many to realize that worship was deeply involved in unwitting forms of social control. Even more important than language were the roles people played in the leadership of worship. Many congregations discovered that they had no good reason for having only middle-aged men as ushers or for hiring men as organists in large churches and expecting women to volunteer to do the music elsewhere. Roman Catholics began having women help distribute communion at a time when some United Methodist bishops were discouraging anyone but the ordained from such a role. As more and more women entered the ministry in most churches except the Lutheran Church–Missouri Synod, clerical garb frequently began to change from a black preaching robe with padded shoulders to the ancient and unisex alb. Efforts were made to understand worship in terms of children's stages of development. The roles played in worship were opened to a greater variety of ages and both sexes.

Language about humans was resolved, for the most part, in the seventies. God language still remains hotly debated. United Methodists (1984 and 1990) and Presbyterians have tried to give guidelines at the national level but with little resulting consensus. The National Council of Churches' *An Inclusive Language Lectionary*[25] provoked much controversy but little agreement in its revision of Scripture.

An important advance has been made in the deliberate attempt to include minorities in the process of revision of liturgical texts and hymnals. Revision committees now are much more representative of all segments of the Church involved. No longer, for instance, can it be assumed that all American Presbyterians speak English as their first language. This new consciousness is perhaps most apparent in music and in the concern to represent Hispanic, Asiatic, Native American, and Black hymns in new editions of hymnals. This also insures that the folksy hymns of Bill Gaither will be represented in new hymnals just as surely as more sophisticated Erik Routley works.

Thus many of the problems encountered, the methods employed, and the resulting rites were remarkably similar. In this period, worship became more and more a source of unity among many Christians rather than a matter of disunity. Still, distinctive characteristics of each tradition persisted. The period of liturgical revision begun in the wake of Vatican II extended for about thirty years after the *Constitution on the Sacred Liturgy* (1963–1993). Its final monuments were *The United Methodist Book of Worship* (1992) and the Presbyterian *Book of Common Worship* (1993). Some occasional services yet remained (e.g., Presbyterian ordinations) and books for some of the

[25](Atlanta: John Knox Press, 1983–1985).

smaller churches. But essentially the United Methodist and Presbyterian books are a testimony to what was accomplished in this period and represented the best of everyone's work. It is instructive to look briefly at the chief denominational achievements in the process of liturgical revision.

In the Episcopal Church the Standing Liturgical Committee had a head start with authorization as early as 1949 to commence the process of revision of the 1928 *Book of Common Prayer*. Thirty years later this action led to a new book, the fourth American *Book of Common Prayer*. Immediately noticeable is the increased length of the new book, from 611 pages in 1928 to 1001 in 1979. If a consensus was reached in the process of prayer book revision it was that there were equally acceptable alternate routes to the same destination and the new acknowledgement of pluralism may be the most distinctive feature of the final product.

The Lutheran process was quite different. In the fall of 1966 the Inter-Lutheran Commission on Worship was organized by the major Lutheran bodies in this country and Canada. The ultimate goal was a joint service book. The result of twelve years of effort was the publication in 1978 of the *Lutheran Book of Worship*, a combination of service book and hymnal. It made music an integral part of the usual services with a variety of stylistic options. On the eve of publication the Missouri Synod withdrew from the process to publish its own *Lutheran Worship*,[26] although some Missouri congregations use the *Lutheran Book of Worship*.

It was more difficult to involve United Methodists in liturgical revision, especially when the 1965 *Book of Worship* and 1966 *Book of Hymns*[27] were still almost new. But by 1970 even those who had just been through eight years of labor on those volumes could be persuaded that a whole new era had dawned. After a long period of trial use services from 1972 to 1989 the *United Methodist Hymnal* appeared in 1989 and the *United Methodist Book of Worship* in 1992.

A similar process ensued among Presbyterians in the 1980s with a series of *Supplemental Liturgical Resources*. This process culminated in 1990 with *The Presbyterian Hymnal* and, in 1993, the *Book of Common Worship*.

[26](St. Louis: Concordia, 1982).
[27](Nashville: Methodist Publishing House, 1966). Originally published as *The Methodist Hymnal*.

Some important consequences are apparent in the revisions of the 1970s and 1980s. Clearly the most successful of the new liturgical books has been the lectionary. Published by Roman Catholics in 1969 for use at the beginning of the 1970 liturgical year, it was immediately picked up and revised by Presbyterians, Episcopalians, and Lutherans. In 1974 the Consultation on Church Union did a consensus (and fifth) version of the four versions then in use. This was adopted for a decade by the United Methodist Church. Clearly the number of varieties was a problem even though the differences among them were minor. Ten years later the Consultation on Common Texts published *The Common Lectionary*.[28] Not only did it overcome the discrepancies between the variants but it made a major advance by introducing a *lectio continua* pattern for the Old Testament lessons after the Day of Pentecost. *The Revised Common Lectionary* (1992)[29] took note of problems in three cycles of use and made many improvements. *The Common Lectionary* was immediately accepted by United Methodists and Presbyterians, more recently the *RCL* by Lutherans (1995) and Episcopalians (1994). Appeals by the American hierarchy to Rome for its use among Roman Catholics have so far been unsuccessful.

The greatest impact of the lectionary has, of course, been on preaching. It is now estimated that sixty-five per cent of United Methodist clergy use the lectionary, an astonishing change from almost none twenty years earlier. The consequences for preaching have been enormous especially in reaching for a more exegetical approach to preaching. Commentaries based on the lectionary such as Reginald Fuller's *Preaching the New Lectionary*[30] or the several series of *Proclamation* volumes have sold widely. It is significant that the lectionary includes the Old Testament each Sunday except during the Easter Season and thereby introduces the thirty-eight books of the Bible (other than the psalter) that had been largely absent from Protestant worship in recent decades.

Anyone who bought into use of the lectionary soon found that he or she had also purchased a much deeper engagement with the Church's year. Festivals such as the Baptism of the Lord,

[28](New York: Church Hymnal Corporation, 1984).
[29](Nashville: Abingdon Press, 1992).
[30](Collegeville: The Liturgical Press, 1974, rev. ed. 1984).

Transfiguration, All Saints' Day, or Christ the King became part of their annual cycle and this led to a greater number of special services such as Christmas Eve, Ash Wednesday, and the Easter Vigil, which, although previously unknown, are rapidly becoming part of the worship life of many congregations. This new approach to preaching has led many preachers to serious wrestling with problems of christology. How do you successfully handle the Transfiguration until you discover all the approaches that do not work?

The lectionary has spread far to the liturgical left and is regularly used in some Southern Baptist seminaries. It has made unexpected inroads in the Church of the Nazarene, Church of the Brethren, and many others on the liturgical left. A grassroots ecumenism has developed with many priests and ministers doing exegesis and sermon preparation together. This is one of the most successful ecumenical ventures we have, achieved without anyone organizing a national committee or setting up an office.

Another major development in recent years has been the charismatic movement. Originating at the start of this century among the culturally dispossessed, it sprang up among Roman Catholic college students in the 1960s to break out among the mainline denominations. After initial panic on the part of many denominations, it has been accepted and even welcomed by Roman Catholic and Protestant leaders, with the possible exception of Missouri Synod Lutherans and Southern Baptists. Charismatics and noncharismatics have learned to live together in many congregations to their mutual enrichment.

Another factor, more difficult to document but equally important, is the gradual move to greater sacramental life among many Protestants. Some of the steps Episcopalians have taken since the 1840s are now being taken by Protestants although without the same controversies over ceremonial. Slowly, many congregations (except for those already having it weekly such as Disciples of Christ or Churches of Christ) have moved from quarterly communion to monthly and then the great festivals. Eventually some move to the new weekly communion. United Methodist and Presbyterian service materials certainly encourage such moves.

The basis of the new sacramental life is recognition of humanity's need for visible signs to relate to other humans and, ultimately, to God. A new anthropology studies the importance of sign acts and raises questions about the sign value of what we do together in worship. This has meant much more attention is being given to the quality of celebration. How can the act of washing signify more in baptism or eating in the Eucharist? This has major consequences for the conduct of worship to say nothing of its architectural setting. The new sacramental emphasis has been closely tied to preaching and the unity of word and sacrament has been generally stressed. Several denominations are now exploring the development of a process similar to the Roman Catholic Rite of Christian Initiation of Adults. This is marked by a serious catechumenate and stages of progress to full sacramental initiation.

Certainly one reason for changes in the use of the lectionary or greater concern for the sacramental life is the new attention in many seminaries to the teaching of worship. Institutions such as Drew University, the University of Notre Dame, and the Graduate Theological Union in Berkeley have produced academically trained Protestant Ph.D. graduates in Liturgical Studies. Their teaching and scholarship have had major impact on the formation of seminarians and eventually on the Church as a whole. Denominational worship staff persons, largely a new phenomenon of the 1970s, have done much through workshops and publications to advance in more thorough and systematic fashion many of the changes already in progress.

It is difficult, of course, to determine the amount of change in many of the churches of the liturgical left. How much has Southern Baptist worship changed in the last fifty years? No one, it seems, knows. Maybe no one can know when each congregation makes all its own decisions about worship. Who can generalize about them? Probably the quality of music has improved. Certainly the newest Southern Baptist hymnal gives reason to suspect this is the case. Some churches have adopted the lectionary; most have not. A few congregations have decided not to rebaptize those baptized as infants in other denominations. Quite a few baptize preschool children on occasion and even more perform some kind of infant dedication. It is not unreasonable to suppose that many of the things that increasingly appeal to United Methodists and Presbyterians will also attract Southern Baptists.

At any rate it seems safe to argue that much of what has happened in Protestant worship in recent years has been centripetal. The nine traditions, once so diverse, have heaped their riches into a common coffer. Without the cover it would be difficult to identify the tradition of many service books by their contents alone. On the theological level much of this coalescence was heralded in the World Council of Churches' 1982 document *Baptism, Eucharist, and Ministry*.[31] That document reflects many of the realities that have been worked out, lived, and worshiped with in the Protestant churches of America during the past half century.

Within the past decade a major new player has entered the field, namely the Church Growth Movement. Under the leadership of Donald McGavran (1897–1990), serious studies using the techniques of the social sciences were devoted to analyzing the process by which churches grow. This has led to a new concern for "people movements" in which minimal cultural and linguistic barriers are imposed to reaching the unchurched. At the local level the priority is given to "discipling," i.e., making converts instead of "perfecting," i.e., pastoral care of the converted. Important studies such as Patrick R. Keifert's *Welcoming the Stranger*[32] have led to a major disjunction in the development of worship in many mainline as well as independent churches.

The new approach, sometimes called "Mega-Church," has taken many forms but fundamental is McGavran's "homogeneous unit principle," i.e., individuals are attracted by those like themselves. This has led to a focus on styles of worship that appeal to a very specific social-economic-educational portion of society (Willow Creek near Chicago) or a series of distinct groups with distinct services (Community of Joy near Phoenix). Music is a prime ingredient in the services, keyed to the styles popular with the target group. "Entertainment evangelism" is a common term and there is very little congregational participation. "Seeker services" are meant to be user-friendly and marketing language is used without embarrassment. Services frequently include very relevant dramatic skits or monologues.

Quite often there are midweek services for the insiders or believers that are somewhat more traditional. These patterns in various permutations have attracted large numbers of worshipers or attenders in the 1990s. Largely it is an urbanized or suburban phenomenon. Critics call it "Christianity lite" and argue that reaching out has too

[31] (Geneva: World Council of Churches, 1982).
[32] (Minneapolis: Fortress Press, 1992).

often meant dumbing down. But in the panic over declining membership even the most confessional of mainline churches have been attracted to the new techniques.

These developments mean a clear rejection of many post-Vatican II mainline Protestant changes such as the lectionary, the Church year, or a sacramental life. Indeed, it has produced a strong counterforce to much that seemed to be dominating the situation in the twenty-five years after Vatican II. Even some Roman Catholic parishes have been attracted to the methods, especially the music, of Mega-Church worship. In any event, it certainly has added a new page to the liturgical diversity of American Protestant worship.

11. Worship in the Age of Marshall McLuhan

Unchanged except for the title, "Worship in an Age of Immediacy," this is as good a reflection as I know of the liturgical atmosphere of 1968 when this was published in *The Christian Century* 75 (February 21, 1968). Used by permission.

We face today a crisis in Protestant worship, one that seems certain to increase in intensity in the years ahead. The crisis is created by the alienation of the usual forms of worship from the modern world's means of perception. If one understands worship as a mirror of reality in which we perceive God, the world, and ourselves at the deepest level, then it is not difficult to speak of worship as an instrument that expands our consciousness by providing a mirror in which we glimpse the depths of reality.

The crisis we face is related to that massive revolution in the modes of perceiving reality, widely known as the communications revolution, which has made—and is making—such a marked impact on contemporary society. In 1953, two television networks chartered planes to race films of the coronation of Queen Elizabeth across the Atlantic in order to be the first to bring the pageantry to American viewers. But five years later we could sit in our homes and actually participate via Telstar in the ceremonies attendant on the funeral of Konrad Adenauer. Indeed, our experience was more immediate and complete than that of the people lining the streets in Cologne.

Marshall McLuhan didn't create this revolution, but he has, I feel, described it better than anyone else—as a revolution of direct participation whereby "the medium is the message." At least for those who have grown up with television, the communications revolution has provided a type of perception radically different from that provided by the spoken or written word—one in which perception of reality is achieved by direct participation, by involvement. McLuhan speaks of it as the "retribalizing" of the race. Some films at Expo '67 bowed to this revolution by making the audience decide on a character's morals or fate, or by putting the audience at the center of 360 degrees of screen. For those who become thus involved in the action, I can think of no word less descriptive than "audience" or "spectators."

Where does all this leave us so far as worship is concerned? That's the problem! It leaves some—though not all—of us stranded high and dry, with the tide rushing in the opposite direction. I say "some" because part of the crisis we face arises from the splits between age levels and between social groups. Many of us are too old to be fully receptive to the changed modes of perception; we grew up on radio, not on TV. For us there may be no acute crisis in worship, for we are largely oriented to verbal forms of perception. The question we have been accustomed to hear from someone who missed church was "What did he say?"—meaning "What was the sermon about?" But we are the minority, or soon will be. Those of the younger generation are more likely to ask "What happened?" For them the problem is that nothing, or very little, happened; the nearest thing to a happening was the congregation's standing, singing some hymns, and going home.

Wrong Medium, Wrong Message

This doesn't much bother those of us over thirty. We are accustomed to perceiving reality by having it described for us. Words may be poor substitutes for the direct experience of realities but many of us knew nothing else in our formative years. We grew up on radio; we read about the events of World War II the day after they happened. But there's no point in reading a newspaper account of Adenauer's funeral if you were there. Today TV may take us on patrols in Vietnam; some of us have even been "present" when a loved one was wounded. Those of us who are over thirty haven't recognized any real crisis in worship because its present forms are based on the mode of perceiving reality to which we are accustomed. We expect others to supply words for us—and this is what we get in worship.

The actual crisis lies in the future since we older folks still constitute the majority in the churches, if not in the population. It is the young who find the present forms of worship so intolerable. They're pretty frank about it: to them worship is basically boring. And I, too, must admit that the dullest hour of the week is the one I spend in church. I'm sure dullness is not intrinsic to worship since some of the most exciting moments of my week are those spent at seminary services. The word-package that constitutes most of Protestant worship just isn't turned on for a generation accustomed to participation and involvement. If "the medium is the message," then much of Protestant worship indicates that the message is not very vital or relevant.

There are groups in our society in which worship is definitely of a turned-on variety: many of the African American churches, the Pentecostal groups and churches retaining a strong revivalistic fervor. There one finds no lack of participation in the worship; the foot-tapping music leaves no doubt about that: you "get with it" in a hurry. And something happens—maybe not just what we might like, but undeniably each service is a happening. Many of the large American denominations once had those qualities in their worship. Whatever we may think about revivalism, its advocates know that to move people spiritually you must move them physically. Most of us long since became too sophisticated for that. Our problems in worship today are often the result of middle class self-consciousness; metaphorically, we got shoes—and our respectability has been pinching us ever since. In a literal sense the most exciting service I've seen in a long time occurred when the celebrant took off his shoes and danced in a procession to music from *Zorba the Greek*.

So we suffer from being locked into middle-class inhibitions about fervent expression in worship. We have lost our innocence and we can't be taught naiveté. Even the music our kids play shocks us— partly because they want it to. I'm not sure that members of the middle class churches can leap the hurdles set up by their inhibitions, can stand and sway where others do. We spend a lot of time thanking God (which is an act of worship) that we are not like other people. But at least we can let others witness that direct participation in worship is for some groups very much a present reality. That for them there is no crisis in worship may well be one reason they are growing so fast today.

The chief problem, then, is that the medium is wrong and, consequently, so is the message. Worship in the mainline adult churches is primarily a diet of words spooned out to us by the minister. That may not bother us too much; we don't really want to get too close to reality anyhow. (Notice that people never sit too close to the pulpit— they might get burned.) But I am afraid that an increasing number of people feel that our present forms of worship provide a mirror of reality much too dim for them to perceive very much in it. They demand a much more vivid representation than the secondhand perception of reality we offer in our worship.

Criteria for Experimentation

It would be foolish of me to pretend that I have any solution to offer for the problem posed by the coming crisis in worship. I do have some hunches, some notions, but these are of little value without experimentation. And whatever we know or will discover will be of value only if worked out through direct experience gained by experimentation. What we must talk about now is experimentations rather than solutions. Obviously it is not enough simply to say we must experiment. Though experimentation is much more difficult in some traditions than in others, many common problems present themselves. Certainly we must begin by drawing a distinction between responsible and irresponsible experimentation.

I would make a preliminary distinction to the effect that responsible experimentation belongs to the whole Church, that it is not private matter. Irresponsible experimentation is often inclined to be divisive, sometimes conflicts with the Church's faith, occasionally is purely sensational. Experimentation growing out of anger breaks the bonds of charity; the message it communicates may be one more of defiance than of anything else. Impatience, despair, frustration, and anger—these are not what we wish to communicate. Augustine had this one out with the Donatists over baptism; what, he asked, was the point of baptism that deliberately broke the bonds of charity? Responsible experimentation leads to the building up of the Church; irresponsible experimentation tears it down.

A more important distinction is that between responsible experimentation, carefully prepared and matured, and irresponsible experimentation, lacking such preparation, often premature, carelessly conceived, inconsequential. But how do you tell when experimentation is based on proper preparation? I would suggest three criteria by which to judge effective preparation: that experimentation be historically informed, theologically reasoned, and pastorally relevant.

At this point Protestant seminaries must, I think, confess considerable guilt. They have done little to make the average pastor knowledgeable about the history, theologies, or sociological dimensions of worship. Perhaps the trouble lies a bit farther upstream: in the graduate schools that train seminary professors, schools that have failed to train specialists in this field. The Church's academic community has simply failed to prepare ministers for a major responsibility the Church now demands of them.

The importance of the historical criterion can hardly be over-emphasized. Santayana, I believe, gets credit for the often-quoted observation that those who do not know their history are condemned to relive it. This is the negative argument: a knowledge of history prevents mistakes. The positive argument is stronger: the past can teach us a great deal about the present by giving us the perspective of detachment. If, as McLuhan suggests, we are moving back to a condition before Gutenberg, the quickest way forward may involve a backward look. One reason that jazz and some other types of music are most modern is that they come out of a preliterate background; the past is always sneaking up on us.

Likewise, history has been the Church's proving ground. Writing some years ago on the "church in the round," Professor Massey H. Shepherd, Jr., pointed out that one had been tried in the sixteenth century and found lacking. Several million dollars later we have tried enough churches in the round to realize that the sixteenth century was right. The past is not just a grab bag of ideas; it tells us why some things were accepted, why others were rejected—sometimes for valid, sometimes for mistaken reasons.

The historical sense ought not be cultivated from too narrow a viewpoint; certainly it should not be limited to formal liturgiology. In liturgical textbooks we will not find mentioned a certain Chicago businessman, A. B. Dick. Yet few people have made as profound an impression on Protestant worship as Mr. Dick did in 1884 when he solved a business problem by inventing a form of stencil duplication and marketed it under the name "mimeograph." Gutenberg made it possible to put prayer books in the hands of the people; Dick made them obsolete. Prayer books are mostly propers that are hard to locate and confusing to most people. Mr. Dick gave every minister his or her own printing press—and a freedom never before imaginable. We haven't realized it yet because the cost is still too high, but new duplicating devices can make hymnals obsolete; when a Xerox 2400 copier/duplicator can make forty copies a minute, only the minister needs a hymnal. We are affected by far more than the information the liturgical scholars drag up in their nets.

The importance of theological reasoning as a criterion for responsible experimentation ought to be more fully recognized than is currently the case. Unless we first engage in thinking through the theological bases of worship, experimentation may turn out to be a lot of fun—but quite meaningless. Protestants are particularly handicapped by a lack of good general theologies of worship. We need not just sacramental theologies or theologies of preaching (though we could use more of each), but theologies of cultic acts in general, discussions of what sense it makes for modern people to worship, clarification of the relation between worship and life. True, we can get hints from Schillebeeckx, Rahner and others, but a great deal of work remains to be done.

But the problem is even broader, for the root question in worship is that of the nature of reality itself: Why being? Serious liturgical experimentation must grow out of basic discussion of the existence and nature of God. I often feel that the best proof of the death of God is the fact that so many congregations worship God in the past tense; both the medium and the message seem to have stopped with the last book of the New Testament. How can we speak meaningfully about a God who acts in race riots, in the United Nations, in the birth of a baby? Until we start discussing this type of question there's not much point to liturgical experimentation. Any meaningful experimentation grows out of a sincere effort to think through the nature of reality. Our mirror of reality is constructed to reflect reality as the Church helps us to wrestle it into our forms of understanding. In other words, until we struggle with the message we shouldn't monkey around with the medium.

The need to make experimentation pastorally relevant is so obvious it's amazing how often we overlook it. Most liturgical conferences and commissions on worship are made up of clergy who think they know what is good for the laity. Maybe they do; maybe they don't. We have long been subjected to suggestions that congregations building new churches should employ acoustical consultants, liturgical consultants, and so on. But has it ever been suggested that they hire sociological consultants to help them understand the people whom the buildings are to serve? We need to relate to people as they are, not just as we imagine them to be.

Most people live in families, yet our liturgies are almost spotlessly "celibate." There are few gifts of God I'm more thankful for than sexuality. But do we get a chance in worship to praise God for this basic gift? You bet we don't! We took sex out of the wedding service—though it's definitely there in Reformation prayer books. And the Episcopalians even got too squeamish for that wonderful phrase: "with my body I thee worship."

It is important for worship to celebrate life as God creates it. We worship a very worldly God, though we seem determined to out-spiritualize God by ignoring God's creation in the orders of nature and the structures of society. Experimentation in worship doesn't develop apart from life in the world; it develops by being immersed in that life. Perhaps the most creative liturgical force in this country in the recent past has been the freedom movement. We got processions into our seminary chapel by calling them "Christian demonstrations" and found out we could worship with our feet as well as with our lips.

All this is to say that significant experimentation must have the immediacy of this morning's newspaper that goes out with tonight's garbage. It must relate to people as they are in the here and now. Obviously this has tremendous impact on problems of language and actions, on the whole mode of perception. We can't have an actual kiss of peace any more than we can baptize in the nude, since we are not the people third century Romans were. But neither are we Elizabethans. Nor are any two congregations identical. We conduct experiments in the context of a concrete congregation, hoping that others may learn from our successes, perhaps more from our failures.

These three criteria—historical, theological and pastoral—would seem to be basic guides in any preparation for responsible experimentation. They certainly will not guarantee the success of experiments—but experimentation is not supposed to prove anything anyhow; that's left for demonstration. And after all, the God whom we worship seems to be partial to the process of mutation rather than to any tidy process of development.

12. Shaping the 1972 United Methodist Eucharistic Rite

This was my Berakah Award address at the 1983 meeting of the North American Academy of Liturgy. Published in *Worship* 57 (July 1983), it is abbreviated here and used by permission. The rite, finally published in 1989, contained many subsequent improvements.

I must confess that I have spent far more time wondering about what I might possibly have to say that would warrant your time and attention than I have expended in actually writing what follows. I finally decided that my experiences in the process and theology of revising the United Methodist eucharistic rite would be of common interest, especially when contrasted with the Roman revision which is more familiar to most of you. In addition, I consider revision of the eucharistic rite the most important work in which I have participated. Such recent history is also the kind most easily forgotten. I want to remember some of it with you and to make my own reflections on what this bit of making history taught me.

Changing the Way We Pray

In the whole process of liturgical revision one question keeps coming back to haunt me: "What right do we have to change the way people pray?" It is the only liturgical question that ever keeps me awake at night. Basically it is an ethical question although I doubt many ethicists lose much sleep over changing other peoples' forms of behavior and educators positively seem to relish promoting new ways of learning. But there is something intimate about prayer, more intimate even than action or education. Do we really serve people by changing the way they pray either in public or in private?

Since prayer is such an intimate act, does another person have a right to interfere in such a personal relationship to God? Familiar ways of praying are unthreatening. Change can make them startlingly frightening. I remember once during the years of liturgical revision at a celebration of the old—basically 1662—United Methodist rite thinking how much I loved that service myself and yet I was working on replacing it. And I wondered, wondered whether what I was doing was beneficial or harmful to others. It seems so presumptuous for anyone to assert that there is a "better" way of praying, to infer that we know a "better" way of praying, to infer that we know a "better" way to address God. Do we know or are we just meddlesome busybodies? These are not questions easily dismissed and yet anyone who refuses to wrestle with them has no right to tinker with the way other people pray.

At last, I can give more certain answers to those questions about serving people through making changes in the way they pray. But this came only after hearing people tell me how the 1972 Methodist Eucharist has shaped their piety and hence their very being. When a few minor changes in the service were suggested in 1980, people began telling us they loved the 1972 rite too much to want it changed. And to be loved is what a liturgy needs to function well although creating it may not make the revisers particularly lovable. Indeed, the more cantankerous the revisers are, the better the liturgy produced may become.

I think one can say "yes, we *can* serve people well by changing the way they pray" but this is only possible after having thought through the reasons for making changes in prayer. I suggest four reasons that, for me, justify interference in the way people have been accustomed to address God. The first is to make liturgical or personal prayer reflect more accurately the true nature of God and God's relation to humans. For example, prayer addressed to God as the purveyor of success needs change. Second, prayer must be made to reflect and teach justice, though it ought not preach. Prayers in former wedding services, which prayed that the woman alone "fortify herself against her weakness," certainly needed replacing. In the third place, the language must be made accessible to all, not just to those who understand what it is to be "sore let and hindered." "Plight thee my troth" always made me think of how we feed hogs, hardly what Cranmer intended! And fourth, the way we pray has to be shaped to relate to the prayer of all Christians. Christian prayer demands the company of many voices, present or unseen. We proclaim the same story and implore God's continuance of the same work.

Apparently we succeeded in accomplishing some of these goals in the 1972 United Methodist Eucharist. So naive were we that we hoped that with luck fifty or sixty thousand copies would be sold to a small number of progressive congregations. Currently over two and a quarter million copies have been sold and about twenty-eight thousand more sell each month, to say nothing of the millions of times it has been photocopied or mimeographed. When one considers what a drastic break the service meant with the traditional Anglican–Methodist pattern of euchology, this is remarkable. It also shows how much we may underestimate our people's eagerness to grow. Even more surprising is that its use seems as common in conservative congregations as in progressive ones, in country churches as in city congregations. Astonishingly, a major change has occurred in the way many of our people pray the Eucharist. It is a change many have welcomed, perhaps for the reasons I have just enumerated, perhaps for others.

The Process of Revision

Some words about the process of preparing the 1972 United Methodist rite will help explain how the theology developed. I was a young assistant professor when the previous rite, that of 1964, was being prepared and no one wanted my advice. I remember being told at that time, when I pled for inclusion of the fraction, that "even the Anglicans have given up that Dix stuff!" My very first association with the Commission on Worship of the Methodist Church was at a service dedicating the 1964 *Book of Worship* in Champaign–Urbana in 1965. Somehow, just five years later, at a meeting in Dayton, a few of us were able to persuade weary members of the Commission that it was already time to start over again.

Out of that discussion came a new project, shepherded by the Committee on Alternate Rituals, and ably chaired by Professor Grady Hardin. And this time around I was chosen to be the writer for the communion service with a committee of ten to supervise my efforts. The choice of members of such a committee, of course, determines in great measure the final outcome. Fortunately that committee included Hoyt Hickman whom I looked on as a co-conspirator at every stage and who always lent knowledgeable support. Most of the others were chosen as representatives of various constituencies within the Church rather than as liturgical experts. One member even claimed that we were not out "to impress Massey Shepherd." Yet I maintained that scholarship was vital, for what would please Massey Shepherd would also serve the Church best. The committees chosen were in marked contrast to the Roman Catholic *coetus* of the liturgy consilium that initially included only one woman and scores of men, all liturgy experts and almost all clergy. We have gone to the other extreme with democracy replacing expertise, representation overcoming specialization. Theology is done by non-theologians, liturgy by non-liturgists. At present there is not a single liturgical scholar in the Section on Worship although there is a most competent staff. Minorities are represented but it is highly questionable whether they are served well by nonexperts. In other words, the patients now vote on how surgery is to be done.

Late in 1970 I began work on the new rite. My second text was mailed out for the Committee on Alternate Rituals to discuss at its first meeting in Chicago, 14–15 March 1971. I well remember how despondent the committee was when it saw the text, partly because some of them had never encountered the Eucharist in contemporary English. They missed the Cranmerian cadences if not the vocabulary. I had to leave before the meeting was over and I understand there was much handwringing about the flatness and unpoetic nature of my prose. Indeed, Albert Outler later told me that in writing it I had loved the Lord Jesus but not the English language.

Be that as it may, I am strongly convinced that it is necessary to get one's theology straight before one can proclaim it with flair. The current Presbyterian attempts at new eucharistic prayers more than confirm that belief. In my lifetime I have only written two such prayers, the 1972 one and one other, written in 1978 and included in *At the Lord's Table*.[1] The latter is obviously better language but was impossible without the theological clarity of the 1972 effort. Actually I am not sure whether the language of 1972 got better or we just got more accustomed to it, but I think it has worn rather well.

Far more important for me than language at that first meeting was that the structure I had proposed was accepted with only minor changes. Those changes were: the *Kyrie* was dropped, the *Gloria in ex-*

---

[1] *At the Lord's Table* (Nashville: Abingdon, 1981).

celsis was not to be printed in full, the offertory prayer was dropped, and an invitation as a spoken rubric was added. But most of the structure I had proposed survived the committee's scrutiny even though some ingredients were unfamiliar. Encouraged by Hughes Old's book,[2] I had deliberately borrowed the use of a prayer for illumination from the Reformed tradition. I had included three lessons and psalmody, recovered the ancient kiss of peace, and highlighted the fourfold eucharistic actions. All these ancient patterns, then just reemerging in the rites of other churches, were accepted, much to my gratification. My recommendation to follow the ICET texts was also agreeable to the members of the committee except to a New Testament scholar who was not content with the ICET version of the Lord's Prayer.

Equally important, the theology I had tried to incorporate was accepted almost without question. As a consultant, David Buttrick was helpful in making us realize what we were doing with language. Another consultant, Laurance Stookey, who was soon to play a similar role as writer in reforming our initiation rites, affirmed our theology.

A third draft followed that spring and a fourth was prepared for the committee's meeting in St. Louis in late May. At that meeting I lost one major battle when the creed of the United Church of Canada was substituted for the Apostles' or Nicene. But by that time I was learning to be obnoxious for the Lord! I could concede the creed if I could hold the line on the eucharistic prayer. I was learning that a person who comes to a committee meeting with mind made up or agenda prepared has a good chance of prevailing. Planning is power. I won on instituting the *Benedictus qui venit* because I could quote Psalm 118; I lost then on the introduction to the Lord's Prayer since I had no ammunition ready. But out of the heated give and take personal crochets and pet phrases were eliminated, greatly improving the results. At the time it was decided to invite Fred Gealy to rewrite the confessional acts entirely and to retool the prayer for illumination and that Grady Hardin should write completely new intercessions. Both improved the synaxis considerably.

Through some procedural unclarity, due to minutes of the meeting not being available immediately, I produced a fifth text in June,

[2]Hughes Oliphant Old, *The Patristic Roots of Reformed Worship* (Zurich: Theologischer Verlag, 1975) 208–218.

unaware that others were also at work on another fifth version. I first saw their version at the third meeting, held in July in Arlington, Vermont. I was stunned by the theological alterations. Some of these, but not all, were compromised before the sixth text was printed for the First World Methodist Consultation on Worship in Denver the next month. By this time the postcommunion prayer had been changed from unison to responsive. I think it has become the most popular part of the entire service even though a novel form for this prayer. At Denver the theology of the eucharistic prayer was inadvertently threatened by the comments of a well-known Methodist ecumenist that the phrase in the epiclesis "that they may be for us the presence of the crucified and risen Lord" was certainly a strong statement of real presence. Some of the weaker brethren quailed at that thought and I was forced to withdraw the phrase.

A new, seventh version was circulated by mail that fall to the members of the committee. On the basis of their written comments a final text, the eighth, was prepared and sent to the printers, incorporating the refinements by Grady Hardin and me. Both of us read proof on it and the service was used officially for the first time by the General Conference in Atlanta, April 1972.

I might add as a footnote that two years later I taught summer school at St. John's University in Minnesota and asked a number of prominent Roman Catholic liturgical scholars present then to comment on it. Interestingly, their comments were almost all literary rather than theological. I was able to propose some improvements, mostly in better transitions in the eucharistic prayer and in removing some of the sexist language that inexcusably had crept back in when we were concerned about other problems. I was forced to probe deeper into the area of discriminatory language and actions and the resulting sacramental injustice. I am considered as indulging in mere trifles by those I regard as insensitive and damned as reactionary by those I regard as irresponsible. This latter conflict arises when I refuse to surrender the name "Father" at certain key points in the Eucharist. But maybe I have succeeded in making a few people angry enough to think about our liturgical sanctions of injustice.

A happy sequel to the 1974 refinements is that I was able to incorporate them in a 1980 revision that appeared in *We Gather Together*.[3]

[3]*We Gather Together* (Nashville: United Methodist Publishing House, 1980).

This time I was also able to design the graphics and edit the booklet. I believe that the way a page appears is almost as important as what is printed on it. We were finally able to eliminate the Canadian creed and to move the acts of confession to a less prominent position. In this case a new committee was open to persuasion on these matters as well as minor retuning on the initiation, marriage, and burial rites. In 1981 Hoyt Hickman's *At the Lord's Table* gave us a collection of twenty-two eucharistic prayers, a book that I think stands unequaled among the other churches and that, along with Don Saliers' book on Lent and Easter, *From Ashes to Fire*,[4] gives me considerable pride in United Methodist liturgy, a new experience for me. I also take much delight in, but no credit for the work of Laurance Stookey and his committee on the reform of initiation. I hope the rest of the dozen volumes now available in the *Supplemental Worship Resources* series will serve the Church as well as these have.

The Product of Revision

When the Methodist–Catholic statement, "The Eucharist and the Churches," was released on 12 February 1982 (*Origins* 2 [25 March 1982] 651–659), it commented on the "surprising convergence" evident in the "remarkable unity and agreement on the structure of the eucharistic celebration and on the central eucharist prayer." I was hardly surprised but certainly was gratified to have my intentions thus recognized in such a document.

At this point I want to spell out those things that I was trying to do theologically in the 1972 service and for which I was obstinate, if not obnoxious. I shall not try to defend my convictions but simply articulate them so I can be understood rather than excused. I am sure it never occurred to anyone else, but I felt at times that I had been entrusted with the most important theological task the Methodist Church could delegate, changing Methodist euchology by altering the language and structure of the Eucharist. I believe I have a responsibility to make explicit what I was trying to do as writer for the 1972 rite. This should be helpful for others who will push us beyond it and, I hope, of interest to you who listen.

I had been prepared for liturgical revision by spending the year 1967–1968 in Rome, looking over the shoulders of the Consilium for

[4]*From Ashes to Fire* (Nashville: Abingdon, 1979).

the Implementation of the Constitution on the Sacred Liturgy, reading all its publications, and keeping up with every issue of *Notitiae* and the *BCL Newsletter* since. I had likewise made and still make it my business to read everything published by the Standing Liturgical Commission of the Episcopal Church, the Inter-Lutheran Commission on Worship, the Presbyterian Joint Committee on Worship, and all publications on worship of the United Church of Christ and Disciples of Christ.

Ecumenism, then, was a basic given of all I tried to do. This was reflected in the nine basic rites I had ever before me, the most recent revisions of Methodists, Roman Catholics, Episcopalians, Presbyterians, Lutherans, the Consultation on Church Union, the United Church of Christ, the Church of England, and the Church of South India. I also made frequent use of the Byzantine rite.

But certain basic decisions had to be made that not all of these reflected. I was convinced that the eucharistic prayer is the Church's central doctrinal statement and key to understanding ordained ministry. The eucharistic prayer proclaims the Church's faith through this form of prayer by reciting and giving thanks for those acts of God that make the community one. But any look at the previous eucharistic prayers in any of these traditions (save the Orthodox) shows how completely this function has been lost. The redundancy of the inclusion of a creed demonstrates how oblivious we all were to this loss.

I had become convinced that as a first step of recovery an Antiochene structure, basically what Robert Taft calls "the ever-so-neat Antiochene pattern"[5] for the prayer would function best. This would incorporate the full breadth of commemoration beginning with creation and ending in the final consummation in Christ's victory. This is quite an expansion from the passion narrative to which we had hitherto limited ourselves. The Antiochene pattern would allow inclusion (for the first time in our tradition) of creation, fall, exodus, covenant, and prophets in the preface, all compressed into fifty words. At the same time the post-Sanctus would be expanded into a much fuller proclamation of the works of the new covenant.

The defects of the 1662 prayer—penitential obsession, the absence of the old covenant, eschatology, and pneumatology, plus a decidedly

[5]Robert Taft, review of Couratin festschrift, *Worship* 56 (March 1982) 178.

negative approach to sacrifice—could be overcome in such a structure. I think now it may be time to try other patterns but the Antiochene proved the best place to begin. At the same time it was possible for us to avoid the preliminary epiclesis that seemed to me an unnecessary intrusion in the new Roman prayers and the recent Church of England efforts. The intercessions, I felt, belonged elsewhere and could easily be heard here as a bit of moralizing.

Having established these prejudices I needed guidance as to content. Two sources seemed most appropriate, John Wesley and Hippolytus. The conjunction need not surprise you. Wesley was a patristic scholar who would have welcomed Hippolytus had he known the *Apostolic Tradition* as well as he knew and esteemed the *Apostolic Constitutions*. Hippolytus provided structure and specific phrases for us. Wesley's contribution was theological: in his 1784 edition of the 1662 eucharistic prayer he had altered only one word, a redundant "one." But the Wesley brothers had provided a marvelous collection of 166 eucharistic hymns.[6] I felt that one has to affirm one's own tradition even while being ecumenical, maybe *especially* while being ecumenical, and that the Wesleys' eucharistic hymns are Methodism's distinctive contribution. John Wesley's patristic interests loom large in these hymns and sing the theology I tried to reflect. Thus I can argue that the 1972 eucharistic prayer is more Wesleyan than Wesley's own 1784 version. The chief exception I made to Wesley's theology was in expanding the breadth of his vision of commemoration beyond just the passion narrative.

Wesley's study of patristics had led him beyond the negativisms of the sixteenth-century Reformation on eucharistic sacrifice. Indeed, a major portion of the eucharistic hymns is entitled "The Holy Eucharist as it implies a Sacrifice" and the imagery of the hymns is replete with Old Testament images of sacrifice. I think it was important that, by using Hebrews 9 and 13, Romans 12, and Augustine, I was allowed to make a strong positive statement of the Eucharist as sacrifice, perhaps for the first time in a Protestant liturgy. This I consider an important ecumenical step that Wesley encouraged.

Another important element in the Wesleyan eucharistic hymns is the frequent use of imagery about the work of the Holy Spirit. Con-

[6]See J. Ernest Rattenbury, *Eucharistic Hymns of John and Charles Wesley* (London: Epworth Press, 1948).

temporary works, especially John McKenna's brilliant book, *Eucharist and Holy Spirit*,[7] show how essential it is that we recover an epiclesis invoking the work of the Spirit in consecrating the gifts and uniting the communicants. Another Wesleyan characteristic is the eschatological dimension, certainly present in the New Testament accounts but long lacking in Western worship until recently. Recovery of this has been strengthened by Geoffrey Wainwright's classic study, *Eucharist and Eschatology*.[8] I think subsequent prayers will need to reflect eschatology even more strongly and to tie it to present efforts for justice.

I felt it important to turn from a rather penitential prayer tradition to a more joyful offering of thanks. If we believe that ultimately everything depends upon God, then less concentration ought to be focused on human efforts and failures. In the 1972 prayer God's work is thankfully commemorated and presently invoked, and God is begged to keep up the good work by bringing it to completion. Human activity is mentioned only at the end of the epiclesis and in the postcommunion prayer as response to God's self-giving.

The fellowship of the gathered community is stressed by the action of breaking bread. We may have erred in 1972 in tying the fraction too closely to the spoken words of 1 Corinthians 10:16-17. Indeed, the fraction may be more eloquent as action alone. And we may need to explore further the ethical dimension of 1 Corinthians 10:21 in which sharing at the table and in the cup excludes us from compromise with the demons of this world. The sense of community is also stressed in the benefits sought in communion: "Make us one with Christ, one with each other, and one in service to all the world."

On the statement of the presence of Christ, as mentioned already, we were forced to compromise but finally managed a more dynamic approach: "Help us know/in the breaking of this bread/and the drinking of this wine/the presence of Christ." (Perhaps a more ontological text such as "be for us" will again be possible in the future.) In the institution narrative Fred Gealy, a New Testament scholar, persuaded us to translate *anamnesis* as "experience anew." To some that sounds too subjective a sense of presence although "recall" and "remember" may be no less so.

[7]John H. McKenna, *Eucharist and Holy Spirit*. Alcuin Club Collections 57 (Great Wakering: Mayhew–McCrimmon, 1975).

[8]Geoffrey Wainwright, *Eucharist and Eschatology* (New York: Oxford University Press, 1981).

My own approach to sacraments as God's self-giving[9] comes out rather strongly in the postcommunion prayer: "You have given yourself to us, Lord. Now we give ourselves for others." It was tempting to push that sense of self-giving farther in the direction of justice but I fear preaching in prayer. And after all, the whole of the liturgy, sensitively celebrated, is a strong statement of the Christian contribution to justice just as, insensitively celebrated, it can be an act promoting injustice in the Church and eventually the world.

Well, these were the chief theological principles that guided our efforts in making changes in United Methodist euchology. Much that was done in the 1970s I think is irrevocable. Things that will endure include reading from both testaments of the Bible, the use of contemporary language, the concentration on Eucharist as action, and the understanding of the eucharistic prayer as thankful proclamation of the Church's faith. In time our words will be refined and exchanged for other words that function more adequately. (In the 1980s a number of improvements were made in the rite, many of them due to Hoyt Hickman.)

It has been a pleasure and a privilege to share in this exciting age in the rethinking and reformulation of how Christians give thanks. This stage in my own life may now be past but it is equally exciting to be moving on to teach those who will be able to improve on what I was called to do when Methodism finally burst out of the tight confines of the Anglican–Methodist liturgical tradition in the early 1970s. There are times when we have an opportunity for *making* history rather than *teaching* history. I am pleased that you have given me this chance to record my perceptions of one such occasion. I hope it will help you in your work of teaching and making history.

[9]See my *Sacraments as God's Self Giving* (Nashville: Abingdon Press, 1983).

13. Evangelism and Worship from New Lebanon to Nashville

This previously unpublished paper was presented as the keynote address at the North American Summit on the Future of Christian Worship held in Nashville, Tennessee, 9–11 December 1994.

This is not the first North American Summit on Christian Worship though it may very well be the second. The first occurred a century and two-thirds ago under circumstances extraordinarily different. Yet the substance of the issues at stake then is extremely similar to those we propose to discuss today, tomorrow, and Sunday. I just hope we can do so with less rancor and antagonism than the first time around.

The first North American summit occurred in the quiet New York village of New Lebanon, hard up against the western border of Massachusetts. Its location was appropriate because it pitted nine Presbyterian and Congregational ministers from western New York against a similar number of their peers from New England and eastern New York state. It consumed the days of 18–26 July 1827 with acrimonious debate over methods of evangelism and worship. Both sides were fervent evangelists; both were fiercely devoted to the style of worship evangelism that they deemed appropriate. At issue was the introduction of "new measures" by the westerners, methods which the more staid easterners found inappropriate and shocking. Those "things which are of a dangerous tendency" included women praying aloud in prayer meetings of mixed gender, something then unthinkable in New England. This issue was not resolved. Other issues were the high octane emotional character of the western revivals, the use of a measure "without regard to its scriptural character," naming people by name in public prayer, and "audible groaning in prayer . . . and violent and boisterous tones."

I cite the New Lebanon conference because it is so relevant to our present concerns. If little was resolved by that strenuous effort at least it did provoke new respect on both sides; Lyman Beecher, leader of the easterners, is said to have remarked on the way home: "We crossed the mountains expecting to meet a company of boys, but we found them to be full-grown men."[1] Mutual respect is essential for us in these days.

What happened at New Lebanon was only a stage in a long process shaping the most dominant American worship tradition, which I call the Frontier Tradition. I shall survey the process in rapid fashion in order to set the stage for what history is made here this weekend. I shall have to move very fast, just waving my hand as I go by most developments.

The seventeenth century was a period largely of importation of European traditions of worship: Roman Catholic, Lutheran, Reformed, Anabaptist, Anglican, Puritan, and Quaker. Each found ways of adapting to a new world. Jesuit missionaries in New Mexico were able to adapt pueblo architecture to build churches with a baroque image of liturgical space. But much that occurred was the transplantation of European cultural patterns along with the worship. New England was founded on the late medieval village pattern even down to details of land ownership. Massachusetts and Connecticut had laws forbidding building a farmhouse more than easy walking distance from the village meetinghouse that often stood on the public green. All were expected to attend church; at least they were taxed to support it. Certainly everyone in the northeast had access to the church.

The eighteenth century brought its share of changes, partly because of the Enlightenment. The Great Awakening shattered religious uniformity and other worship traditions came to compete with the church on the green. Easily overlooked is a shift the Enlightenment mind brought about with regard to sacramental worship. Kant condemned miracle, mystery, and means of grace, and the sacraments came to be seen as human acts to remember those once performed by Christ. If a recent *New York Times* poll is accurate, this approach is al-

---

[1] Quoted by Keith J. Hardman, *Charles Grandison Finney 1792-1875* (Grand Rapid: Baker Book House, 1987) 144.

most as widespread among younger Roman Catholic laity today as among Protestants. Perhaps it is more important to remember that the new American republic was not a particularly religious nation. Despite our own propaganda today, the founding fathers, for the most part, were neither godly, righteous, nor sober. At the time of the American revolution about five per cent of the population were practicing Church members compared to about sixty per cent today.

The nineteenth century saw major social changes as well as worship transitions. For one thing, a large portion of the population moved across the Appalachians into new territories in upstate New York, Kentucky, Tennessee, and elsewhere. By the time of President Jackson a third of the population was beyond the mountains. Here on the frontier they encountered a whole new social order. Emerson recognized this in saying that Europe stretched to the Appalachians; America began beyond them. It was certainly true of Church life. For the most part, the village culture of the East was lacking, let alone churches and clergy. John Wesley noted "for some hundred miles together there is none either to baptize or to administer the Lord's supper."[2]

Conventional forms of Church life simply could not function. Itinerant Baptist farmer/preachers and Methodist circuit riders soon reached out to scattered families. Presbyterians and Congregationalists struggled to minister within more conventional settings. Out of this confusion slowly developed new methods of Church life and worship, methods that eventually led to the Christianization of a continent.

Eventually these crystallized in the form of the campmeeting. It has several sources, especially the sacramental seasons of the Presbyterians and the quarterly conferences of the Methodists. Both climaxed with the celebration of the Lord's Supper. Both brought scattered people together for sessions that lasted several days and involved social contacts as well as religious. The Cane Ridge Campmeeting in Bourbon County, Kentucky, in 1801, attracted maybe as many as twenty-five thousand people to a spot that even today is remote.

Here, at last, was found a means of reaching the unchurched, spread as they were over such a vast landscape. Evangelism and

[2]*John Wesley's Sunday Service* (Nashville: United Methodist Publishing House, 1984) ii.

worship had been fused by the development of a new type of worship shaped to reach the unchurched. Worship of this type preceded baptism. Millions of unchurched came and millions got religion. For them, that was ritualized by being baptized and receiving communion at the sacramental services that terminated each campmeeting. Not everyone did so well; the birth rate often took a sudden spurt nine months past campmeeting! The county fair or agricultural exposition had yet to be invented and little competed with the campmeeting as a social event. Some came for the food; the Cane Ridge campmeeting of 1801 adjourned because the food ran out.

The campmeeting did a rough work in a rough way. Barton Stone listed some extraordinary exercises: falling, jerks, dancing, barking, running, and singing. But along the way it made some very important discoveries, discoveries that reflected an intimate knowledge of its people and their culture. Today we call this inculturation but it began as simple observation and application of the results.

First of all, it was discovered that to move people spiritually one had to move them physically. So the sawdust trail, the altar call, and the anxious bench became important parts of worship that was fully incarnate. Second, the emotions were an important part of life and campmeetings often stressed very emotional preaching and singing. Third, it was soon learned how important music was in stirring heart and mind and preparing people to hear the preaching of the gospel. The campmeeting's success was in large measure due to its ability to reflect the unchurched people it wished to attract. Many of us are here today because it succeeded with our great-great-grandparents.

It was the threat of introducing these wild western patterns to the more staid East that provoked that New Lebanon Summit in 1827. Such easterners as Lyman Beecher and Asahel Nettleton wanted revivals but they wanted them done with decency and order. In other words, they wanted them within the parameters of social life on the East Coast where the sexes and social classes still knew their places. They practiced inculturation but in a considerably different culture. Their fears come out clearly in the measures debated at New Lebanon: women speaking in public, praying for individuals by name, undue familiarity with the Almighty, invading parishes and attacking unregenerate clergy, "disrespect to superiors in age or station," and the reputation for general rowdiness in western revivals.

Two cultures were in conflict here just as much as two concepts of worship and evangelism. To shorten a long story, the westerners won out in the long run. They led to the Frontier Tradition becoming the dominant worship tradition in the U.S., and the Frontier Tradition came to show some specifically American characteristics as it evolved. Charges G. Finney (1792-1875) emerged as the most important spokesman for this tradition as well as being the leading revivalist of the nineteenth century. In his ministry and in his *Lectures on Revivals of Religion* (1835) many of the characteristics of the emerging Americanization of Christian worship are clearly defined. First of all it is an optimistic gospel; all humans are summoned to hear the gospel and "to change their own hearts." The buoyant optimism of the period of manifest destiny is apparent. Second, Finney is convinced that revivalism is a matter of proper technique: use the right methods and conversions will occur. It is a far cry from Jonathan Edwards's *A Faithful Narrative of the Surprising Work of God* (1737). The new measures Finney advocated are simply what had been tried and proven in years of revivals in upstate New York. "A revival," he states, "is the result of the *right* use of the appropriate means."[3] Plant the right seed and a crop is assured.

But one consequence is that liturgical tradition is of little importance. Finney cites the different denominational postures for prayer, or clerical garb, or singing of hymns, or use of choirs, to show that there are no constants. "History," as Henry Ford said (while spending millions to preserve it at Dearborn village), "is bunk." So traditional forms could be used when they worked and discarded when they did not.

Here is the essential American pragmatism at work. If something produces results, i.e., gets converts, then keep it. If it fails, discard it. This allows for plenty of experimentation but unsuccessful tries are quickly eliminated. So pragmatism came to be the essential criterion in worship. The Puritan quest to be free to follow the word of God in worship became an endeavor to be free to do what worked. Effectiveness could be gauged by a head count and few congregations even today can resist publishing attendance figures from last Sunday. One could speak of the Pragmatic Tradition instead of the Frontier Tradition.

[3]*Lectures on Revivals of Religion* (Cambridge: Harvard University Press, 1960) 13.

One of the lessons learned early on was the importance of music. The Frontier had spawned a new genre, gospel songs, that was geared to the educational and musical level of frontier people. Frequent repetition made the lyrics easy to memorize and simple melodies facilitated singing. Finney's cohort was Thomas Hastings (1784-1872) and each of the great revivalists had his or her Ira Sankey (1840-1908) or Cliff Barrows. The message was also simple: it spoke in personal terms about Jesus and me, or rather me and Jesus, and mentioned the joys of present assurance and future bliss.

The Frontier Tradition soon discovered the usefulness of solo and choral music. Choirs, once anathema to the founding fathers, sprouted all over the land. Before 1830 few church buildings allocated space for singers; subsequently almost all did. And they were up front to participate more fully in leading worship.

Finney's new measures, especially protracted meetings, the anxious bench, lay prayers, female prayer meetings, and anxious meetings soon were domesticated on the East Coast as much as inland. The yearly revival became an important part of Church life. And revival style music sang its way into the hearts of Americans.

Perhaps less obvious but even more significant, a standard three-part Sunday service evolved that is followed today with undeviating faithfulness by hundreds of thousands of American congregations. This service consists of 1) prayer and praise, much of it musical, 2) preaching, often calling for conversion, and 3) harvest of those persuaded, usually by coming forward to be greeted or baptized. One can see it every Sunday on televised worship, a term I prefer to television evangelism although it is both. It is the most common worship pattern in this country.

Much of its dominance comes from overwhelming the existing Protestant worship traditions. The Frontier Tradition proved to be an irresistible black hole that pulled other traditions out of their accustomed orbits. It may not be so strange that much of Methodist worship soon conformed to this pattern. It is a bit more peculiar that the Reformed and Puritan traditions felt its pull and frequently yielded. But it is indeed odd that members of the Lutheran tradition, particularly those associated with Gettysburg Seminary, felt the need to develop an American Lutheranism whose worship found the frontier as attractive as Wittenberg. Stranger still was the adoption by Quakers in Indiana of many of the revival techniques of the frontier. Even

Roman Catholic revivals became frequent with Jesuits, Franciscans, Passionists, and Redemptorists taking the lead.

Let us recapitulate. Worship for the unchurched, developed out of necessity on the frontier, succeeded in becoming the norm even among the churched. Once converted, people were put to work in a whole series of social reforms: abolition of slavery, temperance, prison reform, public education, Sunday schools, foreign missions, tract societies, Bible societies, etcetera. The Church itself seemed to function largely as a recruiting agency and almost an option. Worship became a reheating of the fervor of converts. It was basically functional and its function was making converts and keeping them faithful. Romano Guardini's famous discussion of the uselessness of the liturgy, its playfulness, would seem a strange concept indeed. Yet he wrote in 1918 that "when the liturgy is rightly regarded, it cannot be said to have a purpose, because it does not exist for the sake of humanity, but for the sake of God."[4] That is another world from the premises of the Frontier Tradition, which found a definite purpose in providing worship for the unchurched and developed measures to reach them successfully.

Reaching the Unchurched Today

I must fast forward now, bypassing the Pentecostal Tradition which developed largely out of the Frontier Tradition but involved more spontaneity and a broader base of participation. In our own times the Frontier Tradition has continued to grow in variety and skill. I interpret the latest manifestation of it to be the emergence of the Church Growth Movement and the disciples of Donald McGarvan (1897-1990). It passes under names such as the Mega-Church movement or the seekers' service model and I would like to call it high-tech worship.

I include it in the Frontier Tradition with the conviction that no tradition (except perhaps some Quakers and Anabaptists) remains unchanging but that all are in transition. Thus I do not mean it is backward-looking or even very historically conscious. Since we shall be experiencing the seekers' service model of worship here I shall do little to define it but only try to locate it historically.

[4]*The Spirit of the Liturgy* (New York: Sheed and Ward, 1935) 177.

The problem is much the same as the one clergy faced on the frontier: large numbers of unchurched people. The method has much the same approach though infinitely more sophisticated. I cannot imagine frontier circuit rider Peter Cartwright talking about the "homogeneous unit principle." But he did know he had to talk the language of people on the frontier and not the language of the seminarians at Princeton whom he compared to lettuce grown under a peach tree. Some churches such as the Willow Creek Community Church are very culture specific: they reach out to men between twenty-five and fifty.

In this movement inculturation has become a fine science. Perhaps Anscar Chupungco and other Roman Catholic champions of inculturation would have second thoughts if they could visit Willow Creek. The premises are not all that different from those in use at Mobil Oil headquarters down the road and worshipers must feel quite at home on Sunday just as they do at corporate headquarters on Monday. There is not a single Christian symbol visible in the auditorium. Maybe it is time to stop theorizing about inculturation. It is here and the results are dramatic; thousands upon thousands attend Willow Creek. Curiously enough, about thirty percent are marginal Roman Catholics who, after all, constitute the second largest denomination in the United States.

If Willow Creek aims at homogeneity there is another model I call the spectrum model, most conspicuous at the Community Church of Joy in Phoenix. Here there are different services for different groups. What the church calls the "cowboy" service is on Saturday with country western music and casual clothes. Early Sunday morning the old folks service for retired people (the church is near Sun City) has more resemblances to traditional Lutheran worship, especially the hymns for those who have moved down from Lake Wobegon country. But the services get progressively more free until the 11:30 that attracts young adults. By then the only relic of the *Lutheran Book of Worship* may be the offering! When I was there the great Christian festival of St. Valentine's Day was celebrated even though it was the Transfiguration of Our Lord. But even Lutherans have problems relating to transfiguration.

Various permutations of these two models are played out in great variety all over the country. Most have a believers' service during the week that may relate more closely to the denominational tradition (if any). At Ginghamsburg United Methodist Church (near Dayton) there are testimonials in the Sunday service. In some places there are both believers' and seekers' services on Sunday morning.

I speak of this as high-tech worship because there is certainly no reticence about using the latest electronic technology. The control booth at Joy is far more impressive than Finney's spindly pulpit, a treasured relic at Oberlin Church. When the new church building at Ginghamsburg is finished, baptisms will be conducted in a pool in the narthex but witnessed on screens by the whole congregation.

In line with the Frontier Tradition, music is almost half the service. Most avoid the classical music that only three or four per cent of the population listens to. The musical idiom is carefully selected to relate to that homogeneous unit being targeted. Frequently all the music, save a song or two, is done by professionals and not the congregation. In this sense it is much less participatory than the Frontier Tradition has been as a whole. Whatever its idiom, the music is usually very well performed.

In contrast to early revivalism, physical manifestations are not present except among the more charismatically oriented. Depending on the local culture the emotional level may be more or less intense. Drama has been added in many cases, usually professionally done with both substance and humor.

The same fierce pragmatism is apparent. This is worship that gets results. When I visited Willow Creek three hundred candidates were presented for baptism or rebaptism, a good day's work. If practices work they are retained and refined. If they fail they can be replaced. As Finney remarked in 1835, "No person can find any *form* . . . [of worship] laid down in the Bible. It is *preaching the gospel* that stands out prominent there as the great thing. The form is left out of the question."[5] The Church Growth Movement has continued that quest for new forms as authentic members of the Frontier Tradition in worship. Like Finney, who was progressive in theology and social concerns, the mega-churches are frequently moderate or liberal in theology.

Alternative Paradigms

But the Frontier Tradition is not the only tradition in American Christian worship, and to these other traditions we must now turn.

---

[5]*Lectures*, 251.

As we shall see, they too were in transition during this period and continue to be. I shall discuss some common factors among a variety of traditions first, then mention a few specifics.

First and foremost is a different concept of what it means to become a Christian. The Frontier Tradition tended to place all its emphasis on a moment of decision in which one decided for Christ, or accepted the gospel, or got saved. In one blinding flash one's life was turned around and one passed from perdition to salvation. The sharp distinction Calvinism made between the elect and the damned left no room for ambiguity. That clear demarcation remained even while the New England theology opened wider and wider the doors for the saved to enter. Since salvation was offered by Christ, salvation was simply a matter of accepting this new reality. One was snatched from damnation to salvation in an instantaneous fashion. Essentially it was an individual decision in which the Church simply provided the occasion and the incentives.

But there is another older and once more prevalent concept of the process of becoming a Christian. This consists of initiation into a community of faith and was a process of growth in faith rather than an instantaneous conversion. In these traditions the community plays a major role in enabling the individual to become a Christian. Usually it symbolizes the process through ritualizing such passages as baptism, confirmation, reception into Church membership, owning the covenant, or public profession of faith. In each of these stages the Church as supportive community plays a major role.

The role of the community is central not only on the liturgical right wing (Roman Catholics, Lutherans, and Anglicans) but even to the far left where one spoke of birthright Quakers. Those who became Friends by convincement had to pass the scrutiny of the meeting before they could be accepted as members and could be disowned for sufficient reasons such as slaveowning. New England Puritans agonized over those who could not make a public profession of faith, seeking a way to keep them at least at arm's length within the covenant so their children could be baptized. And nineteenth-century Methodists, heavily committed to revivalism, still insisted that newly baptized adult converts would have to pass half a year of probation before they could be received into the Church. The rite of reception into Church membership dates from 1864 among northern Methodists; southerners followed in six years.

In all of these traditions becoming a Christian is seen as initiation into a community through accepting its self-understanding (creed), its behavior patterns (code), and its worship (cult). Stated in another way, the motif seems to be adoption and assimilation more than solitary birth. In these traditions becoming a Christian, in large measure, is learning to worship as a Christian. That is why mystagogical catechesis was so important in the early Church and why being exposed to the full cultus through the rhythms of the liturgical year and the rhythms of the life cycle are so important today. The sacraments are not seen as just an option but as an intrinsic part of the Christian message. The Christian faith is reiterated in the systematic reading of God's word and reinforced in hymn singing, prayer, and preaching. Teaching worship is an essential act in making Christians. Therefore teaching clergy and others to teach worship is a high priority in evangelization.

Implicit in all these patterns is a belief that the Church is a distinctive society with its own code words and actions. It is always in tension with culture and leery of accommodating itself too easily to the society in which it bears witness. It is always too tempting to baptize the American way of life. Jean-Jacques von Allmen says Christian worship is always a threat to the world because it tells the world it is to be judged.[6] That is a far cry from saying that money is a sign of God's favor as some preachers have done. Success is no sign of sanctity.

Historically the 1830s mark a clear sign of resurgence of this approach to worship and evangelism. The 1830s must be called the liturgical decade. All over western Christianity there was a shaking off of too facile inculturation, a recovery of assertiveness about the distinctiveness of Christianity. In the process too-comfortable accommodations with the Enlightenment came to be rejected. Many things in themselves excellent that had been developed in the previous century and a half were discarded because they were insufficiently identified with the central core of Christian worship. Guéranger destroyed many things we recognize as of value in French Catholicism but the point he was making is clear: they were not part of the central core. The destruction of Ignaz Heinrich von Wessenberg's enlightened Catholicism in Germany was part of a similar assertiveness.

[6] *Worship: Its Theology and Practice* (New York: Oxford University Press, 1965) 62–67.

Anglicans defied an age of progress by reverting to the fourteenth century. It took real conviction to build gothic churches in India and Tasmania or even in Rome and Athens for that matter. But they made, and still do make, a statement that the Church is a distinct society. It took real courage to promote what Wesley called the "fiction" of apostolic succession in an age of Jacksonian democracy but it brought people running to the Episcopal Church.

In Denmark, N. F. S. Grundtvig fought a battle for restoration of the sacramental life that had once flourished in Lutheran lands. His preaching and hymn writing worked to restore the traditional Lutheran cultus. In Bavaria, Wilhelm Loehe fought the same battles to restore authentic Lutheran worship that the Enlightenment had largely laughed out of the churches. He restored Saturday confession and a weekly Eucharist and provided service books and missionaries for the churches being planted in the United States.

Nineteenth-century Lutheran worship became a battle between those such as Matthias Loy who longed for a recovery of a distinctive Lutheran cultus and those who had largely accepted the Frontier Tradition. That battle is far from over but successive service books of 1888, 1918, 1958, and 1978 represent movement to a distinctive liturgical form of worship and equating evangelism with learning and liturgy.

They may be less apparent, but we are learning more and more about similar movements within American Presbyterian and Methodist churches, sometimes in unexpected and out of the way places. Thomas Summers in Alabama and here in Nashville promoted the revival of Wesley's Sunday service and led to a monthly Eucharist being mandated in the *Discipline* of southern Methodism. Charles W. Baird and others looked for the day when Presbyterians would have set forms available for optional and voluntary use. That dream took half a century but was realized in 1906.

Among the German Reformed, John Nevin fought a valiant battle against what he saw as the superficiality of revivalism and plugged for a Reformed theology of the Eucharist based on Calvin rather than on Zwingli. Horace Bushnell championed Christian nurture in which the child grew up never knowing itself to be other than Christian. All of these traditions were reasserting evangelism through worship. Worship was a primary form of leading people to Christ in a community that asserted its own distinctiveness.

In many ways these are countercultural movements although much spilled over into the culture. It is said that in Bristol, England, the cathedral looks like a railroad station and the railroad station looks like a cathedral. But many traditions were reasserting themselves as not simply reflections of the culture, and these traditions flourished and continued to do so up through the 1950s.

As early as 1903 a Methodist pastor in Chicago produced a service book in which he asserted that "this liturgical movement is felt in many Churches,"[7] referring to the recovery of Wesley's services. That well may have been the first Methodist use of the term "liturgical movement" but it was far from the last. The term itself had been coined by Prosper Guéranger in nineteenth-century France. For over a century the Catholic liturgical movement was largely the domain of the monks; a Jesuit attacked liturgical renewal in 1913 as a "Benedictine innovation."

The twentieth century saw the recovery of frequent communion after many centuries in which only the most devout practiced it, and it saw the restoration of Gregorian chant become a high priority. From our perspective this was a good run down the wrong road. It was certainly as countercultural as one could get, for the chant, like the rest of the Mass, was resolutely in Latin and the musical idiom equally alien. The period up to *Mediator Dei* (1947) was largely one of restorationism, recovering lost treasures.

A new epoch began soon after World War II in which the central focus came to be participation. In this new atmosphere the campaign for the vernacular came to the forefront. Worship was to shape people's lives by their ownership of it, in what Vatican II came to call "full, conscious, active participation." In the years since the Council active participation in the liturgy has replaced the attitude of the passive layperson preoccupied with such devotions as the rosary. In a significant sense it has become even more intensely insider's worship. Instead of doing one's own agenda one joins with the community in singing, praying, listening, and communing.

Meanwhile the mainline Protestant churches were moving to more formal services. In the first half of the century some of this was motivated by aesthetics. As our people became more affluent and better

[7]Charles LeVerne Roberts, *Divine Service: A Compilation of Collects and Psalms* (Cincinnati: Jennings and Pye, 1903) 5.

educated much of this was inevitable. Not all of it had very solid theological foundations: the most influential writer on worship was a Unitarian pastor who built a large gothic church in Chicago while calling for the discarding of "abandoned concepts." As Methodists and Presbyterians got respectable, their buildings and services got more aesthetically appealing. The architect of East Liberty Presbyterian Church in Pittsburgh boasted that it could be readied "for a Pontifical High Mass" in a few minutes.

One can trace in many of the traditions, be they Lutheran, Reformed, Methodist, or Puritan, the restoration of many items that set Church life apart from the culture in general. The advances of the Church year instead of the secular calendar can be traced in successive worship books of Presbyterians, Methodists, and Congregationalists in the first two-thirds of this century. Each edition took the Church year more seriously. The responsive readings, so popular early in the century on specific themes, eventually yielded to a restoration of the psalter with its difficult passages.

The period after World War II saw a concern with authenticity instead of obsession with relevancy. Signs of this were increased emphasis on confession and creeds as neo-orthodoxy made its impact felt in worship. The keenness to recover the worship forms of one's tradition, Lutheran, Reformed, or Methodist, was a common factor. More and more this was becoming insider's worship.

One must recall that this period of the 1950s and 1960s formed many of the people in our churches today. Sixty-one per cent of United Methodists are over fifty years of age; consequently, these are the worship styles that they know best. This generation became familiar with printed prayers, more frequent Eucharists, and more faithful use of the liturgical year. These people became Christians through the constant repetition of familiar forms that demanded a fairly high level of participation. Certainly it was an insider's service that increasingly came to include distinctive Christian symbols, words, and actions.

Among Methodists much of this was fueled by a Wesleyan revival. This is significant because Wesley's evangelism in the eighteenth century was frequently highly countercultural. To place such a high emphasis on the sacraments in an Enlightenment culture, to stress fasting in a self-indulgent age, to place so much emphasis on sanctification in a time of moral laxity—all these were about as countercultural as one could get. Yet the heroic age of Methodism was an age of enormous growth in adherents both in numbers and in depth of commitment.

Similar practices evolved in other churches in mid-century. As Presbyterians rediscovered John Calvin or Lutherans Luther there was a move to restore many things tossed aside in the earlier centuries: set forms, sacraments, and the liturgical year. A comparative study of the service books or hymnals of the major denominations shows a straight-line progression from the *Methodist Hymnal* of 1905 or the Presbyterian *Book of Common Worship* of 1906.

What seemed like a straight line of progression became a zigzag after Vatican II unfroze Roman Catholic worship. Everyone borrowed from everyone else. Roman Catholics found they could be as folksy as Methodists; Methodists found they could be as solemn as Episcopalians. All were propelled to fresh revision of their liturgical books. The most widely-adopted product was the new Roman Catholic Sunday Lectionary, which led to denominational versions and the *Revised Common Lectionary*. Those who bought the lectionary, whether they recognized it or not, were also buying the liturgical year. I remember when we first observed All Saints' Day at Perkins School of Theology in 1966. Now I suspect half of United Methodist churches observe it and for half of Methodists to agree on anything is revolutionary!

One of the surprises to come out of Vatican II was the Rite of Christian Initiation of Adults. The *Constitution on the Sacred Liturgy* had only mentioned "the restored catechumenate." The new rite was published on Epiphany 1972, in Latin, thus placing it rather late in the revision of the sacraments although ahead of anointing the sick and reconciliation.

Much of the work on it had been done under the leadership of Professor Balthasar Fischer of Trier. The inspiration, of course, was the process of making a Christian detailed in the *Apostolic Tradition*, then believed to have been compiled by Hippolytus in early third-century Rome. The rite, or R.C.I.A., as it is widely called, involves a lengthy process of becoming Christian. The progress is ritualized by three steps: acceptance into the order of catechumens, election or enrollment of names, and a final step of celebration of the sacraments of initiation.

It can truly be said that the R.C.I.A. has emerged in only two decades as an important part of Catholic parish life in this country and has been highly successful in producing new Christians. Much of its popularity in this country can be attributed to the vigorous and eloquent championing of Professor Aidan Kavanagh, O.S.B., a student of Fischer's. I am told that the R.C.I.A. hardly exists in many parts of Europe and is virtually unknown there. I shall make several observations about the R.C.I.A. without going into detail about its structure.

The first premise is that leading a person to Christ is a communal experience in which the whole community has an interest. This has meant that millions of Catholic lay people have been involved in the process. Indeed, with the shortage of priests and religious this has been absolutely necessary. The R.C.I.A. has increasingly become a lay-centered process. This has necessitated training millions of what are in effect ministers of conversion. But just as teaching a subject is the best way to learn it oneself, so the bringing of others to conversion has strengthened the faith of those working with the catechumens. Thus the R.C.I.A. has been a great source of renewal for many lifelong Catholics.

Second, the process is a deliberate and slow one, not an instantaneous conversion. Hippolytus recommended up to three years but even he yielded a bit on that one. Still, it is clear that there is much to absorb, to assimilate, and to accept in the process and it takes at least weeks, if not months. The catechumenate is a training program that involves equipping the brain as well as converting the heart. Though it involves the emotions it also involves the intellect. Much of it is a matter of learning our story, particularly as found in the biblical narratives read and preached in worship.

Much of it also involves acquiring a new culture in which alien ways of doing things become familiar. Much of this is a matter of learning what the community does in worship and why things are done that have no meaning outside of church. In this sense worship is a highly important part of assimilating one into the community. Hippolytus began with hearers of the word in the context of corporate worship and this is still a major part of evangelization. Those constantly absent from worship are hardly promising candidates to move on to the next step. Worship involves full participation in the life of the community as it actually is with nothing held back. The R.C.I.A. is drastically different from the seekers' service model, which tries to soft pedal distinctive Christian words and actions. One is immersed in the real Mass even if not yet able to receive communion.

In recent years a number of Protestant denominations have shown considerable interest in the format of the R.C.I.A. for evangelization. The Episcopal *Book of Occasional Services: 1991* has service materials for "Preparation of Adults for Holy Baptism: The Catechumenate." This includes "Admission of Catechumens," "Enrollment of Candidates for Baptism," and the final sacraments of initiation, including "A Vigil on the Eve of Baptism." Hippolytus would be proud!

The 1982 Evangelical Lutheran Church in America *Occasional Services* provides a rite for "Enrollment of Candidates for Baptism." A rudimentary outline of the catechumenate is indicated in the rubrics. United Methodists and Presbyterians have shown interest in a similar process but have not yet published materials. All the churches have been wrestling for some time with the concept and practice of confirmation but neither the practice nor the term is easily eradicated. More success has been achieved with annual renewal of baptism and this has become common in many denominations.

Two Patterns

Two quite distinct patterns of worship and evangelism seem to be thriving side by side in North America: the Mega-Church with its seekers' services and the various insiders methods in which one is socialized into Christianity, the latest of these being the R.C.I.A. model. Both have brought millions into Christian faith but by using radically different styles of worship and premises about evangelization. Judging from my age and the fact that I spent twenty years of my life helping to reform United Methodist worship you may quickly decide where I feel more comfortable. But I have tried to be fair and to indicate the advantages of each pattern. As a historian I am not called upon to award gold stars but to record what exists and what survives. Certainly both models seem to be doing that at present.

Finally let me quote a statement of John Calvin's that was unfortunately overlooked by his descendants in the sixteenth- and seventeenth-century wars over worship. Calvin noted that God "did not will in outward discipline and ceremonies to prescribe in detail what we ought to do. . . . The upbuilding of the church ought to be vigorously accommodated to the customs of each nation and age." He concludes, "but love will best judge what may hurt or edify; and if we let love be our guide, all will be safe."[8] Calvin is right; ultimately it is not our methods that are essential but our motives. And love, he proposes, is the supreme guide in matters of worship. May we keep this in mind this weekend as we engage in the North American Summit on the Future of Christian Worship.

[8]*Institutes of the Christian Religion* 4.10.30 (Philadelphia: Westminster Press, 1960) 2. 1208.

II. Liturgy and Justice

14. The Eucharist and Justice

Given as an address at a conference of the Kentucky Council of Churches in 1985 and subsequently published by the Council in *Eucharist and Ecumenical Life* (Lexington, 1985), this is used by permission in its original form.

There are many ways one can approach the subject of the Eucharist and ethics. I shall limit myself to one aspect of ethics, namely the area of justice. I suspect this is the area of greatest current interest. And much of what I shall have to say about justice will apply to many other aspects of Christian ethics.

I do not think I need to define what I mean by "the Eucharist," or breaking of bread, divine liturgy, holy communion, Lord's Supper, or whatever name is used in our various traditions. But I may need to specify what I mean by "justice." Justice is attributing to all persons their full human worth: i.e., rendering to each person what is due to that person as a human being. Thomas Aquinas spoke of justice as "a habit whereby man renders to each one his due by a constant and perpetual will" (*Summa Theologiae* II-III, q. 58, a.1). The nature of injustice would seem to be to deny the full personhood by treating some people as of less human worth than others. Obviously there are going to be conflicting claims in many instances, especially when quite different persons are competing for the same ascription of worth. Thus the problem of justice is to mediate between these conflicts so as to render to each his or her due.

For the Christian the exercise of justice is one form in which love is expressed and is not just an abstract, impersonal meting out of rights. Justice is often the discerning of the proper way to act out the Christian imperative to love one another. Power to carry out these actions is necessary to bring that love to fruition and the Christian community itself provides some of that power.

It is particularly significant for Christians that justice be exercised within a visible community, namely the Church. Thus justice is a way of making visible the nature of a community whose whole life is devoted to the expression of love for each other and for the world. Anything to the contrary contradicts the very nature of the Christian community itself.

The Eucharist is a means the community uses to speak and act out the images that reflect the basis of our life together. In so doing the community makes visible and concrete the realities by which it lives. What we believe about our relationship to self, to neighbor, and to God gets expressed in what we say and do in the Eucharist. For example, we discover ourselves as sinners and are led to confession. We receive communion with our neighbor as a member of the same body created through baptism. And we see ourselves standing before God as completely dependent creatures. Thus the Eucharist gives insight into the deepest realities of life.

Much of the power of any formal worship comes from reiteration. The images that the community speaks and acts are rarely unfamiliar to its members but have recurred since childhood for most of them. Week after week the same words are said, the same things are done, all in the same context. Even the rhythms are familiar: the Eucharist takes place at the same intervals at the same time. Novelty, when it is introduced, is often resented because people expect to recapture the familiar when they come to church.

Thus a slow process of formation goes on in the Eucharist. It is rarely a conscious activity, rarely something done deliberately. But becoming who we are goes on week after week. This is not to say that the purpose of the Eucharist is to manipulate or deliberately to shape people but simply to assert that formation is one of the things that inevitably does happen. We should be suspicious of anyone who plans or conducts worship as a means to an end, however exalted. That has always been a temptation, to turn the Eucharist into something useful. The Reformation could not resist making it a means of theological and ethical instruction; revivalism made worship a means to make converts. Both missed the point that, in purpose, the Eucharist is totally useless. And yet it does edify and convert and form our very being.

In this sense the Eucharist remains a constant means of shaping our being by constant reiteration. *What seems normal becomes normative for us in the course of time.* We hardly question the familiar because it has simply become a part of ourselves. The habitual has become an intrinsic part of our being. The way we perceive things, the way we act because of such perceptions, all become part of us by gradual reinforcement through constant repetition.

The Ambiguity of the Eucharist

There is a great deal of ambiguity in the Eucharist or any other kind of worship with regard to justice and injustice. The Christian assembly itself ought to be a strong sign of peace, indeed, a foretaste of heavenly peace. But as many can testify, the assembly often masks internal struggles, various patterns of dominance and oppression. Some will find the gathering of the community for worship liberating; for others it is an occasion of oppression barely tolerated. It would be a mistake to assume that the full human worth of all present is valued and determines practice for most worshiping assemblies.

For example, the roles various people play tend to reinforce the relationships we have with them outside of worship. Children in most western churches are treated as not real members of the community. The United Methodist Church even calls baptized children "preparatory members" although the New Testament is quite clear that baptism initiates one fully into the Church (1 Cor 12:13). Other western churches are only a trifle more subtle. Usually we baptize babies and then immediately excommunicate them. We justify this by claiming one has to know what the Eucharist "is about" before being allowed to partake. What we are actually saying is that one has to talk and think as an adult, i.e., conceptually, before communing.

But if we were willing to adopt a child's mentality and see things relationally we would be ready for communion almost from birth. The adult world has imposed its own concepts of "being ready" as normative for all baptized members. Jesus had some strong things to say about entering the kingdom of heaven as a little child (Mark 10:14) but those words tend to be forgotten at the communion rail. When we do something for children it is usually in adult terms, i.e., a children's sermon, in which children often get exploited for their cuteness. In other words the message is: "You have to worship as an adult or not at all." The Eucharist simply makes our real intentions clear.

Children are not the only group marginalized in much of our worship. It is only recently that women have come to play roles in the Eucharist for which they are certainly competent; ushers, readers, preachers, and presiders. For centuries women sat passively in Christian worship to fulfill a socially-imposed role. There are still plenty of churches in which the ushers are all middle-aged banker-type men who do not seem to enjoy taking up money any more on Sunday than during the week at the bank. Even the preaching robe worn by many Protestant preachers is tailored as a masculine garment with padded shoulders. The robe makes a masculine statement although few would insist that ministry is based on physical stature and strength.

In all these instances the Eucharist is unconsciously used to reinforce cultural patterns by giving them divine sanction. The message is subtle; rarely does it take obvious or explicit forms. The act of assembling together for the Eucharist is a very political activity. It shapes people's perceptions of the roles to be expected of other people. Children should be seen and not heard during worship. Women are to know their place. And it is made quite clear who is to dominate by assigning all the active roles to men, usually those of middle age.

If these patterns are reinforced at the Lord's table, how can we act justly in the world? Life itself is not segmented; we cannot dissociate attitudes cultivated in worship from actions practiced in daily life. Worship has a way of baptizing injustices both inside the Church and in daily life. If one never sees women ministering at the altar-table then women's roles must inevitably be restricted elsewhere. If children never gather about that same altar-table then they are not "ready" to be responsible in other activities. The Eucharist gets deformed when it confirms social injustices by sanctioning them. Thus even the Eucharist can be and often has been a source of injustice.

Tissa Balasuriya, O.M.I., writing from a legacy of colonialism in Sri Lanka, questions whether exploiters and the exploited can even meet at the same altar-table without being mutually destructive due to the indifference of one and the hatred of the other. He says the Eucharist "has been and is being used as a legitimation of cruel exploitation"[1] and adds that "the main problem [is] that the whole

[1] *The Eucharist and Human Liberation* (Maryknoll: Orbis Books, 1979) xi.

Mass is still a bulwark of social conservation and not yet a means of human liberation."[2]

I am by no means making an argument that the Eucharist ought to be suspended because it can support and perpetuate injustice. But these considerations do demand a deeper awareness of what goes on in any gathering for worship. They demand a more thorough examination of the way the Christian assembly behaves when it gathers for the Lord's Supper.

Before we proceed further we must recognize the matter of ambiguity that necessarily adheres to any discussion of justice. If the just act were obvious, most ethicists would be without a job! And it is far more difficult to get any community to agree on what is just than for a single ethicist to determine what is so. Justice, as we said earlier on, deals with the resolution often of conflicting claims. How do we adjudicate between these claims when they involve conflict? This becomes greatly intensified in the Eucharist where the very life together of the community is at stake.

I shall try to illustrate the problem with regard to one of the most perplexing problems currently facing liturgists, the question of inclusive language. A year or two ago, the American Roman Catholic hierarchy got permission from Rome to change the words "it will be shed for you and for all men," certainly key words in the Mass. But if they thought they had finished, they had barely begun. Lutherans avoided language that was bluntly sexist but always used masculine pronouns for the devil in the 1978 *Lutheran Book of Worship*. But what is the just way to name God, not to mention the devil? The matter is clouded with ambiguity. Basically three positions seem current in the churches and adherents of each can and do argue for the justice of their position.

Conservatives defend conventional usage for several reasons. First of all, one's own language is regarded as intensely personal and any efforts to alter that appear to be a form of coercion. With some reason these people argue that one has to change the social reality before the language; hence, as long as blacks were despised, the word "nigger" survived. Second, the only religious language they know is biblical and efforts to change that language inevitably appear to be attacks on Scripture. That certainly is a deep anxiety and one not lightly to be

<hr>

[2]Ibid., 8.

dismissed. If the only known way to address God is taken away, can Christianity survive? And so all conventional use is defended with vigor.

Moderates see the need to make certain adjustments. It is conceded that daily usage outside the Church is in transition, too. Language that implies that maleness is normative humanity is obviously wrong and can be discarded without too much trauma. The moderate even finds it possible to eliminate masculine pronouns for God simply by doing away with any third person pronouns to God. But the familiar ways of naming God are too much to sacrifice. The five little words "Father," "Son," "Lord," "King," and "kingdom" cannot be surrendered by moderates without giving up much that is essential to Christianity.

To radicals these statements seem only proof of how wedded the Church is to a patriarchal mentality. They seek to eliminate these five little words altogether by substituting such terms as "Creator," "Redeemer," "Sustainer," "Sovereign," and "realm" (even though the first three of these are masculine forms). Or they balance masculine terms by use of "Mother" (with "Father") or the ambiguous "Child" (for "Son"). Analogical language is taken literally. For example, to any teenager "Father" implies "finite." The endurance of the symbol "Father" is not based primarily on sexual identity. But that aspect has come to the forefront and caused a great deal of pain.

In any case we have here three quite different conceptions of what is just language for the worshiping community. If it cannot agree on this, how can it do anything together? Traditionally, American Protestants have resolved questions of justice by schism. You do not remain in communion with those whose practices you abhor. Slaveholders are excommunicated; soldiers may be banned. If we cannot share the same history in verbal symbols, how is communion possible? Can we be in communion with the oppressors? Can we afford not to be?

These are indeed serious questions and some of the most pressing that the Christian churches now face. They are issues that come to the forefront at the Eucharist. We are confronted with the ambiguity of the situation and realize just how difficult it is to render to others what is their due when we cannot even agree on what is due.

Here is where the going gets tough. And I do not propose easy answers. Indeed, if we think that spoken language is difficult it is probably simple compared to some of the other dynamics of the Lord's Supper. Spoken language may be less formative than the roles people play in worship, the clothing they wear, and the space they occupy in the church building. It is relatively easy to analyze the texts of prayers and hymns, the words of lessons and sermons. But we have hardly begun to probe the very dynamics of the eucharistic assembly itself.

How do we discover what these dynamics are? This has to be done constantly in making just decisions. We see immediately what a political event the Eucharist is. How do we mediate between competing claims so that we, for example, avoid language that is patriarchal and yet do not destroy the only vocabulary the community knows? Inevitably we have to have a basis for making decisions. Much of worship leadership in planning, preparing for, and conducting the Eucharist is a matter of making decisions. How then can we endeavor to make the most just decisions possible in any given situation?

Functional Analysis

I propose a method for sorting out some of these problems. I do not expect to give answers but rather a means of arriving at the best possible solutions. This will not tell how to avoid all injustices but perhaps how to sense their presence in our worship and therefore to do something about this. I call this method "functional analysis." It consists of four stages of discernment and action. The whole process may seem a cold-blooded approach to worship but it can lead to clear thinking.

One begins by learning to *observe* the full dynamics of what the community is doing when it gathers for the Eucharist. This is not easy for priests and ministers since they have to be concerned not only about their own roles but whether the organist, ushers, singers, and others will do the right thing at the proper time. The best observer might indeed be a happy pagan who wandered in one Sunday and was not aware of assigned roles and common assumptions. Seemingly insignificant clues can tell us much. For instance, how much does the presider sit down during the service? That may tell us whether he or she presides or dominates. If the minister stands for almost the whole service it can mean little leadership is delegated. There is a clear difference between presiding (sitting before) and dominating (lording it over). Observation is an art that needs to be cultivated, to see what is being done and who is doing it.

One moves on from this to *analyze* in ethical terms just what is happening in the gathered community. One can judge the relative degrees of participation, activity and passivity, the expectations of autonomy or conformity, acceptance or neglect of cultural patterns, discrimination or inclusiveness, and a variety of other justice issues. Indeed, the building itself will tell us some ethical things. Does it exclude those who cannot negotiate steps? Are door handles cruel to arthritic hands? Pressures to conformity may discourage those for whom kneeling is painful or conversely those for whom standing is tiring. How accepting is the community of a variety of postures? How tolerant will the people be of other lifestyles in the world?

As one analyzes in ethical terms what is going on, one senses the enormous complexity of the one-hour event. Young children, elderly people, men and women of all ages, all come to the Lord's table with different hopes, abilities, and varieties of gifts. How do we make childrens' wiggles a part of the service when we are more attuned to active minds than active bodies? How do we avoid use of pejorative terms such as "blind, old, midget, black, and small" until we realize whom these terms hurt? How do we retain old favorite hymns without boring those eager for novelty?

But once one analyzes what is actually going on in the assembly, there still remains the third stage of *considering it normatively*. Are we doing what is fair and just? At this point ethical sensitivity becomes necessary. The community may find itself making self-contradictory statements. We may profess inclusiveness but give offense to some by excluding them in roles, actions, or words. Certainly when God is praised entirely in terms of male attributes it can produce genuine self-doubt as to how much value is attributed to the females of the congregation. Do we sing about the "brotherhood of man" when half those present can be neither? Are children allowed to help take the offering? How often is a hymn sung in Spanish or Korean when such languages may be familiar to some of the congregation?

Eventually we have to make normative statements about such worship and make decisions by sorting out the self-contradictions and inconsistencies in our worship that deny the full human worth of some. Most such decisions will involve compromises but they need to be as just as possible.

Having made decisions, we move on to our fourth stage, that of *making reforms* in the worship life of the congregation. All worship reform must be done in dialogue with those we are seeking to serve. This means the worshipers themselves must be party to the effecting of change. Many may relish things that oppress others. Still, it is not just to the oppressors, either, to have familiar patterns snatched away without discussion. One does not take lightly a lifelong practice even when it is faulty.

Thus we have come full circle: from observing what the community does, to analyzing what is happening on an ethical level, to judging these actions in terms of justice, to reforming our celebration to reflect greater justice.

Functional analysis is a recurring process, never ended. Worship patterns must always remain under critical judgment of the command to love one's neighbor. Thus although the *lex orandi* is extremely important for Protestants it is not absolute. Ethical judgments must come into play and sometimes reform practice. This is an ongoing concern as we become progressively aware of injustices of which we had been unaware. Who, in 1960, worried about "mankind" when we still had to rid ourselves of "nigger?"

In this sense, our eucharistic celebrations must be judged rather than be the judge. As our understanding of justice deepens we observe, analyze, judge, and reform what happens in the eucharistic assembly. Otherwise we continue to reinforce roles, perceptions, and actions that may do serious injustice to individuals or groups in Church and the world. Thus there is always danger that the Eucharist, unexamined and unevaluated, will perpetuate unjust social patterns by giving them the illusory aura of divine acceptance. In such cases it can be a source of injustice until reformed.

Eucharist and Eschatology

Fortunately there is a more positive side. I have dwelt at length on the Eucharist as a source of injustice because that aspect is so easy to ignore. But I would be seriously remiss if I did not state the positive side, namely that the Eucharist also provides the Church's greatest single resource for justice. There are many possible approaches to this. I shall sketch out only one very briefly: the eschatological dimension of the Lord's Supper. I should make it clear that this is only one possible way to depict the Eucharist's contribution to the struggle for social justice.

Christian worship has a strong eschatological base although it is often overlooked. Years ago Jean Jacques von Allmen[3] pointed out that Christian worship is always a threat to the world, for it calls the world into judgment. At the same time, worship is a sign of hope for the world for it carries a promise of a better society. Our worship, of course, can become so culturally debased that it becomes simply a paean of praise for the American way of life. If you doubt that, turn on the television next Sunday! Our worship can become a part of the cult of success: ironic, to say the least, for the worship of the Crucified One. But Christian worship can transcend the present social order as something contingent and passing away. Although deeply rooted in past memories of God's actions, the Eucharist always resounds with the *maranatha* cry, looking forward to the final consummation of God's work.

In this sense the Lord's Supper is a constant reminder that the reign of God does not tolerate war and injustice. No doubt eschatology can easily be perverted into what social reformers once ridiculed: "Pie in the sky / Bye and bye / That's a lie!" Such shallow eschatology contributes to injustices in the present because it disallows any human activity to correct them. It is bad theology because it ignores the fact that Christ already has come; that God's rule is begun although not yet completed. Thus through worship we participate in the reign of God but do not yet realize it in its fullness.

Each time the body of Christ gathers on earth to celebrate the Eucharist it is forming a sign of God's reign based on justice. As we have already shown, it is a community that is fragmentary, broken, filled with inner conflicts. But it is still a sign of the peaceable kingdom based on justice. And it is a sign set in the midst of this world, reminding this world that all its premises of success, wealth, and power stand under judgment. The most important thing the Church does when it makes Eucharist is that it comes together to form the body of Christ. It gathers in Christ's name to discern his body in the assembly itself, i.e., among humans. Thus the first contribution of worship to justice is that it brings the community together to discern the body. And failures to do this, as Paul pointed out, are life-threatening (1 Cor 11:30).

3 *Worship: Its Theology and Practice* (New York: Oxford University Press, 1965) 62–68.

There are many other things the body of Christ does when it assembles for the Eucharist. I shall briefly mention only three: hearing God's word, recalling our baptism, and eating the sacred meal.

Traditionally Protestants have tended to look on the sermon as the item that makes the rest of worship relevant. We speak of "prophetic preaching" but never of "prophetic prayer" or "prophetic sacraments." The advent of widespread use of the lectionary and the consequent much more exegetical style of preaching has not lessened the social relevance of worship but given it greater depth. Such practice has forced us to read and exegete unfriendly passages whereas we previously chose user-friendly Scripture texts. Indeed, much topical preaching had discarded biblical texts altogether. But when a lectionary is used, or preaching in course is done, the awkward quirks of the gospel come out in the most unexpected ways.

When the lectionary first became popular among Protestants many preachers exclaimed how relevant they found the passages assigned were to the time and place in their own community. One of the constant factors in a wider exposure to Scripture was that the strange new world of the Bible tends to call into question all the casual assumptions of the world about us. Preaching has become more relevant because it has found a firmer base in the biblical witness to the kingdom of God rather than in the personal opinions of the topical preacher.

When faithful to the biblical witness, preaching has been forced to proclaim the kingdom of God as the central hope of the community. Likewise, the community now hears much more of Scripture read than it once did. Worship has become more relevant by being based on something deeper than human good will. The rule of justice transcends all we can imagine.

It is well said that the Eucharist is the only part of baptism that is repeated. Rarely have we thought through the eschatological dimensions of baptism. But baptism is initiation into a community that lives in hope and focuses on its future in the Lord. We begin in baptism our life together in community. Baptism is a foretaste of the society that is to come and advances that kingdom as new initiates are added to its members.

Baptism also represents initiation into the royal priesthood of Christ. In this it calls attention to the priesthood of all the baptized by uniting them to the person and work of Christ. There is no stronger affirmation of equality in the New Testament than Paul's statement: "Baptized into union with him, you have all put on Christ as a garment. There is no such thing as Jew and Greek, slave and freeman, male and female; for you are all one person in Christ Jesus" (Gal 3:27-28 NEB). All Christians are priests because they have been united to Christ through baptism. Baptism brings to all Christians a call to minister, that love may be expressed in forms of justice.

Hence the call to ordain women has its grounding in baptism. It hardly seems consistent to baptize women and not ordain them. All Christians receive baptism as a gift in which God acts to bring us into the body of Christ. This is done, in most cases, before the new Christian can respond or even speak. It foreshadows a kingdom that is brought in by God's action, not by ours. But baptism helps us live as citizens of that kingdom. Hence whenever we baptize we proclaim that the kingdom is at hand and we must act accordingly. And whenever we celebrate Eucharist we repeat that baptismal insight.

Finally, the sacred meal is a source of justice in many ways but especially because of its strong eschatological character. The Last Supper makes it clear that this sign is meant to inaugurate a new age. Geoffrey Wainwright has shown[4] how thoroughly eschatological the Christian tradition of Eucharist has been, although overshadowed during the last thousand years.

The Eucharist is a foretaste of the kingdom. Like baptism, it is a gift that is not based on merit nor is it preferential or deferential in its invitation of all who are baptized. As equals we share already in the messianic banquet, giving us an image of what life in the present world is meant to be.

At the same time the Lord's Supper is an invocation, a *"maranatha"* of the eschaton. It means a throwing forward of the second advent so that Christ is already present to judge us now in advance of the final judgment. We see ourselves under final judgment as we proclaim his death until he comes again. But our judge is also our advocate, present with us to prepare us for judgment. And so we are enabled to work for justice because we realize we, too, stand under judgment ourselves.

The Eucharist is also the first fruits of the kingdom as we see it breaking into visibility in the gathered assembly. The real tangibility

[4]*Eucharist and Eschatology* (New York: Oxford University Press, 1981).

of bread and wine, the actuality of present action, cause us to experience in our here and now the future reality we simultaneously proclaim. Thus we can work for justice in the world today because we can sample a bit of it in our weekly gatherings, with real and physical human beings. Susceptible as they are to human injustices, our assemblies manifest God's will to justice in our midst.

And so we conclude that the Eucharist, very human as it is, is the Church's chief contribution to the struggle for justice in our world today. Because it looks beyond to the ultimate as nothing else does, the Eucharist can change all things here and now.

15. Justice and the Work of Liturgical Renewal

Originally given as an address at the University of Notre Dame in early 1980, this appeared in Christianity and Crisis *40 (June 9, 1980) and shows the concerns for justice prominent among liturgists at that time.*

Recently when I was speaking to a group of United Methodist ministers in the Midwest I met one who, like myself, had been a candidate for the United States Congress. While swapping recollections of such an effort we came to a basic difference: He still feels his mission is to work for justice outside of Church structures. I, on the other hand, now realize that the struggle for justice has to go on inside the Church as well and have come to believe that my own work can be more productive there. Needless to say, neither of us changed the other's priorities.

But it did make me want to record some of my experiences during the last ten years in which the struggle for justice and the work of liturgical renewal have met in the process of revising the United Methodist liturgical books. "Justice" I shall define, in the words of Professor Joseph L. Allen, as "a recognition of the personhood of each, a refusal to consider any person as of less human worth than any other, and a refusal to reduce anyone to the status of mere means to the good of all the rest. . . . Justice is the expression of covenant love in situations in which rights are involved and a proper balance must be found between competing claims."[1] Liturgy, the Church's most important act, can and often has been a source of injustice when it renders "any person as of less human worth than any other," or when it refuses to recognize the full personhood of some within the body of Christ.

---

[1]Unpublished paper. Later revised in *Love and Conflict* (Nashville: Abingdon Press, 1984) ch. 6.

How have United Methodists reacted to the danger of injustice at the heart of the Church's life together? I shall deal here primarily with liturgical texts, though the struggle for justice in the reform of the liturgy is by no means confined to these. The roles people play in worship are far more subtle and elusive than printed texts, and such roles may often be more significant than the rites themselves. Nonetheless, here I shall list only such types of discrimination as discrepancies with regard to ordination, the institution of acolytes and readers, the right to preach, the selection of ushers, or the usual choice of paid musicians.

Specific actions also reveal biases: preaching robes designed to emphasize physical stature and strength through padded shoulders, the absence before the eighteenth century of church music with women's parts, domineering presidential styles, avoidance of the prenatal and postnatal mysteries of Luke 1 and 2, the giving away of the bride and the garb of the wedding rite, or the unthinking practice of some bishops at ordinations of subsuming the spouse under the personhood of the one being ordained. This list is far from exhaustive, but it does underscore the insidious power of customary roles and actions in undercutting the human worth of some.

My present concern here is with the reform of the liturgical texts themselves, concretely the seventeen-volume United Methodist *Supplemental Worship Resources*. Nine volumes plus the new ordinal are now in print. Throughout the series, ethical concerns about justice are raised on every page. We deal with words as the most obvious reflection of human inner attitudes and feelings. Those who scoff at "mere words" rarely have a response when asked why the term "nigger" has been dropped from "accepted" usage. Even the terms "negro" and "brotherhood" have almost disappeared from the English language. Words do shape and reveal our attitudes to others in according or denying them full human worth. We cannot recognize the full personhood of another and at the same time constantly deny it in the language we use in private or as a worshiping community. *Much of the quest for justice in liturgical reform is a search for the right words.*

Toward an Inclusive Language

Some of our most difficult decisions about words have been in the area of sexist language. How can we consistently employ language that affirms the human worth of both men and women? How can we find that balance "between competing claims" that Professor Allen calls vital in the "expression of covenant love"? Retrospect shows that we have erred in several cases. Indeed, many of the second-generation changes in the newest service book, *We Gather Together*[2] are corrections of previous errors or oversights. (Unfortunately when a committee is concentrating on a particular problem another type of error may enter the text through the solution proposed.)

The Section on Worship was aware when it began work in 1971 that the English language was in the process of change and that such words as "man" or "mankind" are no longer inclusive. The real problem, of course, is not that the term "man" fails to be inclusive but that the culture it reflects has for so long implied that maleness is normative humanity. Quite apart from the exclusiveness that the term "man" has come to signify in recent years is the injustice of its use at any time to represent normative humanity. Early in its work the section decided that all references to human beings must indicate equality for both sexes. This has been relatively easy to accomplish.

Much more difficult is God language. Our tradition, like most of the West except the Shakers, has preferred exclusively masculine names, images, and pronouns for the deity. Yet to imply that God is only masculine limits God arbitrarily and provokes an injustice to all of us, created in God's image. One-sided images of God immediately lead to a defective concept of humanity. Such problems have often been increased by biblical translations that make predominantly masculine language even more common than in the biblical texts themselves. These are not easy habits to outgrow.

Obviously the most difficult term to deal with is that of "Father." It is more difficult to dispute the image of "Son" since the biblical witness is clear as to Jesus' gender. More radical feminists would have had us eliminate the term "Father" altogether. But that position was resisted on several grounds. One could make a case that Jesus was crucified because of this very term: "This made the Jews still more determined to kill him, because he was not only breaking the Sabbath but, by calling God his own Father, he claimed equality with God" (John 5:18). The scandal was in using such an intimate term for God when Jews were not allowed even to breathe God's name. Jesus deliberately told his disciples to pray "Our Father." The term

[2](Nashville: United Methodist Publishing House, 1980).

"Father" suggests an intimacy with God that is a distinctive characteristic of Christianity.

The Section became convinced that there is no equivalent term available to us at present. "Parent" does not convey the personal relationship that "Father" or "Mother" does. Occasional use of "Mother" was considered, but we felt it would accomplish little and disturb people much. The term "Creator" was ruled out as a substitute since it implied that creation was exclusively the work of the first person of the Trinity. John 1:2 indicates otherwise: "The Word, then, was with God at the beginning, and through him all things came to be; no single thing was created without him," and the Nicene Creed affirms: "Through him all things were made." Thus one would have to change Christian doctrine itself were one to substitute the term "Creator" for "Father."

That being said, there are other ascriptions of the first member of the Trinity that are available. In various places we have used "Almighty God" or "Eternal God," for example. Though these terms certainly do not exclude the other two members of the Trinity, for most people they probably do suggest the Father. We decided that there were seven places where such ambiguity was not permissible: at the beginning of the preface of the eucharistic prayer, in the doxology at its conclusion, the parallel doxology at the end of the prayer over the water in the baptismal rite, in the baptismal formula itself, in the Lord's Prayer, in the Apostles' Creed, and in the Nicene Creed. In these instances there was need to be specific for both theological and ecumenical reasons. In a very few other instances the term "Father" appears in passages that may be omitted or used as options.

Despite such constraints we felt at liberty elsewhere to use other ascriptions. In the book on the Church year, *Seasons of the Gospel*,[3] the opening prayers are an attempt to explore some possibilities. We succeeded better in the negative stage, i.e., eliminating exclusively male images, than we did in the positive stage of adding new female images. Phrases such as "Loving God," "God of steadfast love," "God of all history" avoid exclusively masculine images but do little to add feminine. We used "God, our Father and Mother" twice. On the whole we succeeded better in balancing the images of human beings than we did those of God in these prayers.

[3](Nashville: Abingdon Press, 1979).

The other challenge has been pronouns. The Section on Worship long ago decided to avoid masculine pronouns for reference to the first and third members of the Trinity. Of course, frequently "you" is the desirable pronoun in prayer even though we might have a tendency to use "he." The only serious problem in this area is the reflexive pronoun. In my own writing, I have come regularly to use "Godself," which after one year of use becomes perfectly normal. But in liturgical texts we simply avoid the reflexive. There is some loss since pronouns can make a text more personal. Any attempt to balance "he" with "she" makes the reference highly confusing to the worshiper. So we have decided to avoid third-person pronouns except for Jesus Christ.

Other forms of exclusive language pose different orders of problems, especially those with regard to minorities. In these cases the "recognition of the personhood" of these people in order to render them full "human worth" involves cultivating sensitivity to the use and avoidance of key words. It is widely recognized that the term "black" is used in English largely in pejorative ways while the word "white" is used most often with favorable meanings. Obviously it is easy to eliminate those particular words, but what about related terms such as "dark" and "darkness"? For a small number of blacks those terms are taboo, yet to remove them entirely is to discard much of the imagery of the Fourth Gospel. Fortunately, for most blacks darkness-light imagery poses no problems. Our decision was to avoid it when possible but not to dismiss it altogether. Thus in the baptismal prayer over the water the phrase "you swept across the dark waters and brought forth light" (1976) became in 1980 "you swept across the waters of creation and brought forth life." Though images of darkness have largely disappeared, images of light abound, especially in the funeral service.

We slowly developed sensitivity to other terms. For instance, black congregations tend to refer to hymns as "songs." So our 1980 eucharistic rite now refers to a "hymn or song" in several places. This may say nothing to whites but, we hope, it will say to blacks "you count, too."

A deeper problem, for liturgical commissions, is that middle-class whites tend to think of worship in terms of printed texts while blacks (until a certain upward social mobility occurs) do not. One exception is in the form of songbooks. The black Church is, above all, a singing Church. Our recourse has been to give high priority to a black songbook, *Songs of Zion*,[4] to be published in 1981. It will contain three hundred songs most widely used in black churches. We were able to secure highly competent editors who carefully researched black church music in America. We feel they are making a major contribution to music history as well as to actual use.

Here we encountered another ethical problem, that of "competing claims." Many of the texts contain language we now regard as sexist. But some blacks, even women on the task force, were adamant about retaining what was, to them, familiar language such as "Sons of Africa." What right do whites have to force blacks to change their own songs? On the other hand, what right does a national Church have to publish a book that perpetuates injustices against half its members? It puzzles us that some of the victims of so much injustice did not flinch when another sort of injustice was proposed for others. In the end compromises were made, though we retained some lyrics that we would not permit in another volume, *Supplement to the Book of Hymns*.[5] In that book all sexist language has been removed except when copyright owners would not allow it (as in "Lord of the Dance"). In those instances we have provided alternative language in parentheses. The *Supplement* also incorporates representative hymns and songs from Asian Americans, Native Americans, African Americans, and Hispanics as a way of affirming the worth of all peoples. Song books for each of these groups are planned.

We have learned the need to avoid physical allusions. Diminutives are usually derogatory in English. Yet many people are short or small. Nor can we use terms such as "blind," "unseeing," "deaf," "mute," "old" or "aged."

Rites of passage are crucial in affirming minorities. Our attempt has been to encourage as many indigenous practices as are consistent with Christian faith, a procedure the *Constitution on the Sacred Liturgy* encourages in paragraphs 37–40. In the 1980 *An Ordinal*[6] we suggest applause as the people affirm the candidates, as apparently was the custom in our formerly all-black conferences. For the wed-

[4](Nashville: Abingdon Press, 1981).
[5](Nashville: United Methodist Publishing House, 1982).
[6](Nashville: United Methodist Publishing House, 1980).

ding services we mention the giving of "symbols" instead of rings in some cultures (i.e., the necklace in India). Hispanics are encouraged to have the groom give the *arras* (coins) to the bride and for the witnesses (*padrinos*) to place the *lazo* (cord) over the bride and groom.

Different cultures live by different calendars. The Hispanic fondness for the Feast of the Three Kings is an example. For United Methodists there are problems here since many Hispanics are trying at the same time to repudiate their Catholicism and yet affirm their Spanish inheritance. Since Hispanics will soon be the largest minority in this country if not within Protestantism, it is essential to help these people discover what they need to retain and repudiate in order to be themselves. These are not easy decisions, and we need research and more publications similar to *This Far by Faith*[7] and Clarence Rivers' works on black worship.

Language itself is a crucial dimension of any culture. We have made the decision to publish *We Gather Together* in English, Spanish, Korean, and Japanese. This is the only way to say we truly are a multi-lingual Church. It is unfortunate that the non-English versions have to be translations from English, although some deviations are possible. For example in the Spanish version, *Congregados en Su Nombre*,[8] we decided to use CELAM (the Roman Catholic Bishops' Conference of Latin America) texts for the creeds, *Sursum corda*, *Sanctus*, and Our Father instead of those of the Mexican Catholics or our own translations. Not only does this open the possibilities of many more musical settings, but it also avoids saying that Mexican texts are normative when we have Cuban, Puerto Rican, Filipino, and other Hispanic peoples. We have also published two volumes of Hispanic *coritos* (songs), *Celebremos*,[9] most of which are not translations of English texts. It is a joy to discover some things can be said and sung better in Spanish than in English.

Much of what is needed in working with other cultures and language groups is to listen. We have held consultations with African Americans, Hispanics, Asian Americans, and Native Americans. The most visible fruits of these consultations are some articles on

[7](Washington: National Office for Black Catholics, 1977).
[8](Nashville: United Methodist Publishing House, 1980).
[9](Nashville: Discipleship Resources, 1979 and 1983).

Hispanic worship and a collection of Pacific and Asian worship resources, *Pascasiana*.

Anti-Semitism is an especially sensitive area. There can be little question that portions of traditional Holy Week rites verged on anti-Semitism. In our desire to recover these rites for United Methodists we encountered major problems of eliminating anti-semitic references while retaining items of high value for Christian worship. Our solutions occur in the Lent/Easter book, *From Ashes to Fire*.[10] In the readings from the passion narratives, selective use of Scripture made possible elimination of phrases that could be misinterpreted as blanket condemnations of all Jews. No changes were necessary in the essential narration of the passages.

Even more ticklish were the Good Friday Reproaches, a sublime bit of liturgical poetry. Here it was possible to make it clear that it is the Church itself, as the new Israel, that condemns itself rather than the Jews. And it was possible to turn the whole literary form around and to reproach ourselves for inflicting on the Jews "persecution and mass murder." Far from offending Jews, we were able both to retain the Reproaches and to make positive use of them in lamenting past injustices.

My final point deals with the question of the extent to which the liturgy should take an advocacy position on issues of justice. Some of the more impatient would push us in this direction. However, we have some major reservations at this point. Not only does such action force the rest of the liturgy to usurp some of the possibilities of the liturgical act of preaching, but it usually means bad liturgy itself. When liturgy becomes manipulative, homiletic, or didactic, it is usually bad liturgy. For decades many of us have reacted against the psychological approach to worship typical of educators at the University of Chicago early in this century. Their theological stance and social views all too easily turned worship into a manipulative tool.

This is doubly dangerous. Many questions of justice are highly controversial. Christians can with integrity affirm contradictory positions. Refusal to respect these differences within the body is, in itself,

[10](Nashville: Abingdon Press, 1979).

a denial of worth to many. There is a variety of permissible views, and no person should be subjected to being a "mere means to the good of all the rest." *Crusades for justice may affront justice itself by being forced upon people in their liturgy.*

Well, what can be done legitimately without being manipulative, homiletic, or didactic? We have tried to deal primarily in what John Bennett called "middle axioms." There are certain affirmations of broad and general character to which no Christian is likely to take exception. These come between the broad command to love one another and specific directives. Statements can be derived from Scripture that do speak of justice and social action in general terms without getting into controversial specifics. Our general practice has been to incorporate these in liturgical texts.

Thus the conclusion to the epiclesis in *We Gather Together* now reads: "and may the Spirit make us one with Christ, one with each other, and one in service to all the world." The post-communion prayer reads: "You have given yourself to us, Lord. Now we give ourselves for others," and the dismissal reads: "Go in peace to serve God and your neighbor in all that you do." The renunciation in the new baptismal rite begins: "Do you renounce the bondage of sin and the injustices of this world and do you accept the liberty which God gives you?" And new members of a congregation are asked "to strengthen this community of faith and to serve the world as Christ's representatives."

One may find these far too subtle. Maybe they are. But the liturgy itself in its inclusive language and actions is an even more subtle teacher. Still, I note that these scattered references to action for justice and service are more explicit than those in the service books of many denominations. United Methodists would like to think that we have a stronger tradition of fighting for social justice than most other American churches, and there is some historical verification for this. So I would hope that these phrases reflect both a part of our Methodist tradition and the commitment to justice of the universal Church.

We realize that tomorrow will bring new sensitivities to injustices that we do not even recognize today. I have tried to give a survey of where we have arrived today in the hope that we can better understand how the struggle for justice and the reform of worship intersect.

16. Words That Hurt: Language and Justice

Part of the Language and Liturgy Convocation held by the Consultation on Church Union in Nashville in November 1981, this paper eventually appeared in COCU's 1983 book, The Word and words: Beyond Gender in Theological and Liturgical Language. Used by permission.

As Christians we are unable to be indifferent to issues of justice. The worship of the Church and all its other activities are deeply involved in concerns about justice. Without proper care these activities can promote justice or thwart it. For our purposes here we shall define justice as rendering to each person his or her due by attributing to each person full human worth. Language is a most basic element in forming people to express justice. For example, it is impossible to use such terms as "nigger," "wop," "fairy," etc. without implying that a person is due less than full human worth. Not only does the use of such terms reveal unjust attitudes but it also creates and reinforces attitudes and behavior inimical to justice. On this basis, one cannot say "it is only words" but rather must say "it is nothing less than words."

Words can hurt very deeply, especially when they imply that another being or group of beings is due less human worth than others. Words can demean and oppress others in ways that can be very painful to those victimized by them. But those using such language are themselves deprived in that consciously or unconsciously they are denying the Christian imperatives to deal justly with others. Thus a continuing process of education is necessary to make us all aware of what language does to us as well as for us. Only by becoming sensitive can we avoid the use of words that hurt.

There are many other ways in which worship expresses injustices beyond the use of words. Roles people play such as ushers, garb worn such as preaching robes with padded shoulders, the Christian calendar itself, all are examples of actions that reveal discriminatory attitudes. The reluctance of many churches to have a prominent baptismal font (perhaps the most female symbol the Church has) is simply a symptom of a prejudice we may not recognize until confronted by it. The wedding service has traditionally implied subservience on the part of the woman. Our actions and our words are inextricably mixed but they reveal similar attitudes. Fortunately we can analyze words with more ease since they can all be written down on paper and examined. But ultimately our words and actions are one. We shall limit ourselves here to words since they are easier to analyze although we must always remember their linkage to action. We shall look first at language about humans and then see how such language shapes our language about God.

Change in Language

Much of our society has acknowledged rapid change in language about humans. Of course change in language is nothing new. In the fourteenth century Chaucer remarked on how "in forme of speche is chaunge" and words that once had meaning, but now seem strange to us, people once used "and spedde as wel in love as men now do." Words such as "men, mankind, man" no longer mean in American English what they did ten years ago. A decade ago they referred to all humans, today they mean half the human race. The scandal, of course, is that we were not aware of how unjust it was to equate maleness with normative humanity. Our language implied that femaleness was derivative and less than fully human. It is now widely realized that such language is morally wrong and must be rejected. Much of this recognition has come outside the Church, yet the Church dare not lag behind movements for justice in society. Hence school children are no longer taught the generic use of terms such as "man" and many editors now reject such usage in publications.

It is important to recognize that these changes in human language have preceded those in God language. But they have also made changes in God language inevitable.

Many problems occur in biblical translation. In many cases terms such as "if any man" have been used when the meaning is clearly "if anyone." Thus much gratuitous male language has been supplied by translators when it is not found in the biblical languages themselves. Furthermore, in Greek the pronoun is often a part of the verb. Many pronouns, usually of a male gender, have been introduced by the translators. Thus much gender-exclusive language for both humans and God is not in the texts.

Our position is the need to be faithful to the original biblical texts. One does not have the right to rewrite Scripture; one often has the responsibility to retranslate it. Certainly the biblical world was male dominated and this is reflected on every page of Scripture. But that does not indicate that additional male language should be dubbed in by translators when it is not in the original. To a generation conscious of the power of sexual bias in religious language, more accurate translation is a necessity.

This by no means implies eliminating gender from biblical texts when it is present in the original languages. There is nothing gained by a gray neutrality. When sex-specific passages are present they should be rendered accurately. Real life, after all, has varieties of age, sex, and other distinctions. Frequently the Church has tended to submerge these distinctions as in treating children in worship as if they did not exist until they can think as adults. Yet the fact that children think in less analytical fashion does not mean that they are any less parts of the body of Christ. Indeed, they might be a witness to all to the nature of the reign of God!

God Language

Language about God simply reflects the concerns that have arisen about language concerning humans. But there is an important difference: humans are finite; God is not. Thus we need to beware of any language that limits God. God is male and female, old and young, helpless as a baby and infinitely powerful. Exclusive use of one kind of terminology for God distorts our image of the Infinite. Yet personal language is necessary to indicate that God is knowable in whatever form God chooses to reveal Godself. We shall deal with the practical possibilities in language about God in pronouns and nouns.

In the English language, unlike some, most pronouns have gender. Thus when one says "he" the image given is male. When a pronoun is used, the reference to the name or noun it replaces must be clear. Hence "he" refers to a male being. This is not easily avoided. Yet if we wish to use a pronoun for God we have in the past invariably used "he," "him," or "his," subtly suggesting that God is male.

There seem to be two alternatives to limiting God in this way to maleness. The first is to alternate male or female pronouns. The second is to avoid pronouns altogether.

Certain problems arise when one adopts the first option. Good English prose demands clarity of reference whenever pronouns are used. When pronouns alternate in gender clarity rapidly disappears and confusion ensues. Although a commendable balance can be achieved such usage seems impractical, especially in liturgical texts.

The other option is to avoid using pronouns for God. This can be done much more easily than one might suspect. Indeed, there is a benefit in forcing one to reach for ascriptions of God, the Eternal, the Divine Giver, etcetera, that pronouns always eliminate. Some would argue that using the name God over and over gets repetitious although we have long done just that with "he." There may be one exception to the elimination of pronouns. A reflexive pronoun is often desirable when one speaks of God's self giving. It is quite possible to use a new term, "Godself," in such instances. Indeed, it has a certain value in expressing the uniqueness of God's own being. Like most neologisms, after a year's use it becomes perfectly natural just as when we turned from "thou" to "you." Other than Godself, pronouns for God can be eliminated entirely. The same would apply to the use of "she," "her," "hers" for the Church. The Church is just as male as female and the reference to the "bride of Christ" is simply a metaphor.

The names or nouns for God are much more complex. A vast variety of ascriptions for God is available. One list, published by the Section on Worship of the United Methodist Church, lists over two hundred names for God, many of them biblical. Terms such as "Source of All Life," "Israel's Shield," the "Compassionate One" are but a few. Some terms may be offensive, especially militaristic ones or those specifically male. The possibilities are so great that exploration of them is a valuable theological exercise.

The Bible itself provides far more images for God than those we commonly use. Images of God as the one who gives birth, who nurses, who feeds us are present although overlooked. One has to have experienced a brooding hen to know how apt an image for God such a term is in the synoptics. Recognition of these female designations for God becomes a new hermeneutical tool in communicating the biblical message.

Likewise, much of the historical tradition contains references to God in female terms. Theologians as disparate as Chrysostom or Anselm can refer to Jesus as "Mother" or "Sister." Such language comes naturally to some mystics. It is always easier to recognize an existing tradition than to have to create a new one. Sources in Bible and history are there although underutilized.

The most difficult problems occur in Trinitarian language. At times it is necessary, especially in worship and theology, to make explicit references to the individual members of the Trinity. There also are other terms such as "lord" or "king" that are problematic.

The word "lord" is unique to the English language, not being paralleled in other teutonic languages. Often "lord" is used as the English equivalent of *kyrios* or *dominus*. It comes from an Old English source, *hlafweard*, which became *hlaford*, then "lord." The meaning seems to have been "loafward," i.e., "keeper of the bread," a concept found in some modern Scandinavian terms as "meat mother," i.e., "keeper of the food." The word "lady" derives from the Old English *hlaefdige*, kneader of the bread or mistress of the household.

However, the present meaning of words is not necessarily determined by etymology. In feudal usage "lord" meant a noble person with vassals. The female equivalent was "lady." In the case of the sovereign the term "lord" could be applied to a monarch of either gender. Thus one of Queen Elizabeth's titles is "Lord of Man," i.e., sovereign of the Isle of Man.

One can also argue that "lord" is a substitute for the Hebrew *Adonai* or the Greek *kyrios*, neither of which specify gender. On these bases a case can be made for using the term "lord" with a reasonable argument that it is not necessarily a male term except in feudal use. Thus the term can be applied both to the first member of the Trinity in prayer ("Lord have mercy") or to Jesus Christ in confessing faith ("Jesus is Lord"). But one must also be prepared to recognize that many people will understand the term "lord" in a male sense only and that for them it may limit the concept of God by imputing to God only male characteristics. Sometimes one might wish to keep it in Greek as is frequently done in sung liturgy: "*Kyrie eleison.*" But we must live with English and teaching must be done or the term avoided when possible.

The use of the term "king," while equally biblical, is less ambiguous. Again our principle of not rewriting scripture seems best. But when one is writing new materials there are alternatives. In the preface of the United Methodist eucharistic prayer, "king" was changed to "sovereign." Various other substitutes are possible: "reign" for "kingdom," "ruler" for "king." It does not seem feasible to alternate king and queen. There seem to be sufficient words that cover the concept of kingship without indicating a specific gender.

Naming the Trinity

The greatest difficulty occurs when one has to designate a member of the Trinity. The practice defended here is that in certain instances the use of the terms "Father, Son, and Holy Spirit" is necessary for two reasons: the absence of any acceptable alternatives and the positive desirability of such terms in some cases. But of equal importance is the belief that the number of instances when such use is necessary is quite small. Clarity about the restricted number of these necessary instances can and ought to give incentive for the use of other nomenclature. Only when one is clear about necessary usages does one have security in reaching out for other appellations and freedom to use them. Such knowledge is indeed liberating; the uninformed have no choice but to cling to invariable use of traditional terms.

The term "Son" is less controversial. Undoubtedly Jesus was male since there are only two physical ways to be human. This much remains historical fact. Only a docetic Christology would deprive him of sexual identity. The real point, of course, is that he became human. Thus the term "Son" is of more importance in indicating his humanity than his gender. Some terms that are sometimes substituted, such as "Redeemer," point to a role in Hebrew life specifically male, i.e., that of defending the females of one's family. While the term "Son" may be of offense to some, it need only be used in connection with the other members of the Trinity. "Jesus," "Christ," "Messiah," and a host of alternative terms are readily available.

The Holy Spirit seems less problematic as a name. Some would prefer to refer to the Spirit with female pronouns although this violates the principle of avoiding such use.

The deepest problem of all revolves around use of the term "Father." Some find it impossible to use such a male term; others find it impossible to surrender it. We take the position that in certain cases its use is necessary and desirable but that the number of such instances is restricted.

There can be no doubt as to the centrality of the term "Father" in the New Testament witness. Robert Hamerton-Kelly cities Joachim Jeremias: "God is designated `father' 170 times by Jesus, and never invoked by another name in Jesus' prayers" (*God as Father, Concilium* 143, 98). "Father" is, perhaps, the most revolutionary term in the New Testament. At a time when devout Jews would not even breathe the name of God lest they profane it, Jesus chose the most intimate and familiar of all human terms available. Such presumptuous intimacy brought on his death: "This made the Jews still more determined to kill him, because he was not only breaking the Sabbath, but, by calling God his own Father, he claimed equality with God." (John 5:18). To give up the term "Father" altogether would be to give up an essential insight of Christianity, the accessibility of God to all. "Father" then is more than just a name; it conveys meaning. Paul suggests that the Spirit works, "enabling us to cry `Abba! Father!'" (Rom 8:15). The ability to approach God on such an intimate level is part of the essential nature of Christianity.

No other term functions in such a way. The only equivalent is "Mother," which can occasionally be used instead or can be joined: "Our Father and Mother." The term "parent" does not function in this way. No one ever addresses a human person by such a function rather than by name. For many people the term "Mother" will create suspicion or hostility and is open to the same objection as "Father" in restricting the attributes of God to those associated with one gender. Hence "Mother and Father" is probably the most desirable alternative when feasible.

There are, however, seven instances in liturgical texts where the use of the term "Father" seems necessary. That there is only such a small number indicates that we need a major effort to seek other ascriptions in prayer and theological discourse. Such a short list includes passages in which, for theological and ecumenical reasons, unilateral changes are not possible. For example, one cannot alter unilaterally the ecumenical creeds without destroying their special function as testimony to the universal faith of the Church. Other instances derive some of their function from dominical authority and historic usage.

The seven necessary liturgical usages of "Father" are: the address of the eucharistic prayer to the Father in reciting past work of the

Father and in invoking others present and future, the doxology at the end of such prayer that summarizes its trinitarian pattern, the similar baptismal prayer over the font in its doxological conclusion, the baptismal formula itself, the Lord's Prayer, and the two ecumenical creeds (Apostles' and Nicene). Since the eucharistic prayer is the Church's most important theological statement, its trinitarian operation is essential and is echoed in the creeds. (A good reason to avoid many so-called "modern" creeds is that they are usually very sexist with regard to human language.) Although the New Testament Church baptized in other terms, as in the name of Jesus (Acts 2:38), to alter the baptismal formula unilaterally today would be a severe ecumenical blunder. The most powerful expression of prayer known is the first two words of the Lord's Prayer.

Beyond this short list one has the responsibility of creating and seeking out other ascriptions of God. Such efforts expand our knowledge of and relationship to God.

Occasionally, attempts have been made to substitute other appellations for Father, Son, and Holy Spirit even in the seven instances we have mentioned. Yet these efforts cause even more problems. It should be pointed out that the traditional terms are personal names rather than functional distinctions. The Church, as it hammered out its trinitarian theology over the course of centuries, concluded that the Trinity could not be adequately expressed in terms of mutually-exclusive functions. The doctrine of coinherence states the Trinity's joint involvement in their work. Thus creation is not limited to the First Member of the Trinity as John 1:2-4 makes clear. "Creator" is not a substitute for Father. We have already noted that terms such as "Redeemer" or "Maker" have male connotations that make them inadequate substitutes.

The danger of using only such language as "Creator, Redeemer, and Sustainer" is that ultimately it suggests tritheism rather than trinitarianism. That might be an interesting religion but it is not Christianity. The Christian Trinity is differentiated in person but not in substance or ultimately in function. One might speak of "First, Second, and Third Members of the Trinity" in theological discourse but that hardly makes good liturgical language.

It may be that at a subsequent time adequate alternatives to "Father, Son, and Holy Spirit" may be found but such terms have not yet been achieved. It took the Church four and a half centuries to define what it meant by "Father, Son, and Holy Spirit." Unless we appreciate the long agony of that effort we are not likely to do better.

Above all we must learn to be sensitive to the power of words to hurt. Only then will we be concerned to speak justly. But one can change one's patterns of speaking and writing, especially if one has a supportive community to catch one's slips and to encourage one's efforts. Nowhere else is language more intensely communal than in the worshiping Church. Nowhere else can the demand for justice exceed that within the body of Christ.

III. Liturgical Architecture

17. Liturgical Space Forms Faith

This short piece appeared in *Reformed Liturgy and Music* 22 (Spring 1988) and is used by permission.

In the valley of the Mohawk River in upstate New York stand two churches built just before the Revolutionary War. Both were built by recently-landed German immigrants; both were built of the same local stone. But there the similarities end because it was Reformed Christians who built the Fort Herkimer Church and it was Lutherans who erected the Palatine Bridge Church. Both buildings show how far apart in faith their builders had grown in the two hundred years since the Reformation. The Fort Herkimer Church is a preaching church par excellence. Every element in the building focuses on the pulpit, standing about twelve feet high with an elegant sounding board over it. No building is a better witness to the sovereign word of God that shapes both life and worship. The Lutheran Church, by contrast, is a sacrament church, gathered around the communion rail that encircles both altar-table and pulpit. God's presence in, with, and under physical objects is proclaimed by this building.

One comes away from each building with no doubt about the faith of its builders. The buildings are good examples of the ways in which faith can be expressed in stone and wood, plaster and glass. And each has been making its respective witness for well over two hundred years now. We think of Churchill's famous phrase when the rebuilding of the Houses of Parliament was undertaken: we shape our buildings and ever after they shape us.

Certainly these two churches were successful spatial efforts in expressing the faith of the pioneers. In their time these buildings were not only adequate but were probably more satisfactory than the remodeled medieval buildings their builders had forsaken back home in the Rhine Valley. The new buildings were built with an intentionality to express a contemporary faith, not that of a previous age.

The problem for us is whether either of these buildings would be an adequate expression of our faith today. Of course a building need not be old to be out of touch with our faith. In Burlington, Vermont, two cathedrals stand scarcely a block apart. Both were built after earlier gothic-revival cathedrals had burned in the 1970s. In architectural style both are contemporary but the Episcopal cathedral is strangely conservative in that the altar-table and clergy seats are located in a distinct space, removed as a separate volume from the nave where the people and choir sit. The Roman Catholic cathedral thrusts the altar-table into the midst of the congregation and no one sits more than eight seats from it. One cathedral suggests that God is remote and transcendent, the other that God is near and immanent.

What if the building does not reflect our faith today? If not it will fight us, and the chances are that the building will win. I would be reluctant to preach on the priesthood of all Christians at the Episcopal cathedral because the building would shout me down; in the Roman Catholic cathedral I would get a better hearing. Not only does space form faith but it can, and frequently does, deform and distort faith. Thus we are frequently caught in a conflict between the faith we profess and the faith the building proclaims. The most ironic sermon I ever heard was Pope Paul VI preaching against triumphalism in the Church. He preached in St. Peter's Basilica and Michelangelo clearly had the last word. The conflict is not usually that obvious but it happens in many of our churches every Sunday and the more subtle and undramatic it is, the more insidious and dangerous.

The conflict between space and faith is not to be taken lightly. Pastors have to develop a new sensitivity in learning to "read" space. We must learn to ask of any church space the same question we ask when making ethical decisions: "What is going on here?" Church architecture is not some innocuous "muzak" we can afford to neglect. Rather it is an important constituent in forming the faith of the people who gather within it, perhaps the most important single factor in their formation.

Frequently, remodeling or renovating a church is one of the most significant occasions for reshaping the life of a community of faith. Too often such opportunities become mere occasions for redecorating or accommodating a new organ. Renovations ought to be regarded as a vital chance to rethink the mission of the Church and to reinforce that mission by giving it physical form. Careful church renovation is not a luxury; it often is a necessity unless we are to continue in self-contradiction. Unless we are indifferent about the contents of the faith we teach, we have to take seriously the architectural setting of our worship.

At stake here is the sacramental principle that the outward and visible cannot be dissociated from what is inward and spiritual. Somehow Protestants still have trouble with this; the people who sell automobiles take it for granted. They give us power, glamour, affluence, all made of steel and glass. We are not called to be more spiritual than God. Buildings are faith in just the same sense that a kiss is love. Judas could dissemble; actors can pretend; but buildings are very honest statements of faith. In a very real way, space is faith. We have trouble with copulative verbs ("this is") but finally they are the only way to state some truths.

As we become more sensitive to the relationship of space and faith there is a certain grammar we learn as we discover what space is saying. We may note here two forms of speech. One, we recognize that every space in churches exists in relationship to other spaces. This forces us to raise questions about people and how they relate to each other, how they relate to the clergy, and how they relate to God. The arrangement of different spaces is a primary concern. What kind of space is provided for people to come together to discern the body of Christ? Are the clergy alone with God in the remote holy space of a chancel? Does the building suggest that God is somewhere out beyond the east window? The arrangement of spaces makes definite statements about such matters.

The second thing we have to think through is what it is that people do when they come together. Such activities usually focus on a particular liturgical center, a baptismal font or pool, a pulpit, an altar-table. Here it is important to be clear about functions. What happens in baptism? Is it simply a sentimental occasion of Christian cuteness? Or is it grafting a new branch onto the trunk so that the same energy that vivifies every part of the tree gives life to it, too? Does the whole community participate or is it a private ceremony? And is it a genuine proclamation of God's will to forgive and cleanse, or just a dry cleaning? All these questions and more must be asked about the design of the font and its location. One has to make up one's mind about some important theological issues first.

This is why worship reform and architectural renovation have to go hand in hand. You cannot reform the Lord's Supper with the altar-table nailed to the wall. But a freestanding altar-table will not be much of an improvement either unless one is deeply aware of what it means to gather a community about the Lord's table to give thanks.

The baptismal fonts we have in many Protestant churches reveal just what baptism has meant to us. They are an outward and visible witness that baptism has been a short and insignificant ceremony performed from a bowl tucked out of sight most of the time. In a perverse way, those bowls told just how unimportant baptism was in many of our churches. If we had really believed that baptism is union to Christ and incorporation into the Church we would not have been content with such diminutive fonts to proclaim so great a truth. In the South, Baptists tend to speak of being baptized and being saved as synonymous terms. Their baptismal pools are highly visible and important parts of the building, at least when being used.

We do better with pulpits but there are questions to ask here, too. Do we preach "six feet above contradiction" (J.A.T. Robinson) or do we speak on our people's level? Is our preaching biblical or is the Bible visually (and really) relegated to a separate lectern? How do we bring preacher, Bible, and people together in the most meaningful relationship? Our visible signs tell far more than we want to reveal. Liturgical reform must accompany any meaningful reform of space.

One word of caution is necessary. We do not want to tie knots in the future the way many congregations did in the 1950s when they built churches as if nothing in worship would ever change. Now we are more humble; we know that worship does change and so must our space. We shall not always express our faith in the same ways and so the spaces of those who come after us will be different, just as our faith must be expressed in ways different from those who came before us. We can learn from the past but we do not wish to impose it on our present nor on the future.

18. Liturgy and the Language of Space

Originally given as an address to the Federation of Diocesan Liturgical Commissions in 1977, this appeared in *Worship* 52 (January 1978) and was reprinted in several other publications. Used by permission.

Last summer I had an experience familiar to all of us. I was driving along a country highway in southern Illinois on my way to Saint Meinrad Archabbey. As I drove I passed a white wooden country church at a remote crossroads, as all of us have done so many times. Only this time as I whizzed past, barely slowly enough to read the sign, "Mt. Olivet Baptist Church," and to notice the graves clustered about this hilltop church, it somehow struck me that I had just passed a holy spot. Ever since I have been wondering why that one country church spoke to me so clearly despite my hurrying past.

Let me share with you two other places that have said the same thing to me when less hurried. The first is the Santuario de Chimayo, not far from Santa Fe, New Mexico. This primitive adobe building was built in 1816 as an act of thanks. As soon as I first entered this humble building I had a feeling I have never experienced in the most ornate shrines of Montreal and Quebec. And every time I return it has said the same thing to me: "This is an authentic holy spot."

About as different from that place as one can imagine is the Mormon Sacred Grove near Palmyra, New York, where Joseph Smith had his visions just a few years after Chimayo was built. All there is to see is a path wandering through a grove of beech, birch, and maple trees. Fortunately the Mormons have not tried to improve or embellish this spot in any way, though they lacked such restraint at nearby shrines. The Sacred Grove, though, speaks of Joseph Smith's supernatural encounters so powerfully that even my strong doubts about Mormonism cannot shout down the impression that this is a holy place of some sort.

Forgive me for being personal in my recollections, but I suspect each of us treasures such memories. And tonight I ask you to reflect with me on what these drastically different spots have in common so that they can speak to us those words: "this is a holy place." T. S. Eliot said it, years ago, when he called Little Gidding, the site of a seventeenth-century religious community in England, a place "where prayer has been valid." All three locations I have described proclaimed that they, too, were places "where prayer has been valid." But why did they say it so eloquently when many other churches fail to say the same thing? What factors were common to all three: the Baptist church, the Catholic shrine, the Mormon grove?

I am tempted to call it "poverty," not the poverty of destitution but the poverty that enriches so many members of religious communities by freedom from nonessentials. As a Yankee I am also tempted to label it "restraint." It frustrates me that my students in Texas never quite seem to sense what a powerful form of statement understatement can be. Restraint and understatement were there surely. In all three cases the builders or conservers knew when to stop. Less was more in each instance. All three reflected an economy of means. Another way to put it is that "transparency of purpose" made each spot so eloquent. Each place was a window through which to see what Christians do when they gather to meet their God. The clarity of that view was not interrupted by the place itself; it never got in the way; it simply provided a location from which to see. And so "transparency of purpose" may be the least inadequate way I know of explaining the power of these three places to speak so eloquently of holiness. They gave me a glimpse of what we do and experience when we worship God.

What Do We Do in Worship?

We are forced, then, to ask ourselves: "Just what do we *do* in worship?" Good liturgical architecture forces us to look at liturgical action. Just what does happen in Christian worship? In briefest possible terms I shall answer our question: "In worship, God gives Godself to us through words and by human hands." Let's take those in that order.

God speaks God's word to us through the mouths of other humans. That seems a strange way to reach people; it displays a far greater trust in humans than most of us would ever have, but it is God's way. God speaks: "I put my words into your mouth" (Jer 1:9) or "I will help both of you to speak" (Exod 4:15). There can be no doubt that God uses women and men to speak God's word to other humans. God gives Godself to us through those whom God has called to speak God's word. If it was "odd of God to choose the Jews," it was even odder to choose some of us.

There are a few, very few, necessities required for one human being to speak to others. One is that in order to communicate best you ought to be able to see those to whom you talk. When I taught homiletics I used to say: "Don't speak until you see the whites of their eyes," hoping that that was corny enough to be remembered. The point is that you can speak best to those you can see, not to those off to your side, behind you, or listening to a tape. Eye contact is part of reaching out in love to others and is an important part of speech. Mark tells us "Jesus looked steadily at [the rich young man] and loved him." Looking is part of loving.

Spatially this implies a straight line between you as speaker and each of your hearers. The speaker may need to be elevated a few inches so the heads of others do not interfere with sight lines but too great an elevation becomes a visual barrier, a moat of height. Pillars, partitions, and other barriers must not intervene. And the audience and speaker must meet face to face, not in a circle. The best space for face-to-face encounter is organized around a horizontal axis, as if there were a straight line from the speaker to the person in the middle of the audience. What this creates, of course, is a synagogue where people come together to hear God's word or a meetinghouse where Christians assemble to hear the gospel.

God gives Godself, then, to people gathered about a horizontal axis from human speaker to human hearer. If that were all, our job in planning worship space would indeed be simple. But God not only places God's word in our mouths but puts Godself into our hands. I teach my students that there must be a touch of hands when a gift is given. Gifts are not dropped; we touch each other when we give. And this is where organizing space for Christian worship gets complicated. For we must not only provide for receiving the word but also for receiving the sacraments. God gives Godself to us in *both* ways. All good church architecture is a compromise in providing for both types of divine activity. God help us if we think we have to choose between speaking or touching instead of having both. If I can paraphrase from *Music in Catholic Worship*, "Good arrangements of space increase and renew faith. Bad arrangements weaken and destroy faith." The crux of good and bad arrangements comes in how we compromise between space ideal for God's self-giving through *human* words and space ideal for God's self-communication to us through *human* hands.

If the path of the speaking voice is a horizontal axis, the locus of the outstretched hand is on a vertical axis. God has created each of God's ministers small enough so that we can reach out only about a yard. Others have to come to us and they best come in a circle gathered about us. The image is of people gathered in concentric circles about a vertical axis. At the center of the circle may be an altar-table, a font, or simply a person. From there we can reach out, God can reach out through our hands to the standing-around community.

We need, then, an upper room as well as a synagogue. And the upper room is a radically different building type, a cozy, intimate, domestic space different from the lecture hall, the *scholē* that Paul leased in Ephesus (Acts 19:9) or the synagogue in which he spoke in Pisidian Antioch (Acts 13:14). We need space in which we can both project our voice and reach out our hands, whether it be hands washing, hands giving the Lord's body, hands laid on heads, hands uniting the hands of a couple, hands blessing and reconciling, or hands sprinkling a coffin. In each instance God places Godself in our hands so that God can give Godself to others. And we have to be close enough really to touch them. A woman touched the hem of Jesus' garment and power passed to her. We touch others' heads, lips, or hands and power passes to them. But our reach is limited by arms that, unlike our voice, no microphone can stretch. We need intimate concentric space when God places Godself in our hands.

Well, you can see we have problems. How do we reconcile space organized along the horizontal axis with that around a vertical axis? There is something of a paradigm of worship itself in that problem, the God to human represented by the vertical, the human to human suggested by the horizontal. The whole history of church architecture has been that of experiments revolving around the two: the fourteenth-century preaching churches of the Franciscans, the choirless churches of the Jesuits in the sixteenth century, and early Lutheran churches, some built as preaching churches and others as sacrament churches. I understand one Catholic parish in St. Paul finally realized they needed two buildings, one for the service of the word and the other for the service of the table. They were right liturgically if not finan-cially. Eighteenth-century Anglicans experimented with churches with the altar table at one end, the pulpit at the other, and U-shaped box pews between in which one could move about. History can tell us a lot here, both what was valid and what was not. History can lib-erate us by showing us we need not be limited to the captivity of fa-miliar arrangements.

If anything we need to learn that space speaks most eloquently about our worship when we talk worship before we design space. The use of our space must determine its shape; we cannot allow arbi-trary formalistic designs to be imposed on our worship. Talk worship before you build and your space will talk worship when built. Ignore the fundamental uses, build something pretty, and your building will only stutter and stammer. The power of the three places I mentioned is that each one spoke so powerfully of its use as a place where God gives Godself to us through human words and hands.

The Language of Space

We need to be more precise; how does space work to enhance wor-ship? To most of us the language of space comes as a totality; we react to a building as a whole, not to parts of it. But space, like speech, can be broken down into sentences and words. I want you to look with me at the sentences and words through which space speaks. I shall break liturgical space down into six places and three or four objects. We encounter none of these alone but by helping you to identify the words and sentences of liturgical space I hope I can help you become more conscious of what space says.

In recent years we have become much more aware of the impor-tance of *gathering space* as a key liturgical space. The Christian com-munity needs to assemble in order to worship, and this act of coming together may be the most important single activity of the congrega-tion. In the heroic age of the early Church the very act of assembling produced martyrs. In every age forming the body of Christ is the first act of worship, one in which all participate. Therefore space marking the temporary separation of the community from the world outside, space in which individuals become a community, deserves careful at-tention in the design of churches.

The second component of liturgical space is *congregational space*. Basically a church is a people place. The pagan temple was the reverse; they kept the money on the inside and the people outside. We use the money for the world outside and serve the people inside. The most instructive buildings ever built with regard to congregational space are the Quaker meetinghouses of the eighteenth century. There it is manifest that God's presence is in the midst of God's people. There is nothing else, no pulpit, no altar table, no font; the whole building is congregational space. These buildings are terribly stirring places to visit. They anticipate what the *Constitution on the Sacred Liturgy* states when it lists the ways in which Christ is present in the Church's liturgical celebrations. The last one reads: "He is present, lastly, when the Church prays and sings, for he promised: `Where two or three are gathered together in my name, there am I in the midst of them'" (Matt 18:20). Quaker buildings have been saying the same thing for three hundred years.

But even the Quakers are victims of one misfortune here. Only two things of major significance have happened in Christian worship since the fourth century. Both of them were tragic losses. Somewhere about the fourteenth century European Christians began sitting down on the job. Congregational space that had been open fluid space for over a thousand years became jammed with pews. The mobile congregation that ebbed and flowed throughout the nave, gathering wherever the action was, now settled for a congested parking lot. The unencumbered people place became an occupied territory, a furniture place stuffed full of pews. The other major change was that sixteenth-century Protestants, having already lost their legs, now lost their senses of smell, taste, and touch and traded in eucharistic worship for nonsacramental worship. We not only sat down on the job but we went asleep as far as our bodies were concerned. Protestant worship became a head trip. It is not easy to recover congregational space as unfenced open range though a few Eastern Orthodox churches in this country have never been corrupted into comfort. Among them you can still experience how fluid congregational space can be.

A remnant of this freedom remains in the third kind of space our churches contain, *movement space*. Christian worship demands considerable movement. Revivalists in the nineteenth century and charismatics today remind us that to move people spiritually you have to move them physically. After all, we are a restless pilgrim people. Not only do we move about to receive communion, but weddings, funerals, baptisms, offertory and other processions are built about movement. We assemble and we scatter as part of worship.

The importance of movement as a way of worshiping with our whole bodies needs to be considered carefully. Maybe it will reshape our thinking about congregational space. (No one understood this better than the nineteenth-century Shakers. Their meetinghouses completely fused movement space and congregational space. The seven or eight Shaker meetinghouses surviving from Kentucky to Maine ought to be studied carefully.) As a learning experience some day you ought to celebrate Mass without any music or any words, even in the homily. Only then will you realize just how clearly actions do speak louder than words. The congregation, too, ought to be as free to move as the clergy now are (though even clergy rarely sense the eloquence of movement).

We are accustomed to speaking of baptism in terms of a font but less familiar with thinking of it in terms of *baptismal space*. At worst we have thought of baptism as a private ceremony tucked off in a remote corner of the church. A few new Catholic churches have testified to its public nature by placing the font next to the altar table. Every baptism is an act of the whole body not simply because it adds to the body's number but because it witnesses again and again to the nature of our being as those who have gone through the waters of death and resurrection and been united to Christ.

Unlike other acts of worship, baptism usually involves the intimacy of the family, a small church within the congregation, as a focus of love about the one baptized even while the total community joins in this act. Spatially this means we must provide space and access for the candidates and family without blocking the sense of participation of the whole congregation. Baptismal space, then, is people space but it has a concentric focus: first, the candidates and ministers, second, the family and sponsors, and third, the whole congregation. If we thought of this space in terms of people we would have fewer fonts buried in dark corners of churches. If we thought of baptism in terms of proclamation in which, as Luther suggests, for all Christians our baptism is called to mind "again and again and . . . faith awakened and nourished" we would be more concerned about how this space is shaped.

Choir space poses even more problems. Indeed, it may be the most difficult space of all to deal with, partly because we are not sure what the choir is there to do. If you envision the singers' chief role to be that of sharing in the ministry of the word this may dictate a location in full view of the congregation. But if you conceive their function to be that of supporting congregational singing, especially in teaching and leading new music, it may be best that they be scattered throughout the congregation. In this sense choir space would be merged with congregational space. Carlton Young reminds us that we tend to treat the choir as the congregation, whereas we ought to treat the whole congregation as the choir.

In most churches *altar-table* space is so prominent as hardly to need underscoring. What may need to be stressed is how strongly it must relate to congregational space by being both visible and accessible. The role of this space is to serve, not to dominate. What is done there is done for the benefit of the whole community of faith. The word is given, the body is given for the benefit of the whole Church. Thus we need to avoid such barriers as excessive height, the glare of too much direct light, overscaled furniture, enclosure that suggests a room detached from the congregation's room, and all the other barriers that have made altar-table space detached and remote. Believe me, we have almost specialized in ways of making this foreign territory glimpsed across a border barricaded by communion rails and screens. Though the altar-table in the center of the building is not the answer, we need to overcome barriers to hearing and touching.

There are also three or four objects that are vital for use in our worship. Their importance is demonstrated by the modes of Christ's presence as listed in the Liturgy Constitution. *A baptismal font* is necessary because of the sheer physical fact that water demands a container. It can be a hole in the floor, as the earliest surviving baptisteries indicate; it can be a jug, or a basin mounted on a pillar. One thing necessary is that it contain water, though most fonts seem designed to conceal rather than reveal that basic function. Very few fonts give any suggestion of that cold running water the *Didache* so clearly prefers. Our living waters speak more of stagnation and algae than movement. The Liturgy Constitution tells us: "By his power, he [Christ] is present in the sacraments, so that when someone baptizes it is really Christ himself who baptizes." A simple container for water, a font, is necessary to help us experience this presence of Christ.

The Liturgy Constitution also reminds us that Christ "is present in his word, since it is he himself who speaks when the holy scriptures are read in the Church." One could argue in a strict sense that a *pulpit* is not necessary for reading and preaching the word. Once I visited a Hare Krishna commune and the group sat for discussion in a circle on the floor. Without giving it a moment's thought I laid their sacred book on the floor. I was promptly told that that was a "no-no." I wonder just how sensitive we are to the relation between the visual presence of the holy Scriptures and the presence of Christ himself in the reading and exposition of them. Protestants, I suspect, have been a bit more sensitive to this and the Eastern Rite churches could tell us a lot about the high drama of the little entrance. If we really do believe that the reading and preaching of the word is a fresh theophany each time the people of God gather, then we ought to provide physical testimony to the visual aspects of that in the form of a pulpit that adequately displays the Bible. A mere portable lectern is not sufficient. Bookbinding, too, must again become a major art form for the Church.

None of you needs to be told the importance of the *altar-table*, but many of you need to be reminded that it is not there as an architectural focus of the building or even as a symbol of Christ. I believe it was Gilbert Cope who remarked that the huge altar-table in Coventry Cathedral demanded a sixteen-foot tall celebrant and that even the Church of England was not that comprehensive. The altar-table is there because it is used. It holds Christ whom the Liturgy Constitution tells us is present "especially under the eucharistic species." It is there, in short, just as fonts hold water and pulpits hold Bibles, to hold the eucharistic species. I am amazed how small the altar-tables were in the earliest churches. They were ministerial altar-tables, not monuments to fill space nor create an architectural focus. In short, what is holy about them is their use. After all, we cannot conveniently put the eucharistic vessels on the floor though Leonard Bernstein makes a telling indictment about that. But we can reduce the altar-table to the simplicity of our needs and it will reflect ministering better than a monument does.

The amazing thing is that these three objects, font, pulpit, and altar-table, are all that are really needed. Indeed, extraneous objects— lecterns, prayer desks, communion rails—may cause more harm than good. It is extraordinary how direct and simple the needs for Christian worship are.

Some of you will wonder why I have not mentioned the celebrant's *chair*. You will remember that the first mode of Christ's presence that the Liturgy Constitution mentions is "in the person of the minister." But a living person is not identified with the chair in the same way that water is with a font, the Bible with the pulpit, or the eucharistic species with the altar-table. A person can stand and move without an object for support. A chair by itself does not function the way a font, a pulpit, and an altar-table do.

This is particularly true when the chair has become a throne. There are dangers in copying too carefully the early Church. The early Church, after all, was borrowing a pagan building type with the magistrate's throne at the focus. And even though Paul does speak of the magistrates as *leitourgoi theou*, I'm not sure that's the image we wish to invoke. I think we must realize that the primary symbol here of Christ's presence is the person, not the chair. An empty chair reflects nothing but emptiness. I think celebrants' chairs should be designed with extreme reticence. I prefer, myself, to sit with the congregation when I am not on my feet. If you cannot do that maybe you are too far from your people, literally or figuratively. At any rate, I feel the chair has been too readily exalted as a post-Vatican II object and has become more prominent than its function deserves.

Well, that's all it takes. How does space speak of worship? Maybe "poverty" is the best term, after all. It doesn't take much. It only requires an economy of means. But that takes a lot of thought. Artlessness for us has to be an art in itself. But if we build for what we do in worship, our spaces can speak eloquently of what happens when Christians assemble to worship. That is the proper language of liturgical space.

19. Eighteenth-Century Experiments in Liturgical Architecture

This is a portion of the chapter, "Reformation Experiments," from *Protestant Worship and Church Architecture* (New York: Oxford University Press, 1964). Used by permission.

During the seventeenth and eighteenth centuries America served as a vast laboratory for experimentation on the architectural setting of Protestant worship. Every building provided an opportunity to start afresh, to investigate new possibilities. New challenges appeared in the use of materials neglected or scarce in Europe as well as the new functions a building might have in the total life of the community. In some areas churches were the only civic architecture.

It would be impossible to consider here all the experiments conducted in this country during the colonial period. Instead we shall discuss examples chosen from the two largest religious bodies in colonial America, the Church of England and the Puritans as well as (then) smaller bodies, Quakers and Methodists. The Church of England, of course, is represented by the Episcopal Church today; the Puritans most directly by the Congregationalists, though much of what is said of them here applies to the Baptist and Presbyterian heritages. Some quite surprising differences can be seen by comparing the Anglican buildings and the Puritan ones even in the same colonies as each tradition developed its own architecture. The Anglicans, with a fixed liturgy, tried a great variety of experiments; the Puritans, with freedom in worship, show a remarkably fixed pattern in liturgical arrangement.

Anglican Experiments
The Church of England in colonial America remained under the canon law of the Mother Country which provided that "all ministers . . . shall observe the Orders, Rites, and Ceremonies prescribed in

the Book of Common Prayer . . . without either diminishing . . . or adding anything in the matter or form thereof." Although this left a fair degree of latitude in such matters as the frequency of holy communion (once the required three celebrations per year had been held), it did mean that basically the same services would be performed in every church. It is therefore all the more surprising to see the variety of experiments carried on to secure the most appropriate setting for worship according to the *Book of Common Prayer*. During the nineteenth century these colonial experiments were forgotten but they have a direct relevance in the contemporary search for forms in Protestant architecture.

From what little we know of the first few generations of Anglicans in America we can say that they were not particularly venturesome in their church architecture. Information gained from the ruins of the fifth church in Jamestown (1647), the second Bruton Parish Church, Williamsburg (1683), and the still existing St. Luke's, Smithfield, Virginia (possibly built as early as 1632) indicates a strong conservatism. These early churches show an architecture of nostalgia, duplicating as much as possible the medieval parish church even to the extent of having wooden chancel screens across the east end of the building.[1]

Such conservatism was shed in the eighteenth century, particularly after Wren's contributions in England had become known. One can make some general statements about the furnishings of the buildings erected by Anglicans in eighteenth-century America.[2] In almost every instance the altar-table was shaped like a small table in form and reflected the changing styles in secular furnishings. It was usually covered with an altar cloth but was uncluttered by candles and crosses. If anything appeared on the altar-table it was more likely to be handsomely-bound volumes of the Bible and the Prayer Book and the alms basin. In some cases there might be a painting to ornament the east end and the required Decalogue would often be accompanied by the Creed and Lord's Prayer. Other than these features the altar-tables were remarkably

[1]See James Grote Van Derpool, "The Restoration of St. Luke's, Smithfield, Virginia," *Journal of the Society of Architectural Historians* 17 (1958) 12–18.

[2]Many of these furnishings and buildings are illustrated in Stephen P. Dorsey, *Early English Churches in America, 1607–1807* (New York: Oxford University Press, 1952).

simple and unadorned. Almost invariably eighteenth-century Anglican churches had the altar-table enclosed by rails.

Although canon law required that the font be "of stone" and "set in the ancient usual places" the bishop was far away and considerable freedom was exercised. Several wooden fonts have survived and we know that in some churches silver baptismal basins were used, not unlike those of the Puritans. More often than not the font was likely to appear at the east end of the building where the sacrament could be performed in full view of the entire congregation. The font in this position is also found in a number of English churches of the same period, the advantage being that of stressing the congregational nature of the sacrament.

In most churches of this period the dominant liturgical center was the pulpit and reading desk. Frequently this was a single center, the two-decker pulpit, or when combined with a clerk's pew the three-decker as in King's Chapel, Boston (1717) or Trinity Church, Newport, Rhode Island (1725). Pulpit and desk might be separate from each other but usually they remained in close proximity. In most cases they were by far the most prominent liturgical centers of the building and certainly the most used.

The main body of the church was filled with pews, especially the box pews popular in the eighteenth century. Frequently these were sold as private property and decorated according to the taste (or lack thereof) of the owner. Though the shapes could vary they were often square or rectangular with a door opening onto the aisle. Frequently seats ran on three sides of the pew. This gave a certain mobility to the occupants since they could turn to face the opposite end of the building if necessary to look at a liturgical center different from the customary one. It gave the congregation more mobility in orientation than is possible in modern slip pews. It also insured that the family might sit together, enabling the parents to keep an eye on their offspring without other members of the congregation doing so.

Most of the churches erected in the eighteenth century have only a slight recess for a chancel or none at all. When a chancel did appear it was most likely to be a shallow rounded apse or one arm of a cruciform building. No chancel screens have survived, and in every case the space for worship is a single room. Frequently the communion rail defines the liturgical space about the altar and is often returned at the sides to allow pews to be placed to the left and right of the altar-table.

The floor plans that accompany the text in this chapter and the next are simply diagrams to illustrate various liturgical arrangements. They are not necessarily drawn to scale and are only meant to show relationships. The symbols used include: A, altar-table; P, pulpit; L, lectern; D, reading desk; F, font; and C, choir space. Galleries are indicated by dotted lines. In many cases only the main worship space is depicted.

It is possible to detect at least six quite distinct types of experiments in liturgical arrangements in the eighteenth-century churches still surviving in America. One of the most interesting types is represented in St. Paul's Church, Wickford, Rhode Island, built in 1707 (Figure 1). This building is a rectangle with the pulpit and reading desk in the center of one long wall opposite the main entrance. Both

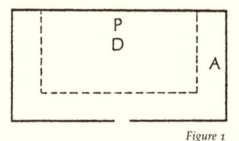

Figure 1

are enclosed on three sides by pews. At one short end of the building stands the altar-table beneath a gallery that is carried around three sides of the church. The placement of the pulpit suggests the Puritan arrangement of the time, but the pulpit and altar-table are at right angles to each other on the two axes of the building. This arrangement probably indicates an infrequent use of the altar-table since it cannot be seen by half the people in the gallery.

A second type appeared in St. James' Church, Goose Creek, South Carolina, a rectangular building erected in 1711 (Figure 2). In this church a tall pulpit stands at the center of one short end of the building. Directly below and in front of it stands the altar-table, enclosed by the semicircular rails. Beside the pulpit and altar-table and also within the rails stands the reading desk. The chief advantage of such an arrangement was that it brought all the liturgical centers together in a place easily seen by the entire congregation. The pulpit, as the dominant center, is in front of a round-headed pulpit window and on

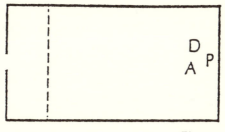

either side appear the Decalogue, the Lord's Prayer, and the Creed. A sub-type appears in Christ Church, Duanesberg, New York (1789), where the altar-table is beside the central two-decker pulpit, both against the east wall. Pulpit-centered arrangements have now almost disappeared from the Episcopal Church.

Only one example has survived in America of a type fairly common in the eighteenth century. In Trinity Church, Newport, Rhode Island (built in 1725) a tall wineglass pulpit, reading desk, and clerk's pew stand in the central aisle of the church directly in front of the altar-table (Figure 3). The building is a rectangle, these liturgical

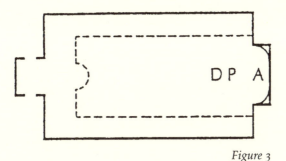

Figure 3

centers appearing at one of the short ends with a gallery around the other three sides. A silver baptismal basin was used in this building instead of a font. Although it might seem that the pulpit would obscure the view of the altar-table this does not happen. The congregation sits in box pews on either side of the central aisle or in the galleries and easily sees past the pulpit to the altar-table. Such an arrangement was once found in Old North Church, Boston (1723) and in some of the early Methodist chapels in England.

A fourth type appeared in the cruciform shape, nowhere more magnificently illustrated than in Christ Church, Lancaster County, Virginia, erected in 1732 (Figure 4). There are box pews throughout this building, neatly divided by two aisles on the axes. The altar-table appears in the eastern arm. By its side is a marble font. The three-decker pulpit is at the southwestern corner of the crossing, facing the crossing. Other examples of the same type of building place the pulpit at the southeast angle of the crossing (Abingdon Church, Gloucester County; Aquia Church, Stafford County; and Bruton, Williamsburg,

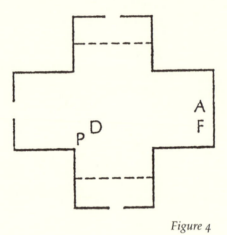

Figure 4

all in Virginia). There are parallels with the cruciform churches in the Reformed churches of Europe except that in these Anglican churches a railed-in altar-table occupies the eastern arm. A considerable number of people can be brought close to the liturgical centers by this arrangement, particularly when three of the arms contain galleries.

Another type appears in Donation Church, Princess Anne County, Virginia, erected in 1736 (Figure 5). In this rectangular building the altar-table is in the center of the east end. Directly in front of the rails is an aisle across the church and the pulpit appears in the north end of this against the wall. Although there is no structural chancel, the pulpit is placed as if it were just beyond where the chancel screen would have been in a medieval church. A similar location evidently occurred in St. Luke's, Smithfield, Virginia, where a chancel screen is known to have existed.

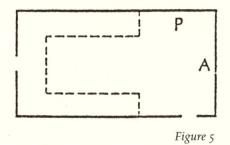

Figure 5

One of the most interesting types appears in only two surviving churches, St. Peter's, Philadelphia, 1758 (Figure 6) and Pompion Hill Chapel above the Cooper River in South Carolina (1763). In both of these buildings, the one a sophisticated city church, the other a remote country chapel of ease, altar-table and pulpit are at opposite ends of rectangular structures. At St. Peter's, box pews made it possible for the congregation to face whichever liturgical center was being used, the pulpit and reading desk in the west or the altar-table and font in the east. At Pompion Hill the slip pews run parallel to the long sides of the building. Some indication of the relative importance of pulpit and altar-table here is seen in the fact that the pews near the pulpit were painted white whereas those near the altar-table were painted brown and used by slaves.

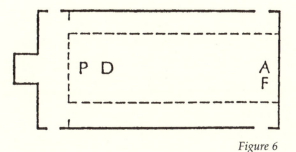

Figure 6

Most likely other arrangements were tried but have disappeared. It is remarkable that so many varieties did appear in the eighteenth century, particularly in light of the uniformity that became a characteristic of Anglican churches throughout the world after the Cambridge Movement of the nineteenth century. In general one sees in the eighteenth-century experiments an attempt to bring the liturgical centers, particularly the pulpit and desk, close to the people so that all may see, hear, and take part in worship.

Puritan Architecture

Among the Puritans quite a different situation prevailed. They succeeded very early in establishing a suitable liturgical arrangement and it was retained with remarkable unanimity though the buildings changed considerably. The Puritan liturgical centers included a tall pulpit with the congregation gathered about it on the main floor and in an encircling gallery. Directly in front of the pulpit was usually a pew occupied by the elders or deacons. Before this stood the altar-table upon which a baptismal basin could be placed. And that was all. It was the simplest and most direct arrangement possible for Puritan worship.

Some generalizations can be made about these buildings. The entire service was led from the pulpit except during the sacraments. Preaching, "being the power of God unto salvation," naturally was a most important part of the service. This importance was reflected in the size of the pulpits, some of them being as much as twelve feet high. There might be a cushion on the pulpit for the Bible and an hourglass to time the sermon. Since everything else in the building was subordinate to the pulpit it formed the dominant architectural focus. Frequently there was a sounding board above the pulpit suspended from the ceiling or projecting from the wall. Round-headed windows behind the pulpit added to its elegance. Some of the most beautiful pulpits were of the wineglass variety though later versions were perched on four or more legs. Occasionally two curving staircases swept up from either side. Many of these eighteenth-century pulpits are esthetic triumphs, far more pleasing than the platform and desk pulpit that replaced them in the next century.

The Lord's Supper was frequently celebrated monthly among Congregationalists and quarterly among Presbyterians. In New England it seems likely that it was received in the pews, the bread and wine being passed to the people in the pews by the deacons. In the words of John Cotton, "ceremonies wee use none" and this simplicity was reflected in the small plain tables, sometimes just a leaf hinged on the elder's pew. Thus the elder could sit behind the table and face the congregation across it at sacrament time. Beautiful examples of communion silver have survived. They include chalices, flagons, and cups, as well as baptismal basins.[3]

One of the most common characteristics of Puritan meetinghouses was the presence of galleries. Their purpose, of course, was to bring the congregation as close as possible to the pulpit. The presence of galleries accounts, in part, for the excessive height of the pulpit. A common form of the gallery was the so-called horseshoe gallery reaching around the sides that did not contain the pulpit. In a few cases there were two tiers of galleries. Though the galleries might have either slip pews or box pews, the floor of the church was almost certain to have box pews.

These colonial meetinghouses were elegant in their simplicity. There were no traditional ecclesiastical symbols but there was a directness in building for a specific type of worship. Clean, well-lighted, they concentrated on the essentials of Puritan worship, the hearing of God's word, with no distractions. For their purposes they were wonderfully successful examples of liturgical architecture.

During the seventeenth and eighteenth centuries there was a series of four stages in the evolution of the New England meetinghouse now so familiar on calendars and Christmas cards. The earliest buildings were evidently quite primitive. Very little is known about these buildings save that they were often fortified against Indian attack. During the seventeenth century they were replaced by larger wooden buildings sometimes square, or nearly so, in plan (Figure 7).

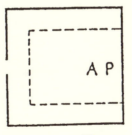

Figure 7

Opposite the main entrance stood the pulpit set in the center of the wall. Galleries seem to have been customary. Only one example of this type of building has survived, Old Ship Church in Hingham,

[3]See *American Church Silver of the Seventeenth and Eighteenth Centuries with a Few Pieces of Domestic Plate* (Boston: Museum of Fine Arts, 1911).

Massachusetts, built in 1681. Enough documentary evidence is available, however, to show that it was not an isolated example. Plain and nearly square, Old Ship Church has a tall pulpit with a pulpit window behind and an old hourglass has been preserved. A pew for elders and deacons appears below the pulpit as does the small altar-table.

In the years after 1700 these buildings were replaced by others that nevertheless retained the same arrangement of liturgical centers (Figure 8). In this third type the building is rectangular with the pulpit set in the middle of one long side. There is a touch of the medieval nave with the pulpit in the middle of one side. Architecturally the

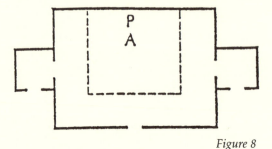

Figure 8

buildings built during the eighteenth century show increasing sophistication. The towers, which rise from the ground, betray the influence of Wren, though in America wood and brick were substituted for the stone used in England. Old South Church in Boston (1729) shows the Puritans seeking to match the elegance of the Anglican Old North Church (1723). Both have towers at one end, round-headed windows, and magnificent interior woodwork, but Old South is true to its tradition in orienting the interior about a pulpit in the center of a long side. Many buildings of this type have a very domestic appearance on the exterior. Galleries made it difficult to provide full-length windows so most of the exteriors have two rows of windows similar to homes of the period. A few examples of this type of building remain scattered in the New England states, particularly Farmington, Connecticut (1771); Amesbury, Massachusetts (1785); Alna, Maine (1789); Newport, Rhode Island (1729); Sandown, New Hampshire (1774); and Rockingham, Vermont (1787).[4]

[4]Illustrations and descriptions of the Connecticut examples appear in J. Frederick Kelly, *Early Connecticut Meetinghouses: Being an Account of the Church*

The final and most familiar type emerged in the buildings built after the Revolutionary War. In these the orientation has been changed so that the pulpit appears in the center of a short side of the rectangle opposite the main entrance (Figure 9). Frequently the rooms

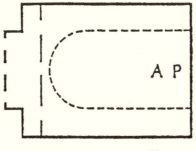

Figure 9

are only a bit longer than wide so that the basic interior is not far removed from a square. However a narthex or portico has been added to the end opposite the pulpit, producing a rectangular building. The portico and tower over it were due to the influence of James Gibbs, an architect who worked in England developing this composition so familiar in many meetinghouses. Galleries were usually present, often in horseshoe form.

It should be noticed that none of these buildings had chancels or even a suggestion of a chancel, quite unlike the modern "reproductions" of them. A single liturgical arrangement, that of central pulpit and altar-table below it, persisted for over a hundred and fifty years before being superseded. Choirs and organs were unknown during much of this period in Congregational churches. The introduction of choirs and a new concept of preaching replaced the traditional Puritan arrangement in the mid-nineteenth century.

A special type of church, the college chapel, shows a distinctive form in both Anglican and Puritan colleges. The chapel built at the College of William and Mary in 1732 may have had the traditional collegiate arrangement: stalls parallel to the long sides and the altar-table at one end opposite the entrance. At Harvard, Holden Chapel

---

Edifices Built before 1830 Based Chiefly upon Town and Parish Records. 2 vols. (New York: Columbia University Press, 1948).

(built 1742–1744) had this seating arrangement but with a reading desk at the end opposite the door.

Quakers and Methodists

Two other Protestant traditions produced distinctive buildings: the Quakers and the Methodists. The Quakers developed the most radical liturgical arrangement of all Protestant groups and held to it with remarkable consistency. Quaker worship actually is one of the most highly corporate forms of worship. According to Robert Barclay, in the silent waiting upon God of Quaker worship

"God reveals himself and draweth near to every individual, and so he is in the midst in the general, whereby each not only partakes of the particular refreshment and strength which comes from the good in himself, but is a sharer in the whole body, as being a living member of the body, having a joint fellowship and communion with all."[5]

Barclay proceeds to liken Quaker worship to the way "many candles lighted, and put in one place, do greatly augment the light." These principles are reflected remarkably well in the Quaker meetinghouses of the colonial period.

No liturgical centers appear but instead the entire building has become liturgical space. All persons present participate fully and equally in the worship of the meeting. Thus the only furnishings are the benches for the worshipers. Frequently the main body of benches faces a bench or two for the elders of the meeting and other rows of benches on the floor level or in galleries may flank the main body of benches.

Perhaps as early as the seventeenth century the Quaker meetinghouse type became fixed. It was usually a rectangle with two main entrances. Since the women sometimes met separately (having different concerns) there was often a movable partition down the middle (width) of the building as in the Medford, New Jersey meetinghouse erected in 1814 (Figure 10). Men and women used separate entrances. The division of the sexes was attempted in many Protestant denominations. The first *Book of Common Prayer* (1549) provided for separation of the men and women at communion; in the eighteenth century

[5]*An Apology for the True Christian Divinity* (Manchester: William Irwin, 1869) 224.

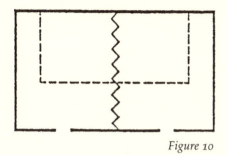

Figure 10

Wesley made an effort to divide them at worship and some Anglicans tried to do likewise in the nineteenth century. But only the Quakers succeeded in accomplishing this supernatural task and they gave it up in the nineteenth century.

The buildings themselves were models of simplicity and their stonework or brick has a very great appeal to modern eyes. In turning the entire space into liturgical space, the Quakers accomplished the abolition of any exclusive liturgical space for clergy and truly made it apparent that all the people of God performed a ministry in common worship.

Methodism dates from the eighteenth century, having originated as a movement within the Church of England under the leadership of John and Charles Wesley. This relationship to the Church of England is important to remember for the early Methodist people conceived of their worship largely as an adjunct to that of the Established Church. Their services were intended to supplement, not to supplant, the Anglican services. Indeed Methodist services during "church-hours" were frowned upon. The *Large Minutes* of the 1770 Conference preferred to refer to the Methodist buildings as "preaching-houses."[6] This indicates their essential function, to serve as the locale for preaching services but not to replace the parish church for the sacraments. In the *Minutes* of 1766, Wesley declared that Methodist worship was "not such as supersedes the Church [Anglican] Service. We never designed it should."[7] The Methodist preaching-houses originally served a function not too unlike the preaching churches erected by the friars in the thirteenth and fourteenth centuries.

[6]*Minutes of the Methodist Conferences, from the First, Held in London, by The Late Rev. John Wesley, A.M. in the Year 1744* (London: John Mason, 1862) 1.540.
[7]Ibid., 1.59.

In a few of the Methodist chapels it became customary to administer communion. Wesley had become convinced by 1764 that no consecration was necessary or lawful other than holding public worship in a building.[8] Accordingly, altar-tables and rails began to appear in the Methodist buildings though they may have had little use during Wesley's lifetime except when an ordained minister was present. The Methodist services centered in preaching, a factor reflected in the invariably prominent pulpit. Hymn singing was an important part of Methodist worship. Anthems were forbidden, however, "because they cannot be properly called joint-worship" (*Minutes*, 1787).[9]

The early Methodist preaching-houses and chapels are a good index to Wesley's ideas of worship since his supervision extended to the architecture of these buildings as well as to their uses. Before any building had been erected for Methodist worship, and long afterwards, field preaching was popular, although the *Minutes* of 1744 caution: "Yet (to avoid giving any needless offence) we never preach *without* doors, when we can with conveniency preach *within*."[10] In many areas the poverty of the Methodist people made it impossible to erect preaching-houses. Private homes, barns, inns, old theaters, and other buildings were used as Methodist preaching-houses. When funds did permit, several distinctive types of buildings were erected.

The most remarkable of these was the octagon. The inspiration for building in this shape seems to have come from Wesley's visit to Norwich in 1757 when he saw the octagonal meetinghouse completed by nonconformists there the year before (Figure 11). With Wesley's powerful authority behind it, this type of building was widely adopted by Methodists. At least a dozen such buildings were erected between 1760 and 1770. The Conference *Minutes* of 1770 and following years carried instructions to "build all preaching-houses, if the ground will admit, in the octagon form. It is the best for the voice, and on many accounts more commodious than any other."[11] These two features—the assumed superiority for preaching purposes and the increased accommodation made possible by galleries on

[8]*Journal of the Rev. John Wesley, A.M.* edited by Nehemiah Curnock (Standard edition New York: Eaton and Mains, n.d.) vol. 5, August 20, 1764 and February 28, 1772.

[9]*Minutes* 1.203.

[10]Ibid., 1.23.

[11]Ibid., 1.612.

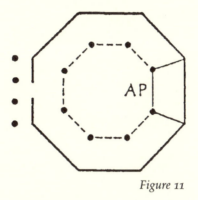

Figure 11

seven sides—were probably Wesley's chief reasons for building octagons. This shape does not seem to have been used much among American Methodists.

Though the octagon had an early popularity in English Methodism, it was eventually replaced by rectangular buildings. Actually the earliest Methodist preaching-house, the New Room in Bristol, 1739 (Figure 12) is of a roughly rectangular shape as are the American

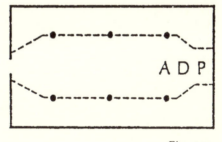

Figure 12

buildings. The Bristol building, still very much in its original condition, has a two-decker pulpit in the center of one short end. In front of the pulpit and reading desk is a platform enclosed by a rail containing the altar-table. There are galleries on the two long sides.

The most famous early Methodist chapel, the City Road Chapel in London, was opened in 1778 (Figure 13). It is significant that it was designated a chapel instead of a preaching-house. In liturgical arrangement it was similar to many eighteenth-century Anglican churches. Evidently it fulfilled for Methodists many of the functions

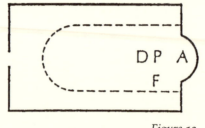

Figure 13

of a parish church, and an episcopally-ordained minister was usually present to administer the sacraments. The presence here of a stone baptismal font at an early date indicates an exceptional development of Methodist independence. In its original form, City Road Chapel was a plain building with galleries on three sides and a shallow apse on the fourth. The apse contains an altar-table and rails. Directly in front of it stands the pulpit, once a three-decker now shorn of the top five feet of its former fifteen-foot height. A few examples of this arrangement survive in Methodist chapels but in most instances the altar-table evidently stood in front of the pulpit. City Road Chapel had a great influence on subsequent Methodist chapels, especially after the ruling of the 1790 Conference, "Every house larger than the Bath house is to be built on the plan of the new chapel in London, both within and without."[12]

After Wesley's death Methodism lost much of its distinctive emphasis on frequent communion. Methodists ceased going to the parish church for the sacrament and it was neglected in the Methodist chapels. There is little to distinguish the Methodist chapels of the nineteenth century from those of other nonconformists except the altar rail. The Anglican practice of kneeling at the rail survived in Methodism.

Since most of the early Methodists were poor, the chapels were often very simple. The *Minutes* of the 1780 Conference ordered, "Let all preaching-houses be built plain and decent; but not more expensive than is absolutely unavoidable; otherwise the necessity of raising money will make rich men necessary to us. But if so, we must be dependent upon them, yea, and governed by them. And then farewell to Methodist discipline, if not doctrine too."[13] Such dangers were

[12]Ibid., 1.242.
[13]Ibid., 1.613.

guarded against in the eighteenth century. Symbolism and decorations were absent. When the image of an angel with a trumpet had somehow been erected over the pulpit in the Halifax preaching-house it was an offense to the weaker brethren and had to be removed and burned.[14] This is a bit strange as such a figure was an appropriate symbol of the preached word and was popular among French Protestants. English Puritanism, however, had dispensed with even this much symbolism. Thus early Methodism combined Puritanical severity with the altar rails of Laud's high churchmanship, a symbol of the combination of these two traditions in Methodism.

Common Factors

In this brief survey some common traits can be seen in the Protestant experiments of the sixteenth, seventeenth, and eighteenth centuries. Foremost of these was a willingness to experiment at least until a completely adequate form was secured. The more complex and varied the liturgical life of a tradition was, the more difficult it was to find the optimum form. Thus the American Puritans early achieved a satisfactory arrangement while Lutherans and Anglicans continued to explore new possibilities throughout this period. In a way this is indicative of Protestant theology, which is unwilling to concede an absolute character to a theological formulation. The fear that according finality to any theological statement would be basically idolatrous is repeated in the continual search for more adequate liturgical arrangements.

One of the dominant characteristics of the buildings cited above is the preponderance of a central type building. Chancels had become largely superfluous in most Protestant traditions by the eighteenth century. The churches erected were one-room churches with a strong focus on the central space. The result was that of combining the liturgical space occupied by the congregation as closely as possible with that used by the clergy. Emphasis was placed on the whole people of God hearing, seeing, and doing the liturgy. It should be pointed out that most of the Roman Catholic churches built in southern Europe during this time were also central churches. The Mass was made magnificent and visible, and some orders built churches designed for

[14]*Journal*, April 15, 1779.

frequent preaching. If the Middle Ages suggested the mystery of the Mass, the baroque era was more inclined to suggest the dramatic qualities of Roman Catholic worship. Although both Protestants and Catholics did build some longitudinal buildings during these centuries, the central church type came into its own during this period.

20. Nineteenth-Century American Liturgical Architecture

> Written before the post-Vatican II revolution in worship, this chapter
> was originally entitled "Behind the Current Stalemate" in *Protestant
> Worship and Church Architecture* (New York: Oxford University Press,
> 1964). Used by permission.

In the nineteenth century two types of liturgical arrangements
came to dominate Protestant church building to the point of becoming standard patterns. So prevalent did these two types become that
until recently [i.e., 1963] further experiments were few and far between and even now their number is only slowly increasing. One of
the two dominant types is the concert-stage arrangement with tiers of
choir stalls behind a pulpit platform at the foot of which appears the
altar-table. The other type is the so-called divided chancel with the
choir stalls and altar-table within the chancel and the pulpit at one
side of its entrance. In both cases the liturgical space allotted to the
congregation tends to be similar: a long, rectangular nave.

It is interesting that these two types have come to have such a
widespread usage in contemporary Protestantism that it is often impossible to tell the denomination for which a building is intended
simply by looking at the interior. In itself this is an indication of indifference to strong denominational traditions in worship. By and
large the nineteenth and twentieth centuries saw the gradual assimilation of each other's traditions in worship by the various denominations. Though they once would have been obviously distinct there is
often little today to distinguish buildings erected for worship by
Presbyterians, Lutherans, and Episcopalians.

The differences that appear in the choice of the concert-stage or divided chancel arrangements more often seem to be byproducts of social and cultural matters than theological ones. Ultimately the
difference is between the relative impact of two nineteenth-century

movements on the culture of a region. Thus the relative importance of revivalism or Romanticism as cultural patterns is often more important than the denominational traditions that have eroded away and been forgotten.

In this respect the nineteenth and twentieth centuries represent a distinct break from the patterns prevalent in the three previous centuries. Previously experimentation had been common except where a well-recognized denominational pattern had been established. Indeed experimentation had become almost a tradition in itself for Anglicans and Lutherans. Yet even these experiments grew out of the denominations' particular traditions so that the relative importance of the liturgical centers helped give a distinct quality to the buildings of each group. The loss of this distinctiveness and the paucity of experiments mark the nineteenth and twentieth centuries off from those preceding.

In a sense what happened in church architecture is symptomatic of some of the profound changes occurring in Protestant worship in the nineteenth and early twentieth centuries. This period saw a tendency toward the breakdown of the emphasis on corporate action in common worship the reformers sought to achieve. The nineteenth century succeeded in overturning many of the principles of the Reformation relating to worship while fervently professing faithfulness to the reformers. One of the cardinal notes of the modern Liturgical Movement has been a reversal of the strong individualism that came to characterize the approach to worship during the last century. In so doing the Movement joins hands with the reformers and the early Church but remains highly critical of the individualism of the nineteenth century and late Middle Ages.

Strangely enough, some of the sources of this individualism seem at first glance to have little in common. Revivalism was a popular movement that rarely concerned itself with much intellectual sophistication. On the other hand, Romanticism was highly sophisticated and was reflected in many of the great minds of the century. Yet in worship both led to a strong stress on the importance of feeling and a tendency to exalt the individual.

At the same time the congregation assumed an increasingly passive role as more and more of the service was performed by the clergy or choir. Although esthetically Protestant worship has improved considerably in the last century and a half it has often been at the expense of congregational participation. An increasing professionalism has shown itself as congregations allow minister and choir to perform most of the acts of worship except for a few half-hearted hymns.

Architecturally this is expressed in the two dominant building types. Both are usually longitudinal buildings with the implicit hierarchical distinctions between clergy and people that this type often involves. In both cases the main liturgical centers are separated from the congregation by both vertical and horizontal distinctions. Both concert stage and divided chancel arrangements remove the leaders of worship into liturgical space to which the rest of the congregation has no direct access except when receiving communion. Thus the congregation is encouraged to assume a spectator role while watching and listening to minister and choir during the service.

It is a bit surprising that such arrangements could have so firm a grip on the imagination of the average Protestant. Unconsciously we have allowed nineteenth-century concepts of worship to lull us, so we are not fully aware of what has been lost. Yet this stalemate continues with the constant repetition of buildings quite inadequate for Protestant worship. The concert-stage and divided-chancel arrangements certainly do not express the concepts of worship held by the sixteenth-century reformers and are equally foreign to the best liturgical thought of our own time. And yet these stereotyped arrangements are repeated in hundreds of new churches each year.

The Impact of Revivalism

Modern American Protestantism is affected in almost every area of Church life by the revivalism of the nineteenth century. Indeed it was mass evangelism of the revivalistic type that changed America from a nation with a Christian minority to a nation in which most of the population belongs to a Church.[1] Though the revival pattern has died out in many denominations, the strengths and weaknesses of this form of evangelism have become a permanent part of American Christianity. This is especially true in relation to worship, where many of the basic presuppositions of revivalism linger on even where revivals are most vehemently repudiated.

Many of the major patterns of nineteenth-century revivalism originated on the frontier. One of the most successful institutions of frontier

---

[1]For an interesting discussion see Franklin H. Littell, *From State Church to Pluralism* (New York: Doubleday, 1962) ch. 2.

revivalism was the campmeeting in which thousands of people gathered from isolated farms, camping on the grounds for several days at
a time. For the rough and exuberant pioneers, campmeeting time was
a time of great emotional intensity, occasionally accompanied by
awesome physical manifestations of the feelings experienced. The
emotional sobriety of the great eighteenth-century evangelist,
Jonathan Edwards, was often forgotten and preachers addressed
their hearers on a highly emotional level as the most direct means of
producing conversions.

At times the campmeeting situation saw a blurring of denominational traditions as evangelists of various churches cooperated on the
same campgrounds. People moved freely from preacher to preacher.
The preaching was similar: a call to repentance and an exhortation to
accept Christ. It is interesting that a celebration of the Lord's Supper
usually climaxed the meetings, the different groups tending to separate for these occasions. Evidently only a minority of those present
communicated, but the sacrament often was the occasion of further
conversions. In the words of one contemporary: "The work is greatest on sacramental occasions."[2] Increasingly, denominational traditions fell victim to the practical expediency of the frontier. At times
this caused schisms within denominations. Several groups broke off
from the Presbyterians and eventually formed another denomination,
the Disciples of Christ. The Lord's Supper became a part of the normal Sunday service of this group. The general practice among the
Disciples of Christ has been to receive communion in the pews and
the altar-table is almost always a free-standing table. A sunken baptistery is usually provided for immersion.

The keynote of revivalism was that of producing a conversion in
which a person's total being was profoundly changed. Francis
Asbury recorded a typical occasion in his *Journal*: "I judge two hundred souls were made the subjects of grace in its various operations
of conviction, conversion, sanctification, and reclamation."[3] It is not
strange that the primary emphasis in revivalism was upon the indivi-

[2]Colonel Robert Patterson, quoted by H. Shelton Smith, Robert T. Handy, and
Lefferts A. Loetscher in *American Christianity: an Historical Interpretation with
Representative Documents* (New York: Scribners, 1960) 1.569.

[3]*The Journal and Letters of Francis Asbury*, edited by Elmer T. Clark (Nashville:
Abingdon, 1958) 2.505–506.

dual and his or her conversion experience. One attended revivals until converted, then labored to convert others. Beside such an earnest concern for producing converts, worship as an offering to God seemed to be only a side issue. Even the Church itself became somewhat of an option except for providing the means to continue the work of extending revivals. It is not strange that in such a situation worship became a means to an end—producing conversions—rather than an end in itself. Worship was utilized primarily for inducing conversion experiences rather than the offering of a sacrifice of praise and thanksgiving by God's people.

Revivalism did not long remain confined to the frontier though many of its characteristics were developed in such an environment. It was the introduction of the revival system among the churches of the East Coast that brought revivalism into the mainstream of American Protestant life. By this time it had developed into a coherent pattern. Probably no one deserves more credit for bringing the frontier practices of revivalism into the Church life of the East than Charles G. Finney. Converted in upstate New York, where he then worked as a revivalist of great power, Finney eventually came to New York City and popularized many of the practices of revivalism despite opposition from his fellow Presbyterians. Finney referred to his methods as the "new measures" though most had not been his invention. In his *Lectures on Revivals of Religion* (1835) he made very clear his willingness to dispense with traditional forms of worship if they did not produce conversions:

"The fact is, that God has established, in no church, any particular *form*, or manner of worship, for promoting the interests of religion. The scriptures are entirely silent on these subjects, under the gospel dispensation, and the church is left to exercise her own discretion in relation to all such matters."[4]

Though one may question whether worship exists "for promoting the interests of religion," there can be no mistaking the clear practical intention Finney had of using those measures that produce conversions and discarding those he considered ineffectual.

[4]*Lectures on Revivals of Religion*, edited by William G. McLoughlin (Cambridge, Mass.: Harvard University Press, 1960) 276.

The consequences are quite clear. One stresses all means available for bringing the individual to conversion. Particularly useful are those that condition him or her emotionally to accept the offer of salvation. Choral singing became an important part of revivalism and song leaders and choirs remain a vital part of contemporary revivals. The approach to the worshiper is emotional, subjective, and individualistic. And very few contemporary Protestant congregations are totally free of the same approach to the public worship of the Church today.

The consequences for church architecture were much more far-reaching than is usually realized. Not only did revivalism lead to a new liturgical arrangement but eventually to a quite new concept of the basic purposes of a church building. Revivalism tended to focus on the development of pulpit personalities, with a lessening of the objective sense of the sermon as an exposition of the Scriptures through which God addressed humans. It is interesting to trace the shrinking of the pulpit and the expanding of the pulpit platform upon which it stood as revivalistic preaching spread. Until the beginning of the nineteenth century, Protestant pulpits were usually of the "tub" type, a rather large structure in which the preacher stood. Often a high sounding board made the preacher seem somewhat diminutive. Yet in a sense these huge pulpits gave a note of authority to the preached word that transcended the individual preacher. (This can be easily gauged by preaching without a pulpit before a congregation accustomed to one and seeing how the sermon becomes a personal talk.) Many great revivalist preachers preferred a small desklike pulpit big enough to hold only their notes. But they relished a large platform on which to make sorties in all directions as they pleaded for conversions.

Certainly the pulpit platform gave room for histrionics and also made it possible for the preacher to kneel at any point on the stage, especially if he found it necessary to pray for the conversion of a particular individual. It also became quite common for several people to lead a service of worship. There might be a song leader and a visiting minister besides the pastor. Accommodation for these was provided by three large chairs that had a much more practical use than representing the Trinity. Some of these chairs from pulpit platforms will be museum pieces in the twenty-first century if not destroyed before then.

A very conspicuous addition was the provision of space for choirs and organs. Puritanism had resisted these innovations throughout the seventeenth and much of the eighteenth century. But revivalism was never prone to turn down any effective measure and it was realized that choirs and organ music could be most useful in inducing the feelings associated with worship. The arrangement adopted for the choir was usually a semicircle of tiers of seats facing the congregation. Musically it was probably as good as any and is familiar today on the concert stage. The organ console usually was at the base of the choir seats and the organ pipes towered over all with their gilt glory.

A further consequence was a growing awareness of the power of a building in creating a worshipful atmosphere. This was to have its fullest expression in the twentieth century when the emotive factors of architecture were used skillfully to induce a mood in which conversion would be encouraged. Pictorial stained glass windows blossomed in every building; painted organ pipes and brass fixtures added to the religious atmosphere. In a way it was an interesting reversal of the Puritan fear of art and music as dangerous distractions from hearing the word of God. Forgotten was the old Puritan reticence that had avoided decorative art and so sternly denounced "the squawking of chanting choristers . . . imitating the fashion and manner of Antichrist the Pope." The congregation was increasingly a passive audience for whom worship was something done for them and to them by experts. The mood-setting beauties of the building and the music conditioned the congregation for worship but they did less and less as active participants. It is no accident that the part of the building occupied by the congregation was designed as an audience chamber much like that of a theater, and the pulpit platform and choir stalls resembled a stage.

In a number of old meetinghouses the old pulpit gave way to a pulpit platform complete with desk pulpit and the sacrosanct three chairs. Often the building had to be enlarged to accommodate a choir and the addition of ornate organ pipes was the last blow to the fine austerity of many of these buildings. The Victorians, like nature, could not stand a vacuum.

It was not long, of course, before churches were built specifically under the influence of the revival system. They are often referred to, even today, as the "auditorium" and the term is expressive. As the term suggests, they are largely used as a place where the congregation hears worship. The concept is far from that of Wren's auditory church where the congregation was meant to be actively engaged in the acts of the liturgy as well as hearing the sermon.

Finney himself took a hand in designing Broadway Tabernacle in New York City. It was a large building with a gallery encircling the interior and a platform projecting onto the floor of the lower level. Tall organ pipes provided the backdrop for the platform. The size of many such buildings made any real sense of intimacy impossible. Hundreds of people had to be accommodated so they could see and hear the preacher. Generally galleries were necessary to seat worshipers in the larger churches. Pulpit platform and concert choir became standard arrangements (Figure 1). In the case of Baptist churches provision had to be made for a large baptistery, often at the rear of the platform. This usually took the form of a sunken tank with steps leading down into it. Below the pulpit stood the altar-table, an inconspicuous furnishing.

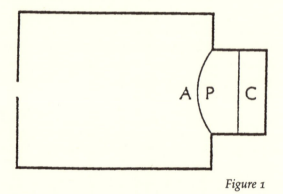

Figure 1

One of the most prevalent subtypes developing out of the concert stage arrangement was the so-called Akron plan. Originated soon after the Civil War, it seems to have been the invention of a Mr. Lewis Miller and was first used in the First Methodist Episcopal Church of Akron, Ohio. It was the product of an effort to provide a setting for Sunday Schools in which "opening exercises" could be conducted and then separate classes held. The Akron plan consisted of a hall with a horseshoe gallery. Both ground floor and gallery could be divided into classrooms by sliding partitions or opened for worship.

Through the "opening exercises" the Sunday School came to have its own worship, often becoming a church within the church. Usually the Sunday School unit opened directly into the auditorium by means of sliding doors and often the gallery might be carried through into the auditorium. In its most common form, the Akron plan included a pulpit platform wedged into one corner of the building (Figure 2). On this stood the pulpit and the inevitable pulpit chairs, and behind rose the concert choir and the organ pipes. On the

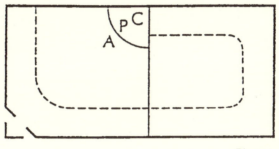

Figure 2

lowest level stood a small altar-table, upon which a baptismal basin might be found on many Sundays. Usually the floor sloped downward toward the pulpit platform. On overflow occasions the partitions were opened and worshipers could sit in the Sunday School rooms.

An enthusiastic writer wrote half a century ago: "Church architecture in America—more especially that of the non-ritual church—has been completely revolutionized by this influence."[5] Certainly the Akron plan had a tremendous influence for half a century or more. Books were published illustrating its arrangement and singing its praises.[6] Many of these buildings are still in existence but since World War II hundreds have been remodeled so their original arrangement

[5]Marion Lawrence, "The Akron Plan—Its Genesis, History and Development," *Thirty-Second Annual Report of the Board of Church Extension of the Methodist Episcopal Church, South* (n.p., 1914) 270.

[6]Cf. W. H. Brearley, *Architect's Plans, Specifications, and Builders Estimate for an Improved Bible-School Building and Church Edifice Combined* ([Detroit?], 1881); and Sidney J. Osgood, *Churches* (Grand Rapids: Dean Printing and Publishing Co., 1893).

is unrecognizable. Indeed a number of articles and chapters in books on church building have raised the question, "what to do with the Akron plan?" Actually, for the type of worship for which it was created the Akron plan was admirably suited, much more so than the building type that has so frequently superseded it. As one of its champions pointed out, "The strong point of this building—and this is the essential test of any building—is its utility in the highest sense. . . . Such completeness and comprehensiveness is almost without parallel among the inventions of man."[7] Divorced of its eclectic styles the Akron plan is quite adequate for those groups whose concept of worship is hearing the minister and the choir, though many contemporary Protestants may care to question such a concept of worship.

In the last fifty years the Akron plan has been almost completely superseded by churches that place the Sunday School in separate rooms or even separate buildings, and quite different concepts influence the design of classrooms. The auditorium is now usually a rectangle. At one short side is the pulpit platform and choir seats. The chief change seems to be that the choir robes are a bit gaudier and the organ pipes more subdued. Yet the question remains whether there is any real advantage in the congregation's being able to see either choir or pipes. Usually a small communion table appears on the floor of the church below the pulpit. Increasingly it is laden down with brass candlesticks and a cross or flowers. In Methodist churches an altar rail encircles the platform. So persistent had this become that Methodists who build divided chancels still place the rail outside the chancel even though the altar-table has retreated in the opposite direction. For Baptists and other groups a large baptistery may be located behind the pulpit or behind the choir. It seems to be virtually impossible to secure a location for the baptistery that will not be awkward on the numerous Sundays when it is not used. It is usually treated as an occasional liturgical center and concealed by drapes or by other means when not in use. It calls baptism to mind only when actually being used. The problem is compounded since all that the congregation can see during baptism is the empty space above the tank. Further experiments as to the design and location of the type of baptistery used for immersion are necessary.

[7]Lawrence, "The Akron Plan . . ." 271.

Many of the concert-stage type buildings being built today are well decorated and provided with emotive factors, particularly those involving the control of lights. This, of course, is in full keeping with the tendency of the revival tradition to emphasize the subjective approach to worship as basically a matter of feeling.

The liturgical space allotted to the congregation is most often the conventional theater arrangement. The pulpit platform tends to be a stage and the congregation occupies the place of an audience. The congregation rarely has any direct access to the liturgical centers themselves. No better example could be given of the passivity of the congregation than that they are willing to assume the role of spectators rather than be actors on stage. In itself this is an architectural denial of the ministry of all the faithful and a symptom of what has happened in much of Protestant worship.

Romanticism's Influence

It would seem at first glance that Romanticism had little in common with revivalism yet both were imbued with the same spirit of individual expression. "The folk religion of the exuberant, optimistic, and undisciplined frontier represented a bizarre, but nonetheless genuine, expression to the spirit of romanticism."[8] Yet the Romanticism that finally found its expression in American church building came from the opposite end of the ecclesiastical spectrum from that of revivalism. The total effect of both, though, has been a stress on worship as a subjective matter of feeling affecting people as individuals.

Romanticism in church architecture is usually associated with the revival of gothic architecture. It is interesting to trace the course of this period in the history of taste because it gives a good index of the concepts of worship. One of the first gothic churches in America was built by John Henry Hopkins as rector of Trinity Episcopal Church in Pittsburgh, Pennsylvania.[9] The new building, erected in 1823, replaced

[8]Ralph H. Gabriel, "Evangelical Religion and Popular Romanticism in Early Nineteenth Century America," *Church History* 19 (1950) 39.

[9]For more detail on Hopkins see James F. White, "Theology and Architecture in America: A Study of Three Leaders," in *A Miscellany of American Christianity; Essays in Honor of H. Shelton Smith*, edited by Stuart Henry (Durham: Duke University Press, 1963), 362–371.

an earlier octagonal church. The arrangement of Hopkins's new church reflects the experiments of the eighteenth century. The building was basically a rectangle with galleries on three sides. In a slight recess at one end stood a central pulpit with a prayer desk, altar-table, and font all directly in front of it and each progressively lower. The ceiling was painted in imitation of fan vaulting though perfectly flat. The gothic details had a toy-like quality and the building had more in common with Georgian churches than with later gothic revival structures.

Frequent requests for designs led Hopkins to publish his *Essay on Gothic Architecture* in 1836.[10] The plates, done by Hopkins (who had in the meantime become the first Bishop of Vermont), illustrate a number of gothic churches. In many of these appear his favorite arrangement—pulpit, desk, altar-table, and font, all on the main axis of the building. Chancels are absent, as are pictures and altar crosses. Hopkins suggested instead "adorning the walls of the Churches only with the appropriate architectural enrichments, and with judicious and edifying selections from the word of God."[11] Hopkins's real attachment to gothic is certainly not for the medieval arrangement but because he felt the "solemnity and repose" of gothic gave a greater "impression of sublimity" than other styles. He chose gothic not because of liturgical requirements but because of its effect upon individual worshipers. Emotive factors here dictate the style.

In a decade or so Hopkins's toy-like gothic had become obsolete. A new orthodoxy reigned and has continued to rule in many denominations up to the present. The revolution that came to affect thousands of American Protestant churches from the mid-nineteenth century to the present occurred in a most unlikely fashion. More than any other single cause it was the work of a group of undergraduates at Cambridge University in the 1840s banded together as the Cambridge Camden Society.[12] Their professed object was "to promote the study of Ecclesiastical Architecture and Antiquities, and the

[10]*Essay on Gothic Architecture, with Various Plans and Drawings for Churches: Designed Chiefly for the Use of the Clergy* (Burlington, Vermont: Smith and Harrington, 1836).

[11]Ibid., 15.

[12]For a detailed account see James F. White, *The Cambridge Movement: The Ecclesiologists and the Gothic Revival* (Cambridge: Cambridge University Press, 1962).

restoration of mutilated Architectural remains." Behind such an innocent program lay some startlingly new ideas. For the real leaders of the Cambridge Movement, almost without exception, were men inspired by the theology of the Oxford Movement with its strong emphasis on the authority of the clergy and the importance of the sacraments. The Cambridge men were also convinced that the Middle Ages represented the height of Christian piety and worship and concluded that medieval church buildings should be reproduced. One of the leaders declared "that the same shell which contained the apparatus of medieval worship was, speaking generally, suited to contain that of modern worship."[13] Now this is little short of incredible if one recalls the pains to which the Anglican reformers had gone in adapting medieval churches for worship according to the *Book of Common Prayer*.

Nevertheless, the Cambridge Movement prevailed. The writings of John Mason Neale, Benjamin Webb, and others appeared in numerous pamphlets and in their periodical, the *Ecclesiologist*. They succeeded in convincing a large segment of the Church of England not only that "GOTHICK IS THE ONLY CHRISTIAN ARCHITECTURE," but that the common arrangement for a late medieval village church was the only acceptable one for Anglicans to use. Their most important rule was that "every church, of whatever kind, size, or shape, should have a distinct Chancel *at least* one-third of the length of the Nave, and separated from the latter, internally at least, if not externally, by a well-defined mark, a chancel arch if possible, or at least by a screen and raised floor."[14] Against the east wall stood the stone altar-table. Westward of this were the stalls for choir and clergy. The Cambridge men fervently advocated a roodscreen for "the separation of the Clergy from the Laity." In the nave appeared a lectern facing the congregation, a pulpit on the other side of the chancel arch, and a font at the western door (Figure 3). It was the entire medieval arrangement reintroduced in complete reversal of the auditory tradition prevalent in the Church of England from the time of Wren. One of the most famous publications of the Cambridge Camden Society was *A Few Words to Churchwardens on Churches and Church Ornaments: No. 1.*

[13]Beresford Hope, "Mr. Hope's Essay on the Present State of Ecclesiological Science in England," *Ecclesiologist* 7 (1847) 87.

[14]Editor's note, *Ecclesiologist* 1 (1842) 45.

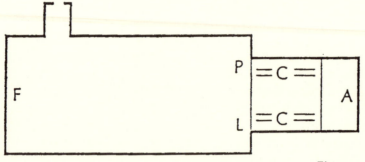

Figure 3

Suited to Country Parishes,[15] surely one of the most influential publications ever on church architecture. It contained the full orthodoxy of the Cambridge Movement, ideas that ever since have dominated a large segment of Protestant church building. The new Coventry cathedral is only the most recent example of the neo-medieval arrangement advocated by the Cambridge Camden Society in the 1840s. One only needs to note that in the 1940s an influential book by an American Methodist advocated the same arrangement to see what a wide circulation these ideas have had.[16]

One can sympathize with the Cambridge men in their distaste for the barrenness of churches of their time, particularly those built in one of the classical styles. It is so easily forgotten that most of the furnishings and decorations of Anglican churches today were absent in Anglican churches in the 1840s. The introduction of such items as crosses on bookmarks or candles and crosses on altar-tables could and did cause riots. The Cambridge men boldly championed the introduction of an immense variety of furnishings and decorations copied from medieval patterns.

One of the unfortunate consequences of the Cambridge Movement was the wholesale adoption of elements of medieval symbolism in arranging and decorating buildings. Thus the roodscreen was justified as signifying the separation of the Church on earth from the Church in heaven. There is a tremendous danger in this type of

[15]First to thirteenth editions Cambridge: Cambridge University Press, 1841 to 1843; fourteenth edition London: Joseph Masters, 1846.

[16]Elbert M. Conover, *The Church Builder* (New York: Interdenominational Bureau of Architecture, 1948).

thought that still plagues church building today. Thinking in symbolic terms can easily obscure functional thought. Far too many churches have adopted items because of a symbolism usually read into them long after their original function had been overlooked. Candles were introduced into churches for the same reason as electric lights and were not commonly placed on the altar-table until about the twelfth century. Even then the number of candles varied according to need and finances, but two candles have become almost orthodoxy today. Thinking in functional terms often takes one back to earlier traditions than symbolic thought, which usually represents a later development.

Another basic mistake of the Cambridge Movement was the belief that medieval buildings were suitable for Anglican worship. The whole tradition of Anglican church building since the Reformation had stressed the unity of clergy and laity in offering their worship in such a manner that all was visible and audible. The return to the medieval double rectangle of chancel and nave was a reversal of almost two hundred years of Anglican church building. A very pronounced clericalism is seen in the publications of the Cambridge Movement. It was constantly reiterated that the clergy should sit in the chancel and the laity in the nave "exhibiting, what is so wholesome for both to remember, the distinction which must exist between the Clergy and their flocks."[17] Such concepts are far removed from the tendency we see increasing in our times of stressing the positive priesthood of all the faithful. Clericalism is derived from a defective doctrine of the Church that tends to equate the Church with the clergy and to assume that the laity are passive in worship. The neo-medieval arrangement of chancel and nave advocated in the Cambridge Movement seems as foreign to the Spirit of the *Book of Common Prayer* as it does to that of the early Church.

A further difficulty arose for which the Cambridge men were not directly responsible. Although at the beginning of the Victorian era churches had small choirs in western galleries, the modern choir dressed in robes and sitting in chancels was not found in parish churches. Such choirs were found in cathedrals where the choir and clergy composed the entire congregation on most occasions. Thus the cathedral service could be both fully choral and congregational. In 1841 Walter Farquhar Hook took the advice of his friend John Jebb

17"On Sedilia and Altar Chairs," *Ecclesiologist* 2 (1843) 91.

and introduced the cathedral form of choral service into his new church in Leeds, placing a choir of laymen in the chancel.[18] This was a radical step in a parish church since it confused the functions of a cathedral and its residential choir with those of a parish church and its congregation. The choir, which was usually the entire congregation in the cathedral and collegiate church, now became an addition to the congregation in the parish church. The consequences are apparent today in many churches: the choir often monopolizes worship almost as much as it would were no other congregation present. The chancels the Cambridge Movement provided became the natural location for such choirs and ever since they remain physically (if not symbolically) between the congregation and the altar-table.

A further consequence of the Cambridge Movement is the idea that there was only one proper form for a church building, the neo-medieval arrangement with chancel and nave. The publications of the group hammered home the idea that there was such a thing as "correctness" in church building, and experimentation was unnecessary and dangerous. We have seen how many experiments had been conducted to find good liturgical arrangements for Anglican worship before the Cambridge Movement. Since that time a single pattern has dominated the Anglican communion for over a hundred years. The concept of correctness has led to sterility in church architecture and the discouragement of attempts to break the current stalemate.

The gothic churches built under the influence of the Cambridge Camden Society were usually splendidly decorated. They used abundant stained glass, colored floor tiles, wall paintings, and carved woodwork. This was natural since the leaders of the Movement thought of worship largely in terms of individual response. It was not strange that they should place such importance on the emotive factors of the buildings, for providing an atmosphere was a means of cultivating the aura of awe and mystery that they associated with worship. By contemporary standards their concept of worship seems too subjective and individualistic.

The ideas of the Cambridge Movement were effectively promoted in this country by the New York Ecclesiological Society founded in

---

[18]Cf. John Jebb, *The Choral Service of the United Church of England and Ireland: Being an Enquiry Into the Liturgical System of the Cathedral and Collegiate Foundations of the Anglican Communion* (London: John H. Parker, 1843).

1848. The first real landmark was Trinity Church, New York City, finished two years earlier by the architect Richard Upjohn.[19] This building had a deep chancel with a prominent altar. Evidently the depth of the chancel and the cross atop the spire were opposed by the building committee but the architect championed ideas similar to those of the Cambridge men. Its completion, coming only ten years after Bishop Hopkins's book on gothic architecture, shows the rapid changes under way (which Hopkins readily accepted). Trinity has a chancel two bays deep, containing the altar-table with reredos and choir stalls, and immediately beyond are a lectern and pulpit facing the nave.

Such forms became increasingly prevalent in Episcopal churches in nineteenth-century America though not in all. In the years ahead the popularity of gothic was often eclipsed by other styles. Other arrangements appeared too. Trinity Episcopal Church in Boston, consecrated in 1877, was of Romanesque architecture, though planned as no Romanesque church had ever been. Trinity, the church of Phillips Brooks, was designed with the requirements of preaching in mind. A cruciform building, it has galleries in the transepts and accommodates many people close to the preacher. Evidently the chancel was something of an embarrassment for as first designed (by H. H. Richardson) it contained a small altar-table in table form, a D-shaped rail around it, the baptismal font, pulpit and lectern. This arrangement was changed considerably in 1902 and 1938.

The real triumph of the neo-medieval arrangement in Protestant churches dates from what might be called the "second gothic revival." Without much doubt the leading figure in this movement was Ralph Adams Cram (1863–1942).[20] Cram and his associates built a number of churches for most of the major Protestant denominations. An Anglo-Catholic himself, Cram had some reservations about using gothic for Protestants but eventually consented to do so. He emphatically believed that gothic was the style that best expressed the worship of Catholicism. He was scarcely less emphatic in championing the medieval arrangement of the building. "I need hardly say that the chancel and sanctuary are not only the most sacred portions of a

[19]Cf. Everard M. Upjohn, *Richard Upjohn: Architect and Churchman* (New York: Columbia University Press, 1939) 47–67.

[20]Cf. *A Miscellany of American Christianity*, 371–381.

building consecrated to the service of God, but also almost *the* church, the nave being but an adjunct of more or less size provided for the shelter and convenience of worshippers."[21] With Cram's powerful influence gothic churches with large chancels and the full neo-medieval arrangement became popular among Presbyterians, Congregationalists, Methodists, and Unitarians. Frequently the language was Georgian but the arrangement continued to be medieval. No one seemed troubled by the anomaly of a chancel on a Georgian building built in the twentieth century. The romantic influence of the magnificent Episcopal cathedrals begun early in this century and the great gothic university chapels erected in the 1920s was felt in Protestant churches all over the land. Every big congregation tried to build a cathedral.

Perhaps even more important than the actual arrangement of these buildings was the subjective concept of worship that informed them. As Cram put it, an important aspect of church architecture is

"the creation of spiritual emotion through the ministry of all possible beauty of environment; the using of art to lift men's minds from secular things to spiritual, that their souls may be brought into harmony with God. . . . Not in the barren and ugly meeting-house of the Puritans . . . were men most easily lifted out of themselves into spiritual communion with God . . . but where they were surrounded by the dim shadows of mysterious aisles . . . where was always . . . the still atmosphere of prayer and praise."[22]

Rapturous language this is indeed, but it is redolent of the same type of individualism one finds in the revivalism Cram abhorred. Cram's effort to provide all manner of means to help people escape "out of themselves" follows the same subjective concept of worship as one finds in the earlier gothic revival. A modern liturgical scholar criticizes such buildings:

"Such edification as it communicates is always individualistic, rarely corporate. For it does not aim to call attention to the action of the liturgy—indeed, it frequently obscures or obstructs the action—but

[21]Ralph Adams Cram, *Church Building: A Study of the Principles of Architecture in Their Relation to the Church* (3rd ed. Boston: Marshall Jones Company, 1924) 89.
[22]Ibid., 8.

rather to stimulate the contemplation of personal prayer by evocative symbols that surround and adorn, but do not necessarily inhere in the action of the liturgy."[23]

Such subjectivism was a common characteristic of both Romanticism and revivalism. Among many twentieth-century Protestants it was expressed as a kind of estheticism. One might be too sophisticated to relish the outward emotionalism of revivalism, but the same stimulation of the feelings might be secured with a "dim religious light" and all the adornments of gothic architecture. In the twentieth century we have seen a great adoption of the neo-medieval arrangement, now referred to as the "divided chancel" among Protestants of every denomination. Very frequently it was couched in gothic terms; otherwise it was likely to appear wearing Georgian clothes. Since World War II it has worn contemporary dress. In any case it is still an arrangement designed primarily for worship by medieval people who were mainly illiterate and could not or would not join in worship with the clergy.

Von Ogden Vogt and others helped domesticate the gothic revival among Protestants. Vogt, a Unitarian, found "the intimations of Gothic building, then, are not chiefly intellectual . . . but emotional and mystical."[24] Removed from their association with Catholicism, gothic buildings and all their ornaments were eagerly built by Protestants before World War II put an end to most building activities.

The gothic style itself was a casualty of the war and the rising building costs thereafter, but the same divided chancel arrangement has remained as one of the two standard Protestant arrangements of our time whether built in pseudo-Georgian or in contemporary idiom. Some indication of how standardized this arrangement has become can be seen in *The Church Builder*, published in 1948 by Elbert M. Conover, director of the Interdenominational Bureau of Architecture. The illustrations alternate between neo-gothic and neo-Georgian, Conover having little patience with "modern." On successive pages appear Congregational, Methodist, Presbyterian,

[23]Massey H. Shepherd, Jr., *The Reform of Liturgical Worship: Perspectives and Prospects* (New York: Oxford University Press, 1961) 25.

[24]Von Ogden Vogt, *Art & Religion* (New Haven: Yale University Press, 1921) 189. On Vogt see *A Miscellany of American Christianity*, 381–390.

Christian, Lutheran, and Baptist churches each featuring similar divided chancels. No one would have guessed that the Cambridge Movement could have been so successful that its dictums of correctness would be widely imitated by twentieth-century Protestants. It is indeed ironic to read Conover's discussion of a roodscreen, piscina, and sanctuary lamp[25] and then to reflect upon the reaction of sixteenth-century Protestants to these same items.

The Present Dilemma

The contemporary stalemate in Protestant church architecture consists of the uncritical acceptance of two alternate liturgical arrangements as if these were the only possibilities. Actually it is difficult to tell whether the concert-stage or the divided-chancel arrangement has less to recommend itself for Protestant worship. For the purposes of the present discussion style is irrelevant since both arrangements have been tried in every possible style. The drawback to the concert-stage arrangement is the suggestion that the choir sing to the congregation to stimulate its worship or to exhibit their own skill. No one has ever considered the choir an edifying spectacle to look at even during a long sermon, yet this arrangement makes them the dominant visual center of the building. Such an arrangement almost always dwarfs the altar-table and the font or baptistery so that they become insignificant centers buried beneath or behind the pulpit. It also calls excessive attention to the preacher whether he or she is sitting or standing. The same is true of the organist or choir director, although one gets a view of his or her back instead.

The divided chancel has other liabilities. The arrangement of a choir on opposite sides of the chancel makes it difficult for them to sing together. After all, this type was invented for antiphonal singing and chanting. The altar-table's being far removed from the congregation suggests a hierarchical concept of the Church that most Protestants do not acknowledge theologically. The remoteness of an altar-table at the end of a chancel makes the action of holy communion seem like a clerical performance. The acts of worship done at the pulpit and lectern tend to seem quite detached from those at the altar-table despite the unity of the visible word of the sacraments and the preached word.

[25]*The Church Builder*, 60–64.

The underlying difficulty in both arrangements is that neither is suitable for Protestant concepts of the Church as the whole body of faithful people. In either arrangement the congregation is separated from the clergy and choir by an arbitrary distinction that gives the liturgical centers to the clergy and choir and isolates the congregation from them. The implicit hierarchical distinctions of the longitudinal church would be repudiated by many Protestants if they were put into words, but unconsciously these divisions have been readily accepted.

It may indeed be that our churches are mere reflections of the passivity of modern Protestant congregations with their willingness to let clergy and choir perform the work of common worship for them. Most congregations seem content to seek a worshipful feeling and let the emotive factors of the building and the music waft them into some form of personal devotions. But such a subjective and individualistic approach to worship neglects the importance of worship as the common act of the whole Church. The basic difficulty with the concert-stage and the divided chancel arrangements is not simply the practical problems (which would occur to some degree in any type of building) but that they contradict the very nature of the Church itself. These arrangements impede the people's realization of the Church as the body of Christ and thus interfere with worship, evangelism, and all other aspects of the Church's life.

21. Theology and Architecture in America: A Study of Three Leaders

This chapter was written for *A Miscellany of American Christianity: Essays in Honor of H. Shelton Smith* (Durham: Duke University Press, 1963) and is used by permission.

The architectural movement known as the Gothic Revival can now safely be called a matter of the past, but it cannot be said that all of the ideas of its exponents have vanished. It may well be that some of the concepts developed in conjunction with this particular period in the history of taste have found a permanent place in the life and thought of American Christianity.

This essay does not pretend to be a history of the Gothic Revival, but rather an outline of the lives and theological concepts of three important figures whose work in one way or another influenced the course of American church architecture. These men can hardly be called typical or representative, but it would be difficult to deny that the work of John Henry Hopkins, Ralph Adams Cram, and Von Ogden Vogt mark prominent episodes in the history of American church building and worship.

John Henry Hopkins

Bishop John Henry Hopkins (1792–1868), a native of Ireland, came to this country in 1800. Largely self-educated, while still a young man he found a position supervising an ironworks near Pittsburgh. The decline of business after the War of 1812 led him to seek a career as a lawyer. In the midst of a successful practice in Pittsburgh he was asked to play the organ at Trinity Episcopal Church, although he was at the time a Presbyterian. Shortly he became a communicant at Trinity and, in the absence of a rector, the parish persuaded him to accept the vacant position. Ordained by Bishop William White in 1823, Hopkins gave up an income of five thousand dollars, a sum that was three hundred dollars in excess of his future salary as bishop of Vermont.

As he was the only Episcopal minister west of the mountains, Hopkins busied himself organizing seven new parishes and guiding the destiny of his growing parish in Pittsburgh. His versatility was soon tested: there was a demand for a larger building to replace the existing structure—a brick audience room of octagonal shape. His sole architectural training consisted of copying by hand the plates of some of the "works of Britton."[1] According to his son, John Henry Hopkins, Jr., "in this manner he became more thoroughly a master of that noble style [Gothic] than any professional architect who had as yet appeared in America."[2] This preeminence was by default, as very few gothic churches had been built in America at the time. Hopkins put his amateur training to work and designed the new Trinity Church, a building erected in 1823 which seated a thousand people. By later standards, it was a terribly crude effort at gothic. Galleries surrounded three sides of the building, the fourth being occupied by a central pulpit with a prayer desk, altar, and font all directly in front of it and each progressively lower. The slight recess for the pulpit was flanked by two chairs. A "perfectly flat" ceiling was painted in imitation of fan vaulting.[3]

Whatever the defects of this building it was a token of the future, more remarkably so because of its location beyond the Appalachians. Few, if any, professional architects of the time cared to design in gothic, preferring the more popular classical style. Applications for church plans came to Hopkins from various parts of the country, and the demands soon exceeded the time he could expend in answering them. Nor was architecture his only interest: Church music also received his attention, and he began to compose. Before he left Pittsburgh the rector had composed much of the music used at Trinity Church. More or less for recreation he also took up the paint-

[1]Presumably John Britton's series on the *Beauties of England, Architectural Antiquities of Great Britain,* and *Cathedral Antiquities,* well-illustrated volumes that caused quite a publishing sensation in England, 1800–1835.

[2]*The Life of the Late Right Reverend John Henry Hopkins, First Bishop of Vermont, and Seventh Presiding Bishop* (New York, 1873) 71. Cited hereinafter as *Life.*

[3]John Henry Hopkins, *Essay on Gothic Architecture, with Various Plans and Drawings for Churches: Designed Chiefly for the use of the Clergy.* (Burlington, Vt., 1836), Plate VI.

ing of religious scenes. At the same time he began a careful study of patristics, a pursuit he kept up throughout his lifetime.

In 1831 Hopkins left Pittsburgh to become assistant rector at Trinity Episcopal Church, Boston, Massachusetts, and to accept a teaching position in a new theological school in Cambridge. These activities were cut short in 1832 by his election as the first bishop of Vermont, a position he occupied for thirty-six years. During much of this time he was also rector of St. Paul's Church in Burlington.

Though elected with the favor of the Low Church party in Massachusetts, Bishop Hopkins was always somewhat suspect of being a High Churchman. While laying the cornerstone of his church in Pittsburgh he had vindicated "the use of a gorgeous ceremonial in the worship of God."[4] This tendency toward the ceremonial manifested itself in his crusade of thirty years for the wearing of the surplice during the daily offices and sacraments. Hopkins championed the wearing of the surplice because of his conviction that it was the garment used by the priests in the Old Testament and that its use was retained by the Apostles.[5] He found it no more Roman Catholic than the black gowns commonly worn during services by ministers of the Episcopal Church at the time. Vestments were reintroduced much later.

Although he felt it necessary to apologize for such a diversion from his "more strictly spiritual duties," Hopkins in 1836 issued his *Essay on Gothic Architecture*. It was a response to the continuing requests for church plans. In subsequent years a reviewer lauded it for being "the earliest work, (so far as our inquiries extend,) issued from the American Press for the furtherance distinctly of Ecclesiastical Pointed Architecture; and . . . [for] laying down Ecclesiological principles with a clearness and firmness then new among us."[6] There seems to be no reason to doubt the priority of Hopkins' book. The

[4]*Life*, 72.

[5]*The Primitive Church, Compared with the Protestant Episcopal Church, of the Present Day: Being an Examination of the Ordinary Objections Against the Church, in Doctrine, Worship, and Government, Designed for Popular Use; with a Dissertation on Sundry Points of Theology and Practice, Connected with the Subject of Episcopacy, & c.* (2nd ed. Burlington, Vt., 1836) 160.

[6]"Review," *New-York Ecclesiologist* 2 (September 1850) 161. The term "Ecclesiology" is here used (with its original English connotation) in the sense of "the science of the building and decoration of churches." *Oxford Dictionary of the Christian Church*, ed. F. L. Cross (London, 1957) 436.

lithography of the thirteen plates was done by the bishop himself. Avowing the work as that of an amateur, Hopkins concluded:

"Well knowing the want of some plain and simple directory of the kind, I lay it upon the altar of utility with the hope that it may be found acceptable to some of my brethren, and save them from many of those perplexities which commonly attend an attempt to erect the earthly sanctuary of God."[7]

Much of his information on gothic had obviously been gained from the works of John Britton and from Augustus Charles Pugin, author of *Specimens of Gothic Architecture* (1821–1823). Architectural history was still in its infancy. Hopkins found a remarkable affinity between gothic and Solomon's temple and considered the gothic style "the most ancient in the world which has been applied to sacred purposes."[8] Fourteen years later the better informed writers of the *New-York Ecclesiologist* found Hopkins' work

"not now a safe guide. . . . In other words, the *historic* as well as the artistic claims of the Parish Church of England, to be received and acknowledged as the Christian 'Type,' for us Americans at least, was either not perceived or not recognized, and thence the grievous want in our author's plans of *settled* proportions; of *distinct* chancels; of definite ritual arrangements. . . . Now, we doubt not, on most if not all these points, the views of our author, as of all of us, have since that time greatly matured: that we all see many things in a very different light than we did; and are now willing in all these matters to acknowledge a *Law* having reasonable authority over Churchmen, as well as *Principles* of Taste having intrinsic truth and beauty."[9]

The very reasons that in only fourteen years made the *Essay on Gothic Architecture* "not . . . a safe" guide are those that make it most interesting today. Hopkins' thirteen plates illustrate many details taken from genuine medieval examples (via Britton and Pugin) but these details have been used to garnish simple rectangular structures. Chancels do not appear because Hopkins saw no need for them. The

[7]*Gothic Architecture*, 46.
[8]Ibid., 9.
[9]"Review," *New-York Ecclesiologist* 2 (September 1850) 166.

most common liturgical arrangement is typified in a plate representing the "interior of a plain village Church." It is described in these terms:

"Below the pulpit, is seen the desk; on each side of which are the doors of the screen. Below the desk appears the communion table, and at each end of the chancel is a gothic chair. In front is the chancel railing, in the center of which is placed the font for baptism."[10]

A similar arrangement was used in his own church, St. Paul's Episcopal, Burlington, Vermont. In an alternative scheme that appears in Plate VI, "the pulpit and the desk are at each side, and the altar in the middle."[11] Several of the plates locate a vestry where one would expect a chancel.

The chief adornments in these buildings are sentences from Scripture, a decoration beloved of the Puritans. One example includes the letters "IHS" with a cross rising out of the "H." Hopkins hastens to advise us: "Many pious people are afraid of this figure of the cross, because it is used so extensively by the Church of Rome; but this is a weak and unworthy argument for laying aside any thing, which, in itself, possesses an edifying and wholesome character."[12] He had already cautioned against the use of pictures since in the early Church they "led the way to a species of idolatry, at least among the ignorant and superstitious," and he suggested "adorning the walls of Churches only with the appropriate architectural enrichments, and with judicious and edifying selections from the word of God."[13] Hopkins later changed his mind and painted some pictures for churches, but it is noteworthy that in 1836 an Episcopal bishop with a reputation for High Churchmanship could entertain doubt regarding the propriety of a cross as ornament, or consider pictures so used actually dangerous.

Hopkins makes it quite clear that gothic gives "an impression of sublimity more exalted than any other sort of architecture can produce."[14] He prefers dimly lit interiors, suggestive of "solemnity and

10*Gothic Architecture*, 36.
11Ibid., 39.
12Ibid., 36.
13Ibid., 15.
14Ibid., 1.

repose." His attachment to the style seems to have been primarily because of its subjective conditioning on "devotion." He chooses gothic not because of any liturgical requirements, but rather for its effect on individual worshipers. Emotive factors dominate. In short, his preference seems to be based largely on gothic's ability to condition the individual rather than on any role in corporate worship.

In 1838 Hopkins traveled to England. While he was there he went up to Oxford and met John Henry Newman and E. B. Pusey. He also visited Newman's chapel in Littlemore and sketched it carefully, noting the chancel arrangements. Although he found himself in almost complete accord with the theology of the Tractarians he was, in the years and conflicts ahead, to maintain "his sensitive and conscientious determination not to be identified with either party in the Church."[15] Indeed, his faith in the Oxonians was shaken by the secessions to Rome. After Newman embraced Roman Catholicism, Hopkins wrote that "the meaning of the Church must be gathered, not from the *bare letter of her written law* but from *that and her practice together*."[16] On this ground he discouraged the recovery of vestments, altar candles, monastic vows, and other practices associated with the Catholic Revival, though on some of these points he later changed his mind.

By 1840 Hopkins had become certain that "the modern custom of making the pulpit the principal object in the Church, instead of the Altar, is altogether unsupported by any authority in Scripture, in antiquity, or in the Mother Church of England."[17] Meanwhile American interest in gothic architecture was growing steadily. The completion in 1846 of both Trinity Church and Grace Church in New York, almost a generation after Hopkins' first efforts at Pittsburgh, marks the coming of age of the Gothic Revival. There were also many less pretentious structures, such as the Chapel of the Cross, Chapel Hill, North Carolina, that were being erected. The movement was aided and directed by the New York Ecclesiological Society founded in 1848 in conscious imitation of the Ecclesiological Society then flourishing in England. The New York group promulgated explicit laws as to correct church building and campaigned for "the adoption of the old Parish Church of England as our fixed type—with its lengthened

---

[15]*Life*, 198.
[16]Ibid., 271. His son noted: "My Father grew wiser as he grew older" (272).
[17]Ibid., 215. Quoted from the 1840 Convention Journal of his diocese.

Nave and ample Chancel."[18] On several occasions Hopkins was invited to become a patron of the group. "This, however, he thought it wise to decline, though expressing `the most friendly feeling towards its objects and its labors.'"[19] His son was an active member of the company.

Perhaps because of the influence of this society, perhaps for his own reasons, Hopkins in 1851 undertook the rebuilding of St. Paul's Episcopal Church in Burlington. Previously there had been no chancel in the building. Now one was added in accordance with the mandates of "correct" ecclesiology. It was divided into choir and sanctuary by a communion rail and provided with a wooden altar, prothesis, altar chairs, and a pulpit and lectern west of the choir stalls. Purists deplored the fact that the church still had no central aisle and lamented the galleries that remained.[20] But the finished structure was in remarkable conformity to the laws and principles of the New York Ecclesiological Society.

Bishop Hopkins subsequently designed two other stone Gothic churches: St. Thomas' in Brandon, Vermont, and Trinity in Rutland, both of which still stand. He painted tablets and religious scenes for several churches. The University of the South at Sewanee, Tennessee, employed him to make "plans for buildings." By this time Bishop Hopkins was no longer a pioneer. In fact his son reported with condescension: "My Father's means for keeping up with the progress of the revival of Pointed architecture were, however, very slight; and his preference for the four-centre arch remained during his whole life."[21] This was not correct dogma, as his son knew, for "the stronger and purer style of an earlier age" had become the orthodoxy of the New York Ecclesiologists.

Similar traits of heterodoxy appeared in the bishop's rebuilding of St. Paul's Episcopal Church, Burlington, in the last years of his life. In 1866 he provided plans for a new enlargement incorporating transepts. A basilican arrangement of the chancel was introduced into the new cruciform structure. The altar stood on the chord of the apse

[18]"Address," *New-York Ecclesiologist* 2 (May 1850) 135.

[19]*Life*, 269.

[20]"St. Paul's Church, Burlington, Vermont," *New-York Ecclesiologist* 14 (November 1852) 192.

[21]*Life*, 72.

with the bishop's throne and a semicircle of priests' seats behind it. Evidently Hopkins had not become convinced that English medieval arrangements were mandatory, though he liked the more emotive aspects of gothic. "No one," his biographer writes, "was more conscious than its architect of the points in which the building is open to professional criticism," but one wonders whether the more orthodox son might not have been an exception to this statement.[22]

By virtue of seniority of consecration Hopkins became Presiding Bishop of the Episcopal Church in 1865, and his great popularity helped to reconcile Northern and Southern bishops after the Civil War. Nevertheless, Hopkins' publication of *The Law of Ritualism* in 1866 was the cause of considerable consternation among the bishops. The book appeared at a time when some suspected that ritualists were exploiting architecture and the arts in the interest of Roman Catholicism. Bishop Coxe of Western New York was perturbed since he felt it was "'a serious thing, as it opens the door for experiments which are not unlikely to be made in respectable Churches, if not in some of the most important seats of the Church's dignity and strength.'"[23] Today it is difficult to understand the vehemence of the controversy, but by 1866 Ritualism had become a burning issue on both sides of the Atlantic. Hopkins had begun his book with a statement that he would "propose nothing which is not derived from the Bible."[24] Accordingly he affirmed that the Christian Church of the apostles followed the ritual of Moses. His chief concern, a passion with him for thirty years, was the use of the surplice rather than the black gown in preaching. He felt the Ritualists were on a safe legal position in their new practices. *"Personally,"* he remarked, "I prefer the more simple ceremonial to which I have been accustomed all my life, and men can hardly be expected to adopt new tastes and habits at the age of seventy-five."[25] Nevertheless he did try a few experiments himself beyond the use of the surplice. On Christmas day 1866 he wrote his son that he had placed

[22] Ibid., 305.

[23] Ibid., 380.

[24] *The Law of Ritualism, Examined in Its Relation to the Word of God, to the Primitive Church, to the Church of England, and to the Protestant Episcopal Church in the United States* (New York, 1867) 4.

[25] Ibid., 76.

"two lights on the Altar [at St. Paul's]. Quite an advance for Ritualism! But St. Paul's is so dark that I really could not see to read with the wall lamps lighted by gas as usual. Thus I have had a very good *practical* argument for the remedy, which I intend shall be a permanent improvement in the right direction."[26]

The Law of Ritualism concludes with a prediction "that this Ritualism will grow into favor, by degrees, until it becomes the prevailing system."[27]

Actually the Ritualism of which Hopkins spoke would be considered normative Low Church today. In 1867 he went as a delegate to the Lambeth Conference. On this journey, while attending St. Michael's, Brighton, Hopkins "for the first and only time in his life, saw a really high ritualistic service of the Anglican rite."[28] Evidently he approved of it but never had an opportunity to imitate the advanced practices. He died shortly thereafter while on a winter visitation of his diocese in 1868.

Bishop Hopkins' lifetime spanned the period of the introduction of gothic architecture and medieval ceremony in American churches. By the time of his death gothic had become widely accepted among Episcopalians as the correct style for a church. Very explicit regulations had been worked out to create the standard Episcopal church arrangement of the nineteenth century. Characterized by a deep chancel, impressive altar, and separate pulpit and lectern at the west end of the chancel, it has since become common in every part of the country.

Ralph Adams Cram

The budding of the Gothic Revival that appears in Bishop Hopkins' work comes to full flower in the career of Ralph Adams Cram. Born the son of a Unitarian minister in 1863, Cram lived as a child in various New Hampshire parsonages. His formal education never went beyond that provided by Exeter High School, but his father's library opened other doors. It was here he discovered and read "everything that Ruskin had written."[29] Ruskin, Wagner, and William

[26] *Life*, 386.

[27] *Law of Ritualism*, 94.

[28] *Life*, 439.

[29] Ralph Adams Cram, *My Life in Architecture* (Boston, 1936) 9. Cited hereinafter as *My Life*.

Morris were Cram's heroes when he was a young man, though in later years he found Ruskin "quite the most unreliable critic and exponent of architecture that ever lived."[30]

At the age of seventeen Cram sought his fortune in Boston, working at various positions including, for a period, the post of art critic for the *Boston Evening Transcript*. During the 1880s he spent five years working in the office of an architectural firm, his "only professional education." On reflection Cram judged that the time had hardly been propitious for good architecture. He compared his arrival in Boston with "being plunged in the infusion of false principles, horrid methods, and shocking bad taste that marked American architecture and architectural practice in the year 1881."[31] American architecture, he felt, had fallen "to a lower level than history had ever recorded." What had happened was that the earlier Gothic Revival had been swallowed up in a morass of stylistic revivals, especially imitations of H. H. Richardson's Romanesque or Charles F. McKim's Renaissance. The earlier Gothic Revival of Richard Upjohn and James Renwick seemed forgotten.

Cram burned with desire to "get to Europe to see the old work Ruskin had taught me was so supremely good."[32] His wish was granted, and the next few years brought two opportunities to visit Europe. He made a pilgrimage to the sites Ruskin had taught him to revere, particularly Venice. In 1890 Cram established his own architectural firm in Boston in collaboration with Charles Francis Wentworth. The talented Bertram Grosvenor Goodhue soon joined the firm, remaining until 1913. At Wentworth's death in 1899 he was replaced by Frank Ferguson, who died in 1926. Artistic problems were left to Cram and Goodhue; the other partners dealt with engineers and contractors. As Cram expressed it, Ferguson's task "was to keep the buildings Bertram and I designed from falling down."[33]

Far more important for Cram than the buildings he saw in Europe was his conversion. Before his trips overseas he considered himself devoid "of all religious superstitions of every sort." But on his second trip his friendship with Henry Randall, a layman of the Episcopal

[30]Ralph Adams Cram, *The Gothic Quest* (New York, 1907) 149.
[31]*My Life*, 27.
[32]Ibid., 47.
[33]Ibid., 83.

Church, brought a transformation. Cram was persuaded to attend a Christmas Eve Mass in Rome, and of this experience he confessed *"I understood."* On his return to the United States he was baptized in the Church of St. John the Evangelist on Beacon Hill and continued a devout Anglo-Catholic for the remainder of his life. He remained closely associated with the Society of St. John the Evangelist. His partner, Bertram Goodhue, on the other hand, showed "no particular interest" in religious matters.

The thirty or more books that came from Cram's pen show how closely associated his theology and architectural practice became. He was convinced that only a man "in loving sympathy" with Catholicism could build a good church. Catholicism, as he saw it, had been the fountainhead of the best art of the West. Cram took for his motto the phrase: "`Art is a result, not a product.'"[34] As he surveyed the great art of the past he concluded that Catholicism had been the source of all that was great in every art form. Protestantism, on the other hand, brought a deadly blight. It could destroy or imitate, but only Catholicism possessed true "creative force." The ethos of Catholicism was friendly to the arts; that of Protestantism, however, enjoyed no such rapport. Much of this difference was, in Cram's opinion, due to sacramentalism. According to him, "sacramentalism is . . . the essential element, of the very *esse* of Catholic faith and Catholic philosophy."[35] The absence of this principle in Protestantism had caused irreparable harm in the destruction of genuine art and in the creation of an abundance of ugliness.

In order to explain the excellence of art at various periods Cram developed a theory of history. He found that periods of crisis had occurred at intervals of about every five hundred years since the time of Christ. Culture flowered in the intervals between these moments of regression. In everything Cram wrote "mediaevalism" was the greatest of these ages, the one to which modern humanity must return. "Back to mediaevalism we must go, and begin again."[36] No great religious art had developed since the fall of Constantinople. "The civilization of Mediaevalism," he found, "was more nearly perfect than that of Athens, far nobler than that of Rome, and separated

[34]Ibid., 284.
[35]*Gold, Frankincense, and Myrrh* (Boston, 1919) 34.
[36]*The Ministry of Art* (Boston, 1914) 240.

by the entire diameter of being from the repulsive barbarism of the High, or Pagan Renaissance."[37] Cram did much to promote the study of this golden age of mediaevalism. He helped found the Medieval Academy of America, and he persuaded Henry Adams to publish *Mont-Saint-Michel and Chartres*.

As one might expect, the spirit of the Middle Ages found expression in its art, particularly in gothic architecture. Cram was not content simply to recover the forms of this art but felt that "if we would have back the old art (in its essence and its relation to life, not in its forms), we must have back the old life in its unity, in its joyfulness, and in its human scale."[38] One might fairly say that Cram, to borrow Chesterton's phrase, saw the Middle Ages "by moonlight." This romantic glow of the "great thousand years" ended with the fifteenth century, followed by the threefold catastrophe of "Renaissance, Reformation, and Revolution." The Renaissance, to Cram, was nothing more than "a brazen affectation of all the vices and evils of paganism; to express this new spirit in the world recourse was had quite properly to the very forms of pagan art."[39] Renaissance architecture was only "neo-pagan," and though perhaps appropriate for Protestants, completely wrong for any branch of Catholicism. As one might expect, Protestantism appeared to Cram as a culprit of history, being incapable, in his eyes, of producing "vital art of any kind."

Not until the nineteenth century did there seem to be hope of an end to the "artistic dark ages" of Protestantism. The new hope broke out in the Oxford Movement, but its prophet was a Roman Catholic architect, "the immortal Pugin" (Augustus W. N. Pugin), whose ideas Cram's duplicated constantly. The Gothic Revival had flourished in England ever since the Oxford Movement. Its first practitioners, Cram pointed out, "saw at first only archaeological possibilities, . . . copying with scrupulous exactness."[40] But the late nineteenth century had produced such leaders as John Sedding, whose principle was not imitation but "development." Gilbert Scott's Liverpool cathedral was perhaps the best expression of this new approach. America had not

---

[37]*The Gothic Quest*, 40.
[38]*My Life*, 306.
[39]*The Gothic Quest*, 42.
[40]Ibid., 130.

been so fortunate as England in this respect, for the movement had bogged down in eclecticism. By the turn of the century, however, there was hope, and the restoration of gothic was proceeding rapidly. An epoch was ending but Cram wondered "whether the next step is into five centuries of Dark Ages or into a new era of five centuries of a restored Christian commonwealth."[41]

This was the exciting period in which Cram and Wentworth began their architectural practice in 1890. The new "cathedral age" was still in its infancy, the Episcopal cathedral in Albany, New York, having marked the new beginning during the previous decade. Gothic, though used occasionally, had vigorous competitors in the Richardsonian Romanesque and in other styles. There was none of this uncertainty in Cram's mind. In words reminiscent of Pugin he declared: "There is one style, and only one, that we have a right to; and that is Gothic as it was when all art was destroyed at the time of the Reformation."[42] It must be remembered that gothic was far more to Cram than simply a superior architectural style; it was "less a method of construction than . . . a mental attitude, the visualizing of a spiritual impulse."[43] Classical architecture lacked these spiritual qualities; hence it was to be avoided as a "visible expression" of Christianity. He illustrated his creed in his first church, All Saints', Dorchester, Massachusetts—a stone gothic structure—and in many similar buildings that followed. Cram made it quite clear that he had a definite principle in his work:

"The obvious inference was that the thing for me was to take up English Gothic at the point where it was cut off during the reign of Henry VIII and go on from that point, developing the style England had made her own, and along what might be assumed to be logical lines, with due regard to the changing conditions of contemporary culture. This of course meant using English Perpendicular Gothic . . . as the basis of what we hoped to do. As for its development, the course was laid down and the precedent established by John D.

[41]*The Substance of Gothic: Six Lectures on the Development of Architecture from Charlemagne to Henry VIII* (Boston, 1925) 200.

[42]*Church Building, A Study of the Principles of Architecture in Their Relation to the Church* (2nd ed. Boston, 1914) 43.

[43]*The Gothic Quest*, 57.

Sedding, at that time the most vital and inspiring of contemporary English ecclesiastical architects."[44]

The principle of "development," thus conceived, was later modified in some details. As Cram admitted, "I was so anxious to demonstrate the continuity of tradition (theologically as well as artistically) in Christian culture . . . that I tended naturally, at first, to reproduce rather than to recreate."[45] As his work matured, Cram's interest in the different phases of gothic broadened and he showed increased influence from Continental varieties rather than just the sixteenth-century English "of our earliest amatory experience."

The struggle to secure enthusiastic acceptance of Gothic was not an easy one. Few contemporary architects accepted Cram's conviction of the absolute superiority of gothic, and even fewer were persuaded that the Middle Ages had been a better period in culture. The Columbian Exposition of 1893 in Chicago had caught the imagination of the American people with its impressive classical buildings. The École Des Beaux Arts in Paris, where many American architects were trained at the time, vigorously promoted classical architecture. All of this was based on wrong principles, Cram felt, for it ignored the far superior work of the Christian civilization of medieval Europe. It was a conflict between paganism and Christianity, and there was no doubt on which side Cram himself stood.

Hardly less disastrous in Cram's opinion was the "débâcle of contemporary modernistic art." Though all of it was not entirely bad, most of it disgusted him. German churches built in the contemporary fashion before World War II he found revolting. The style might be appropriate for garages and movie theaters, but for Catholic churches it "must absolutely be eschewed." Cram did not live to see widespread use of contemporary architecture by American churches, a development that hardly began until after World War II.

The Church had a particular right and obligation to gothic, Cram felt, because Christian art (which could be only gothic) would serve the Church "as a language and as a mighty missionary influence, winning back the world from heathenism."[46] Christian art was to be

[44]*My Life*, 73.
[45]Ibid., 78.
[46]*The Gothic Quest*, 49.

one of the mighty tools in restoring Christian civilization, and the work of gothic architects was all part—an important part—of beginning a "new Reformation, the second Renaissance, the Restoration."

Cram stressed the subjective elements of gothic: "We must realize that the first desideratum of a church is . . . [that the occupant] shall be filled with the righteous sense of awe and mystery and devotion."[47] But he had very definite ideas about the arrangement of the building. This for Catholics, Anglican or Roman, was to be the neo-medieval arrangement with deep chancel, remote altar, and the various *instrumenta ecclesiastica* of the medieval church. Cram scoffed at Roman Catholic churches built without this design. All of this was necessary for "the Fine Art of religious ceremonial." As might be imagined Cram preferred elaborate ceremonial, the proper settings for which are illustrated in *Church Building*. One cannot escape the impression that much of worship for Cram was largely a subjective matter of individual devotion. This had also been true to a marked degree among the gothicists of the nineteenth century. A modern liturgical scholar criticizes their architecture:

"Such edification as it communicates is always individualistic, rarely corporate. For it does not aim to call attention to the action of the liturgy—indeed it frequently obscures or obstructs the action—but rather to stimulate the contemplation of personal prayer by evocative symbols that surround and adorn, but do not necessarily inhere in the action of the liturgy."[48]

The charges made against those churches that Cram built for Catholic worship could as easily be laid against gothic churches built for Protestants.

There can be no doubt as to the powerful emotive factors involved in Cram's buildings. There is hardly space here to go into a detailed analysis of any particular building. We are concerned, of course, only with his religious work, not with such major landmarks of the later Gothic Revival as buildings at the Military Academy at West Point, Princeton University, and other schools.

[47]Ibid., 101.

[48]Massey Hamilton Shepherd, Jr., *The Reform of Liturgical Worship: Perspectives and Prospects* (New York, 1961) 25.

Some of the outstanding examples of the later Gothic Revival are the great school and university chapels erected in the 1920s and 1930s. Cram designed one of the largest for Princeton (1928), as well as school chapels for St. George's School (1928) and Mercersburg Academy (1926), and worked with Goodhue on the chapel at West Point (1910). Other universities soon raised magnificent gothic chapels under the direction of different architects, Duke (Trumbauer, 1932) and Chicago (Goodhue, 1928) being the most remarkable.

The same period saw the full flower of the cathedral movement. For Roman Catholics this had begun early in the nineteenth century. Among Episcopalians the work of the New York Ecclesiological Society finally bore fruit in the last decades of the nineteenth century. Albany was begun in the 1880s but finished much later. More ambitious projects were soon under way in New York, Washington, and San Francisco, with smaller buildings projected in Cleveland, Detroit, Baltimore, Spokane, and many other cities. The Cathedral of St. John the Divine in New York was begun by Heins and LaFarge in a Byzantine-Romanesque style; Cram was appealed to in 1911. He rebuilt a portion of the apse, added one chapel and the baptistery, and constructed the largest nave in the world in a manner reminiscent of French Gothic yet with many original features. Cram designed the Episcopal cathedral in Detroit himself. He was also briefly involved in the design of the Swedenborgian cathedral in Bryn Athyn, Pennsylvania, perhaps the most exquisite product of the twentieth-century Gothic Revival.

Cram shuddered at the suggestion that the National Cathedral might be built in Renaissance or French Gothic. The former was a threat to the Church for Cram insisted on "the necessity of preserving the continuity of architectural idea, in order that we may adequately show forth the perfect continuity of the Church."[49] In this case French Gothic was forbidden "from ethnic and historic reasons." After all, the Episcopal Church was English in its succession and traditions. Fortunately both Renaissance and French Gothic were rejected in favor of fourteenth-century gothic, the style in which the National Cathedral was eventually built. Cram announced with pleasure that two of the architects who took over this work, Robb and Little, "had been largely educated in our offices, while Frohman had previously

[49]*Church Building*, 207.

declared himself as a follower of our leading."[50] The three most ambitious structures begun in the cathedral movement, New York, Washington, and San Francisco, remain [1963] unfinished. Whether this is a sign that the cathedral movement has vanished like a romantic dream, that gothic is no longer considered appropriate, or simply the consequence of the income tax is an open question.

Far more important in many respects were the numerous parish churches Cram and his partners built all over America. St. Thomas' in New York and Calvary in Pittsburgh are perhaps the best known, but they had many companions. Most interesting of all was the demand of such denominations as the Congregationalist, Presbyterian, Baptist, and Methodist for gothic of the same quality as that represented by Cram's work.

Cram's comments on this new development are interesting. Concerning the beginning of his career, he wrote:

"We began to experiment in Colonial work, both for Protestant churches and for schools. . . . We held, or I did then, that there was something incongruous in using Catholic Gothic to express the ethos of that Protestantism which has revolted against all things Catholic and had done its best to destroy its architectural and other artistic manifestations, so we did our best to induce our `Nonconformist' clients to let us do Colonial structures for them."[51]

Without any doubt he was sincerely convinced that while Georgian might be adequate for a Congregational church, medieval art was altogether inappropriate. But it was another matter to convince clients of this:

"Protestant congregations declined pretty generally to admit our Colonial premises, and increasingly demanded good Catholic art, refusing to accept any substitute, so we had very promptly to abandon our original position and do just as good Gothic as we possibly could for Presbyterians, Congregationalists, Baptists and even Unitarians."[52]

[50]Ibid., 96.
[51]Ibid., 96.
[52]Ibid., 96–97.

The result was that Cram decided that even here art might have a missionary force as it had in the spread of Catholicism among pagans in medieval Europe. He concluded that his firm was justified in "being as Gothic (and as Catholic) as we liked" even when building for Protestants. Numerous other firms soon began building gothic churches for Protestant clients, frequently with full medieval arrangements.

Throughout the 1920s and 1930s Cram observed with increasing delight the progress of the gothic movement. Strangely enough the Roman Catholic Church, though certainly as Catholic as Cram desired, stood "chained hand and foot by utter artistic depravity, ignorance, and self-satisfaction."[53] Its barbarism was matched only by that of the Baptists and the Methodists. Even these benighted groups began eventually to improve. In the 1900 edition of *Church Building* Cram confessed that he saw little good gothic architecture outside of the Episcopal Church. In ten years' time he discovered that Congregationalists and Unitarians "were beginning, quite clearly, to see the light." And before another decade had passed he found that "Roman Catholics and Presbyterians . . . demanded, and obtained, the best architecture and the best arts of every kind."[54] Soon Methodists and Baptists were repenting of their ugliness. Cram was delighted that his East Liberty Presbyterian Church in Pittsburgh "could be prepared for a pontifical High Mass" in a few minutes simply by adding a crucifix and six candles. There was sweet satisfaction in this: "It would have surprised and even horrified Doctors Calvin and Knox in their day, but we are permitted to believe they are better informed now!"[55]

It is possible to overestimate the role of Ralph Adams Cram as a writer and architect in bringing Protestants to a deeper desire for beauty in their churches. The 1920s in this country were a period of developing sophistication and prosperity with correspondingly greater support of secular art as well as religious. But one cannot deny that Cram's contribution was large. He wrote in 1936: "Fifty years ago none of this beauty would have been imaginable in any branch of Protestantism."[56] Certainly a major reorientation had oc-

[53]*Church Building*, 269.
[54]*My Life*, 133.
[55]Ibid., 255.
[56]Ibid., 256.

curred in the half century of his architectural career. With Cram's death in 1942 and the wartime cessation of church building the Gothic Revival came to an end, but the demand for good art and architecture on the part of all sections of American Christianity has continued.

Von Ogden Vogt

Von Ogden Vogt, the third leader here considered, links the Gothic Revival to the present day. [He died in 1964.] At first glance his work seems less directly involved in the Gothic Revival, but his writings combine both an advocacy of historic architecture and an attempt to develop a theology relevant to the concerns of modern people. His earlier writings exhibit the Gothic Revival becoming domesticated among liberal Protestants; his later writings reflect the subsequent rejection of gothic and the search for a contemporary style with few historic roots.

Vogt, who is now [1963] living in retirement in Florida, was born in 1879. Most of his lifetime was spent in the Midwest, though after graduating from Beloit College Vogt attended Yale, where he earned a Master of Arts and also a Bachelor of Divinity degree. He spent five years in Connecticut as minister of a Congregational church and then went to Chicago to become pastor of the Wellington Avenue Congregational Church. After nine years at Wellington Avenue he was invited to become pastor of the First Unitarian Church, Chicago. As pastor of this congregation he was responsible for building the magnificent gothic structure on the edge of the campus of the University of Chicago. During his pastorate there (1925-1944) Vogt was intimately associated with Chicago Theological Seminary as lecturer in liturgics and in Christian art and architecture.

In examining Vogt's work it is well to note his place in the development of Protestant worship and theology. The 1920s were a period of a great deal of church building. Hundreds of congregations erected impressive gothic or Georgian buildings. In these dignified structures spontaneous prayers and unstructured services seemed out of place. Numerous books appeared giving the needed instruction in worship. Naturally, few Protestants could accept the Catholic forms of worship Cram advocated. Much of the new Protestant literature on worship was avowedly liberal in its forms as well as in its theology. One of the products of this interest was the psychological approach to worship, a field explored by such individuals as George A. Coe. Henry Sloan Coffin remarked of this school: "Most of the psychologists were pragmatists in philosophy, and regarded worship as a means of achieving results in those who worshipped."[57] Naturally others sought to redress this utilitarian tendency and Dean Willard L. Sperry of Harvard Divinity school published his *Reality in Worship: A Study of Public Worship and Private Religion*.[58] This work together with Vogt's *Art & Religion* (1921) and *Modern Worship* (1927) have had as much influence on Protestant worship as anything published between 1900 and 1945. The ideas of both books remain current today [1963]. Indeed it would be quite difficult to understand the contemporary situation in the worship of American Protestantism without a knowledge of these works. For present purposes, however, we will limit our attention to Vogt's writings.

Vogt's *Art & Religion* was first published in 1921. Subsequent reprintings in 1929, 1948, and 1960 attest to the continuing popularity of the book. It was followed by *Modern Worship* in 1927, a work both theological and practical. The more theoretical *Cult and Culture*, which appeared in 1952, attempted to find a unifying factor in culture. Vogt's most recent book, *The Primacy of Worship* (1958) opposes worship to dogmatism.

Without exception Vogt's writings contain a vigorous polemic for liberal theology. On page after page one discovers the hallmark of liberalism, especially in the continuing effort to make religion relevant to modern people. Consequently there is a rejection of any form of ecclesiastical or theological authority. "We cannot enter the new age," he writes, "until the old churches give up their concepts of an authoritative faith 'once delivered to the saints' and freely accept the spirit of modernism."[59] Vogt's outlook on human nature is optimistic, the natural person being in his opinion "great in capacity and in natural endowments." Moreover, Vogt believes that "Jesus was so

[57]"Public Worship," *The Church Through Half a Century: Essays in Honor of William Adams Brown*, ed. Samuel McCrea Cavert and Henry Pitney Van Dusen (New York, 1936) 191.

[58]New York, 1925. Sperry had not read Vogt's *Art & Religion* before writing this book.

[59]*Art & Religion* (New Haven, 1921) 3. Unless otherwise noted, references are to this edition.

wholly absorbed in his great task of the imitation of God and sonship to God by loving ministry that he put nothing higher. . . . This is the highest conception he held of himself and the highest conception that may be held about him."[60]

For Vogt, this belief implies the end of dogmatism. *The Primacy of Worship* contains a vehement chapter on "The Damages of Dogmatism" which Vogt considers guilty of obscurantism, aggression, and duplicity, and repugnant alike to genuine education and to devoted seekers. He concludes that "the way out is to abandon creedalism altogether and undertake the practice of immediate religious experience and action."[61] Theology, Vogt argues, has usurped the place of experience. "The essence of religion," as he sees it, "is a form or pattern of religious experience and action rather than a specific content of ideas and usages."[62] From first to last he has contended that "the primary effort of all religion is communion with the Final Powers."[63]

With religion so interpreted it is not strange that worship is much more important to Vogt than theology. Worship for Vogt becomes the inclusive category. *Modern Worship* begins with the statement: "For the sake of simplicity and clearness I am proposing abruptly to consider worship as the celebration of life."[64] Some idea as to how inclusive the element of celebration (with its overtones of Schleiermacher) becomes is seen in a subsequent statement: "Religion celebrates nothing less than the whole of man's existence and all his faiths about its source, nature, duties, and destiny."[65] Worship is primarily celebration, but Vogt hesitates to try to analyze too precisely the events or ideas it celebrates. Being very sensitive to the modern person's difficulty in seeking religious belief, he is most reluctant to confuse the "celebration of life" with any specific theological definitions about "the Object of our devotions."

It is not surprising, then, that Vogt advocates the use of modern materials in worship, even a "substitute scripture reading taken

[60]*Primacy of Worship* (Boston, 1958) 144.

[61]Ibid., 69.

[62]*Cult and Culture: A Study of Religion and American Culture* (New York, 1951) 223.

[63]*Art & Religion* (Boston, 1960), 245.

[64](New Haven, 1927) 3.

[65]Ibid., 12.

from modern sources." The deliberate attempt to make worship relevant to modern life in all its complexities is an outgrowth of his concepts. This appears most strikingly in the series of vocational services Vogt conducted at the First Unitarian Church, Chicago, during the course of his ministry there. Typical examples include services in honor of teachers, bakers, railroaders, and lawyers. The various orders of worship composed by Vogt featured symbols of the trades or professions involved, a Psalm of Labor, and addresses concerning the group honored.

At the same time, Vogt made constant use of historic materials. He found that it was desirable for ministers to select "from the materials of the past those treasures which are least burdened with abandoned concepts."[66] It is noteworthy that the chapter in *Art & Religion* concerning "The Order of the Liturgy" is closer than one might expect to the traditional sequence of Christian worship. The single "Order of Worship" appended to the first edition includes an Introit, a Prayer of Confession, an Anthem of Praise, a Scripture Reading, a Confession of Faith, and a Sermon, as well as hymns and prayers. In Vogt's terms the normal pattern of worship includes "Vision, Humility, Exaltation, Illumination, Dedication."[67] Of course many of these elements have undergone a metamorphosis, particularly the confessions of faith. These vary from service to service, sometimes making no mention of God though stressing a belief "in man, and the worth of all persons."

One sees in Vogt's services and in the patterns he advocated in *Art & Religion* an openness to historic materials but a determination to avoid anything offensive to moderns. In the 1948 edition of *Art & Religion* he mentioned that "some of the best new liturgical composition is now being done by the more radical bodies, including several so-called humanist churches."[68] These were not the only ones to share Vogt's ideas. Similar principles soon pervaded the worship of the Methodist Church and many of the larger Protestant bodies that had no fixed liturgical forms.

Perhaps even more influential were Vogt's ideas concerning the architectural setting of worship as advocated in *Art & Religion*. Indeed,

[66]*Modern Worship*, 39.
[67]*Art & Religion*, 152.
[68](Rev. ed. Boston, 1948) viii.

no other American book on these subjects rivals this volume in importance. The first edition was introduced with a declaration that "beauty is desirable and good" and that "the religion of Protestantism stands profoundly in need of realizing it."[69] Chapter 3, on "The Unity of Religion and Art," points out the similarities between "the experience of Beauty" and "the experience of religion in its essential assumptions or demands in the realms of thinking, feeling, and willing."[70] The two were united by "Origin, Subject Matter, and Inner Experience." A further common element was the desire for "a composition that will harmonize all things." As Vogt saw it, art had a need for religion "to universalize its background of concepts" and to improve its "moral content." Religion, on the other hand, needed art in order "to be impressive, to get a hearing." As he expressed it: "The assistance of various arts can be brought to bear upon the worshiper in church in such a way as to help him to be reverent and to display to him the larger cause of religion over against which his own life may be seen to be unsatisfactory."[71]

With such hospitality to the arts it is interesting to see the forms art took under Vogt's direction. One of the conditions for his call to the pastorate of the First Unitarian Church of Chicago, several years after the first publication of *Art & Religion*, was that he undertake the erection of a new building. The result was the present impressive edifice, a masonry structure of gothic design. The building was the gift of Morton Denison Hull. Denison B. Hull was the architect and shared with Vogt the determination of the iconography. It remains an excellent example of the very best of the later Gothic Revival buildings erected by Protestants.

In his writings of the 1920s Vogt indicates the features of gothic he found attractive. His interesting article on "The Art of Ralph Adams Cram" raises questions as to how the Gothic Revival could be justified in twentieth-century America. Vogt attempted to answer his questions: "I venture to suggest three lines of consideration along which lie the justifications of this movement: the cultural contribution of Gothic, the plasticity of work on the Gothic base, and the

[69]Page ix.
[70]Ibid., 23.
[71]Ibid., 53.

intimation of new catholicity in Mr. Cram's own most recent work."[72] In 1929 he was more outspoken:

"Work in the Gothic mode has become predominant. It has two important justifications. As a people, we are aware of our inheritance from the Greco-Roman world through the classical character of the most of our civil buildings. But we have not yet so appropriated our proper share in the thousand years of western culture from the fall of Rome to the Italian Renaissance. Gothic buildings enable us to incorporate this also. The other reason is that a Gothic structure emphasizes primarily religion itself rather than ideas about it or ethics that flow from it. There is ample evidence in the most recent developments of the pictorial and plastic arts in churches, that they may intimate new theologies and new ethics caught up into and enlivened by the abiding psychological forms of the religious experience realized in a great building of the Gothic lineage."[73]

As originally written *Art & Religion* had expressed some reservations about the adaptability of gothic design. The use of gothic by those churches that refused to "revive also at least some important elements of mediaeval worship" Vogt considered unfortunate, and on the other hand he saw that gothic suffered from its too close association with the Episcopal Church, a "sectarian lineage . . . inadequate for the new age."[74] If these faults could be overcome gothic would be most appropriate; otherwise Colonial would be more suitable. The buildings that illustrate the early editions of *Art & Religion* are both gothic and Colonial. At the same time Vogt looks forward to the development of a "new architecture."

One of the most interesting developments of the later Gothic Revival in the various Protestant churches was the conscious attempt to use a historic style and yet to make it relevant to the conditions of modern life. In Vogt's church in Chicago a row of symbols around the nave represents various occupations in industry, commerce, and agriculture. Representations of nature, the state, and the Church appear about the chancel. The various emblems representing "man's

[72]Originally published in *Arts and Decoration*, June 1926. Quotation from typescript copy furnished by Vogt.

[73]*Art & Religion* (New Haven, 1929) x–xi.

[74]Page 200 (1921).

vocations are to teach the ethics of productivity, the mutuality of human toil, the social point of view for every man's labor, and to recognize the social worth of every man's daily work."[75] Vogt felt that such recognition was doubly needed in an age of mass production in industry.

Despite the introduction of novel subjects into religious symbolism Vogt pointed out that "culture is a continuum" and that the churches must guard against being "cut adrift from the inestimable treasures of devotion that are our Christian inheritance."[76] One sees in a large number of churches built during the 1920s and 1930s a deliberate effort to develop a symbolism that was relevant to modern people and yet reflected "our Christian inheritance." At the University of Chicago Chapel (1928), the traditional Christian saints were joined by symbolic figures representing the artist, philosopher, statesman, scientist, merchant, craftsman, and others. A Committee on Iconography at Riverside Church (1930) carried this concept of vocation even farther in sculpture and stained glass. Chancel screen, portals, and windows unite Charles Darwin, Albert Einstein, Matthew Arnold, John Ruskin, Booker T. Washington, and countless others whose influence on modern life has been great. They are accompanied by biblical figures, Greek philosophers, and figures as varied as Mohammed, St. Thomas Aquinas, and John Calvin. Less impressive buildings introduced equally varied figures, particularly those representing different occupations. It was a gesture at once appreciative of the past and eager to relate the life of the Church to contemporary people.

It might seem that a medieval style such as gothic would appear totally irrelevant to twentieth-century American Protestantism, but this was not the case. Indeed, Vogt's favor for the medieval arrangement with full chancel was apparent in 1927 when he wrote: "The possibilities of helpful worship are much increased by the adoption of the traditional chancel plan of building, where also the choir can be disposed about the altar."[77] His fondness for the chancel rests as much on its success in creating "an atmosphere of worship" as on its liturgical function. The neo-medieval or divided chancel arrangement has since become the most common one in many large denominations.

[75]Ibid., ix (1948).
[76]Ibid., 127 (1921).
[77]*Modern Worship*, 116.

A major reason for the appeal of Gothic seemed to be its emotive powers. Gothic attracted Vogt because of its subjective elements much more than its operation in the actions of liturgy. Vogt cherished gothic for its mystical intimations that, he felt, elevated unchanging processes of worship above less stable structures of belief. He wrote: "The intimations of Gothic building, then, are not chiefly intellectual . . . but emotional and mystical. . . . The high vaulted aisles . . . lead the imagination to find some communion with the infinite unknown."[78] Such interpretations of gothic made it acceptable to Protestants of every denomination.

The domestication of gothic architecture among Protestants occasioned some harsh criticisms. Cram, the acknowledged high priest of the later Gothic Revival, wrote Vogt a long letter after reading *Art & Religion*. He found much to praise in the book, but Cram could not help reflecting on a basic difference between his theology and Vogt's:

"What you are trying to do, I think, is just this, i.e. get back all the richness and beauty and symbolic content of a Gothic church with nothing of the informing force that made it live. That is to say, you would get back the richness of ceremonial, the opulence of the old liturgies and the poignant devotions but without the very things they were developed to expound, express and enforce, i.e. the Real Presence of God in the Blessed Sacrament, the Sacrifice of the Mass and the intercession and communion of saints with the Mother of God as chiefest of these, and veritably, Queen of Heaven. . . . A book like yours will do . . . good, and every step along the way you have indicated is so much clear gain, but the end is the Catholic Faith, not the plenitude of Catholic worship without the Faith."[79]

Here are two distinct theological positions. For Cram "Catholic plenitude" includes particular beliefs; for Vogt it simply means full devotion to the ultimate reality, however defined. Architecturally, though, both parties sponsored buildings remarkably similar.

Cram and the Gothic Revival both died in the 1940s. Vogt had long ago predicted the advent of a "new architecture." In the 1920s he felt it would be connected with the past but would be "freshly saying

---

[78] *Art & Religion*, 189.
[79] Letter from R. A. Cram to Von Ogden Vogt from Seville, April 3, 1922.

what we newly experience and feel about life."[80] In 1948 Vogt noticed that the central pulpit had become almost a thing of the past in new churches. The illustrations of the 1948 edition of *Art & Religion* recognize the new architecture with several examples. Full recognition of the modern movement in architecture appears in the long Epilogue added to the 1960 edition of *Art & Religion*. Vogt finds himself inclined to agree with the current criticism of the "recent revival period" but points out in its defense that "it came before the means of new design were available; it rescued us from the dreadful chaos which just preceded it; and it affords us a visible connection with the best of the past not otherwise realized."[81] Nevertheless he enthusiastically accepts the modern movement, listing some outstanding examples and illustrating others.

Though the Gothic Revival may be a thing of the past, much more of it lives on in contemporary [1963] Christianity than may be apparent at first glance. With few exceptions most contemporary churches have adopted the neo-medieval arrangement of the chancel containing altar and choir stalls, divided from the nave where the congregation worships.

Much more significant is the persistent tendency to evaluate buildings on a subjective basis whatever the style. This is reflected in the constant concern for emotive effect, so frequently referred to as creating a "worshipful atmosphere." Worship, in this sense, is largely an individualistic and subjective matter conducted within the privacy of one's soul. Unfortunately this viewpoint often overlooks the more fundamental actions of the Christian community in common worship.

The Gothic Revival is a thing of the past, and yet the same subjective approach to church architecture it expressed so successfully is very much present. Only the future can tell how permanently established this attitude will be.

[80] *Art & Religion*, 201.
[81] Page 243.

IV. Pastoral

22. How to Eat

This bright reflection of happy family life appeared in *Liturgy* 22 (May 1977) and is used by permission.

I know of no more common act of blasphemy than a family keeping television on during dinner time. Apparently this is a frequent occurrence in American homes today. It indicates that we have forgotten how to eat.

Liturgists have worried for years about how to get a parish to understand itself as a community and especially how to make the Eucharist a communal meal. Perhaps we have begun at the wrong end. If we don't understand how to eat together as a family, that small ecclesial community, how can we possibly comprehend what it means to eat together as a congregation, that larger ecclesial community? Each family is a congregation in miniature. If we can't share a meal at home how can we possibly do it in church?

The basic problem seems to be that many families simply have become insensitive to what a family meal is and in the process have forgotten what it means to be a family. I would like to share in a simple and personal way how our family eats so that others may learn what a precious event a family meal can be.

How do we eat? The obvious so easily eludes us, but the first thing a family must realize is that mealtime is important. After all, we can always find time to do those things we really believe are significant. A family meal happens only when we place high priority on it and commit to it our most precious and limited resource—time. Why is the meal important? It is important because this is when the family happens if it ever happens at all. Every meal shared with others is a social occasion, but with those whom we love it is also a sacred occasion. When we eat together we are both making visible the love that is the key to family life and building up that love. This is why it is necessary deliberately to provide daily occasions for the family to happen. This is far too important to leave to chance, but I'm afraid that is what occurs in many American families today. All agree that love is good but without the daily rhythm of eating together love has infrequent opportunities to be made visible and to be built up.

The family meal occurs only because we value it and insist on protecting its time. In practice this means a certain understood discipline. Everyone is expected to be present and everyone remains until excused. This is only possible when there is a real consensus that eating together is important. Teenagers sometimes need to have a chance to discuss why this matters when there are so many other attractions for their time. Younger children are more apt to understand it instinctively. Feeding is obviously an act of love in infancy. But as children grow older, occasional discussions of why we eat together become more and more necessary. Churches do the same thing—though maybe not too much listening goes on and even less dialogue happens.

Pius XII was profoundly right when he remarked that spiritually we all are Semites. Probably no other peoples have sensed so profoundly what a sacred occasion a meal is. And their insight is essential—that one ought to begin any meal by remembering God by blessing God for providing food. I grew up in a family that, for some unknown reason, always had the blessing at the end of the meal when one was sometimes a bit less optimistic than initially. One does better to have grace at the beginning of the meal before trying to persuade the children to eat their spinach. The basic idea that food is received as a gift and that God is a party to the meal event is underscored by the blessing.

Fathers have few privileges left but one I cherish is the sense of presiding to the extent of asking one of the children or my wife to begin the meal by saying the blessing. (The children long ago decided that the "male chauvinist chair"—with arms—had to be rotated around the table.) The important thing is that throughout the week each person be given turns in saying grace. On Sundays and special occasions we join in singing the Wesley grace or other doxologies. This also provides an opportunity for teaching some of the texts and music we use in church.

Mealtime needs to be protected in other ways. It is not a time for discipline. We don't gather to fight, to lay down the law, or to compete with each other. Since it often is our only time together, we want to make it pleasant. Outside intrusions such as phone calls we try to avoid. During political campaigns, I admit, this is a sacrifice I don't always make graciously. Mealtime after all is fun. It is the only time of the day that none of us is working. So why not make it pleasant and enjoyable? Any church can, too.

But it is more than just fun. It is a time for edifying conversation. This means a responsibility for both parents and children, a responsibility to bring up topics of conversation that are of value. We strictly exclude recounting television or movie plots. We encourage reminiscing about what we have done together in the past and anticipating things we hope to do together in the future. We often encourage each other to share with us the day's activities or what we have of real interest. And religion creeps in occasionally. If anyone wants an example of how edifying and varied this type of conversation can be, read Luther's *Table Talk*. But it doesn't happen just by accident. Parents, especially, have to look for topics and encourage the worthwhile ones that pop up spontaneously. And sometimes a presider is necessary to make sure everyone gets a chance to be heard.

There is a sense of place about the dining table. It is where an important event occurs, the family happens. Each person has a place at the table, our surest evidence of belonging to each other. I must say I get upset when school books or anything not related to meals gets thrown on the table. It has a place of importance in our lives and this tends to be reflected in the way we treat it. Outward and visible signs can do that.

In short, maybe if we learn again to eat together at the family table we can some day learn to gather at the Lord's table as communities. If the family can happen despite all the pressures against it in our culture, let us hope the Church can happen too. After all, it all began with a group of friends eating together in an upper room.

23. Coming Together in Christ's Name

This piece from *Liturgy* 1 (Fall 1981) reflects what we had learned in the 1970s about the act of assembling. This is embodied in the new United Methodist and Presbyterian services which begin with "Gathering." Used by permission.

Worship is the most important thing the Church does, and coming together in Christ's name is the most important thing that happens in worship. It may also be the most overlooked.

One can trace in detail the evolution of the entrance rite of priests, but what about the entrance of people? Church interiors are designed with care; most people, however, arrive through a side door from the parking lot. Their gathering is treated as something to be hushed or smothered under loud organ music. Neither time nor space is allocated to signify the importance of coming together in Christ's name.

When we gather to meet our God we first meet our neighbor. Thus before anything is said or sung a very important event occurs; the Church is formed by the gathering of those called out from the world to be the body of Christ. They gather to recognize the body of Christ in their midst (1 Cor 11:29); their gathering creates the body itself, the Church. And they know that their risen head has promised to be with the body of Christ: "Where two or three have met together, there I am in the midst of them" (Matt 18:20).

An Important Reality

Ministers everywhere panic at the thought of the electronic Church. They fear that everything done on Sunday morning—prayer, preaching, music—will be done so much better by the highly skilled professionals on television that they and their congregations will be compared and found wanting. Most ministers forget that the incarnate Church has gifts that can never be matched by the docetic Church of the media. For the incarnate Church assembles face to face.

It is a meeting of real people who speak to and touch each other. In that speaking and touching in Christ's name the Church happens. Our fears of the media show how little we have valued our assembly in Christ's name. The television set can never duplicate the experience of Christ's presence in the midst of people. Christianity is a religion of real people, not the chimera of dancing light images. I like to speak of Christian worship as speaking and touching in Christ's name, a definition that may not be very abstract but does catch an important reality. Only in the assembled Church are both speaking and touching possible.

Christians in other times have sensed the importance of coming together. Indeed we meet, assemble, convene, gather, collect, congregate, or confer together and the richness of our language serves to highlight the importance of our act. In Judaism the "synagogue" was both a place of assembly and the congregation itself. Christians could apply the term too (Jas 2:2). For Quakers the term "meeting" serves as a synonym for worship itself, namely "go to meeting." In Puritan New England the meetinghouse was the building in which the church met for worship and the town for town meeting. In some colonies it was illegal to build a home more than a mile from a meetinghouse. New England developed little civic architecture until well into the nineteenth century because the meetinghouse served as the place where both Church and state happened.

A Royal Priesthood, a People Fully Human

Why is the act of meeting so important? Robert Barclay, the seventeenth-century Quaker theologian, compared meeting to the way "many candles lighted, and put in one place, do greatly augment the light." If anything Christianity is the flight of the together to the Together. John Wesley preached that "Christianity is essentially a social religion . . . to turn it into a solitary religion is indeed to destroy it." This is not to say that personal devotions are unimportant, but it is distinctive of Christian worship that we need to gather together to serve God through serving each other.

Baptism has made all of us part of a royal priesthood, a priesthood we exercise when we assemble. As Paul says, "When you meet for worship, each of you contributes a hymn, some instruction, a revelation, an ecstatic utterance, or the interpretation of such an utterance. All of these must aim at one thing: to build up the church" (1 Cor 14:

26-27). Our present gifts may be considerably less dramatic but they all contribute to one aim: by praying together, by singing with each other, by listening to God's word we build each other up. Priestly people come together to minister to one another.

Another aspect may be less obvious. In my village most of my neighbors spend the week on the seat of a tractor, in the cab of a truck, or at home with the children. Most of them see few people other than family during the week. They come to church on Sunday to be human. Church is a humanizing experience for many people in our society, certainly not just for the elderly who look forward to "getting out to church." Gathering for worship is an important socializing occasion; its humanizing function ought not to be overlooked.

As we gather to recognize the Lord's body, we also learn what it is to be fully human. The body that takes shape on Sunday morning is a body already discerning the presence of the Lord in the flesh even as it gathers for worship. Therefore, let us not be disturbed by the noise and shuffle of people arriving. Meeting is important; assembling is part of Christ's work among us. It deserves to be recognized with sufficient time and space.

Apportioning the Time

A few examples of such recognition can be cited. In the 1980 United Methodist service book, *We Gather Together,* even the name indicates an understanding that was carried throughout the basic services of worship that constitute the book. The first portion of each service—"A Sunday Service" (with or without the Eucharist), weddings, and funerals—begins with a section labeled "Entrance and Praise." Within this section the first act of worship is designated as "Gathering." In other words gathering is not just a necessary evil, as it has so often been treated, but is specifically designated as part of worship itself. How much this understanding is shared by most ministers and church musicians is another question. Some still feel compelled to drown out all footsteps and conversation with loud organ music.

Word and Table, the manual of instruction for "A Sunday Service," suggests several possible ways of enhancing the act of gathering: conversation, informal singing, welcoming by the pastor, and rehearsal of new music or other unfamiliar service materials. It is hoped that pastors and musicians will begin to consider gathering an important part of every service—as worship rather than as a preliminary to worship. In certain types of services assembling has long been recognized as an important act of worship. The wedding procession is far more than a mere preliminary. Since it demands a significant number of participants it receives considerable time. A procession with the coffin is also often part of the funeral service. Strangely, our arrival at the church in death may be granted more significant time than it was week after week in life.

The new services in *We Gather Together* should help communicate the importance of coming together in Christ's name. The "basic pattern" indicates that "Entrance and Praise" is a portion of worship in which "the people come together in the Lord's name." Creative use of this portion of the services will depend largely on ministers, musicians, and worship committee members. Once they grasp its significance they will be limited only by the horizons of their imaginations. Their first step will be to consider gathering as a time of importance, as a meaningful time well spent.

A Space for the Gathering

But even the most imaginative worship planners are going to be frustrated if the building says that coming together in the Lord's name is insignificant activity. The quality of human interaction that occurs in the movement from the impersonal space of the car in the parking lot to the personal space of the pew in the church depends largely on the organization of space. If "good celebrations foster and nourish faith," surely careful planning of gathering space strengthens good celebrations.

We come together by various means. Most of us are brought to our baptism; all of us are brought to our funeral. We are ushered into other types of services: in the company of intimate friends at our wedding, in consort with our contemporaries at first communion or confirmation, and with all our fellow Christians at the Lord's Supper. Thus the designing of space for assembling is a complex matter.

The basic problem, of course, is that rarely have architect or building committee given it much thought. Absent from their minds is any recognition of how much the design of congregating space shapes the nature of human interaction as the Church assembles for worship. Usually the worshiper is left to his or her own devices to make a beeline from parking lot to pew. That may save some energy, but if so that is its only advantage. European church builders have long recognized the importance of a transition space in which people can move from the world (street) to the kingdom (church). The magnificent atrium before St. Ambrose's in Milan is a prime example of space in which to gather, to cleanse one's hands, and to reflect as the church congregates. The columns of the arcade provide a magnificent alternating rhythm of light and shadow, beckoning one forward. Trees and shrubs can do the same thing in creating a processional path. It is important to sense in a processional path the rhythm of objects along the route: sculpture, benches, trees, or columns. Too often these are treated as luxuries only, to be considered after the building is paid for.

Interior space for coming together is also usually considered of minor importance. What happens in the lobby or narthex is not often considered part of worship. Provision is made for cloakrooms and restrooms but not for forming the body of Christ. "Get inside the church as best you can" is the usual message. Fortunately nothing new is quite so bad as the eighteenth-century prison chapel I saw in Lincoln, England. Absolutely demonic, it was so designed that no prisoner could see any other prisoner while entering or while worshiping. After that, who can doubt that the devil takes architecture seriously?

I have found it a marvelous exercise for seminary students to observe a service, ignoring what is said or sung, but noting all human interactions and movements, especially when people arrive and leave. Most students think worship is just saying the right words but this exercise opens their eyes as well as their ears. Many learn that the quality of a community's life together is largely determined by the space they share in worship. Even the parking lot is important; we impatient ones can lose most of our Christianity before even reaching the street!

Three particularly well-thought-out buildings deserve our attention. One of the most successful new churches of the 1970s is the Church of Saint John the Evangelist, Hopkins, Minnesota (George Rafferty of Rafferty, Rafferty, Mikutoski and Associates, architect; Frank Kacmarcik, consultant). Here an interior gathering space pulls people together from all parts of the church building and the world outside. They are led together from a rather dark space past a mammoth granite baptismal font with the sound and sight of moving water and thrust into the well-lit church space.

An entirely different approach appears in a remodeling project at St. Peter's Catholic Church, Saratoga Springs, New York (Frank

Kacmarcik, designer). The front entrance of a conventional gothic revival church was sealed off, the chancel walled up to create a small weekday chapel, and the interior reoriented to face one of the long walls. To enter, one comes from the main street of the town into a walled courtyard, beautifully landscaped with trees and flowers, then turns right to enter through what once was the easternmost bay of the nave. Thus long before one enters a door something has happened: One has been brought into a people place and induced to mix with other worshipers. The various members of the body come together to be one in worship before the door is reached.

Edward Sövik has designed several churches with a "concourse." In First United Methodist Church, Charles City, Iowa, this is a rectangular space with chairs and tables such as those found in old ice cream parlors. This design invites people to come early and linger late after worship. It is obviously processional space; it leads into the worship space, but it has a low ceiling and an air of informality. Again it is a people place, bridging the transition from car to pew.

Other architectural possibilities can be envisioned, but they will only materialize as we realize that coming together in Christ's name is itself a vitally important part of worship. Once we realize that we gather to form the Lord's body we will find the resources to facilitate and enhance the act of coming together. A body needs space and time.

V. Pedagogic

24. Some Lessons in Liturgical Pedagogy

This article, with a valedictory tone, appeared in *Worship* 68
(September 1994). Used by permission.

One of the advantages of teaching liturgy for thirty-five years is
that I have discovered, bit by bit, what not to do. What follow are
both personal observations and some reflections on the lessons
learned by the first generation of full-time seminary professors of
liturgy. Modern liturgical scholarship began more than a century and
a half ago; the teaching of liturgy as a major subject in North
American seminaries is a phenomenon largely dating from the 1960s.
It reflects paragraphs 15 and 16 of the *Constitution on the Sacred
Liturgy*: "Professors who are appointed to teach liturgy in seminaries,
religious houses of study, and theological faculties must be properly
trained for their work in institutes which specialize in this subject.
The study of sacred liturgy is to be ranked among the compulsory
and major courses in seminaries and religious houses of studies; in
theological faculties it is to rank among the principal courses. It is to
be taught under its theological, historical, spiritual, pastoral, and juridical aspects."

These paragraphs represent an impetus already underway in 1956
with the establishment of the Paris Institut Supérieur de Liturgie.
Bernard Botte tells of the Institut's early years and his apprehension
at the news a similar institute was to be established at Sant' Anselmo
in Rome in the early 1960s.[1] A decade later, in 1965, a doctoral program in liturgy began at the University of Notre Dame, built on the
foundations of the M.A. summer program begun by Michael Mathis,
C.S.C., in 1947. Thus the intentional training of liturgy professors for
seminaries is of relatively recent origin.

Today we see the beginning of the end of the careers of the first
generation of scholars trained in these new institutes. The recent

[1] *From Silence to Participation* (Washington: Pastoral Press, 1988) 104–106.

flood of *Festschriften* for such distinguished scholars as H. Boone Porter, Thomas J. Talley, David N. Power, and Robert F. Taft are well-deserved tributes. I would like to speak *for* myself, *of* my generation, *to* the next generation, many of whom I have had the privilege of training.

About two-thirds of my career was spent teaching at the seminary level. When I began teaching in 1959 liturgy was indeed a lonely field; even Massey H. Shepherd, Jr., the preeminent professor of liturgy at that time, once told me he considered himself primarily a teacher of patristics. I was told I was much too specialized inasmuch as I taught nothing but worship, albeit the whole scope of it. Now I teach western liturgical history after 1500. In the early 1960s Notre Dame was still importing much of its summer-school faculty from Europe. Today [1994] Notre Dame has produced fifty-four Ph.D.s in Liturgical Studies. The Catholic University of America, Drew University, and the Graduate Theological Union have added dozens of others. Exactly half of the Notre Dame Ph.Ds are Roman Catholic; half are Protestant and Orthodox. About half are now teaching in seminaries; many others are college professors or liturgical bureaucrats. The second generation is much more numerous and has the support of many more colleagues. Liturgy as a major subject is now firmly established in Roman Catholic, Orthodox, and most Protestant seminaries. It took thirty years, but by 1992 each United Methodist seminary had a faculty member who had been admitted to membership in the North American Academy of Liturgy.

My generation has helped to shape the discipline and mold its North American contours. Now we know what a seminary course in liturgy looks like; in 1959 we did not. Two of my books reflect what I have learned in this process, the textbook *Introduction to Christian Worship* (Abingdon, 1990) and the sourcebook *Documents of Christian Worship* (Westminster/John Knox, 1992). More important is what I have learned from directing or co-directing sixteen doctoral dissertations in liturgy at Notre Dame. Ten of these students are currently teaching in seminaries. So what can I say that will benefit them and their students?

General Observations about Teaching Liturgy

Courses in liturgy at the seminary level usually seem to have three components: historical, theological, and practical. Much of the uniqueness of teaching liturgy is that theory and practice are more closely linked here than anywhere else in the seminary curriculum. That is one thing that makes it a joy to teach. One touches both the *Apostolic Tradition* and next Sunday. Before discussing the historical, theological, and practical I want to make some general observations.

It often occurs to me that much of teaching worship is searching for analogies. One looks for the familiar to express the unfamiliar. The homely analogy becomes a means of acquainting the student with that which he or she has not experienced. By discovering the appropriate analogy we help the student experience the *agape* of the early Church or the love feast of another contemporary tradition.

One of the first needs in a beginning course in liturgy is to acquaint the student with a new vocabulary and the concepts these terms express. The same is true of any academic subject. A student must be able to distinguish between concomitance and contrition, between epiclesis and epiphany. Indeed, the process of acquiring a basic liturgical vocabulary is the first step in liturgical knowledge.

Unfortunately we have not done very well with the visual and musical vocabularies that future presiders need to acquire. It would seem that liturgists of all people would be most advanced in these areas. Liturgy, after all, is a visual and aural experience and words only describe these realities. The technology for teaching these aspects of worship is certainly available but aside from a video that S. Anita Stauffer did for The Liturgical Press on baptismal fonts and pools none has yet come to my attention. Edward Foley has made fine use of the print medium in *From Age to Age* (LTP, 1991) for presenting the visual and I have attempted a chapter of photographs in *Documents of Christian Worship*. But we should be well beyond print by this time. There should be videos on church architecture, the liturgical arts, and various types of celebrations. And CDs on the history of and present options in Church music should be available. This would seem a natural arena for liturgists but we have not had the imagination or time to take advantage of it.

In the print medium I have come to realize how much information can be compressed into a single page through the use of charts, tables, diagrams, and maps, and these have some unexpected advantages in making manifest relationships that do not appear when materials are treated serially. Diagrams not only present available information, they create new information. It is possible to bring together both time and space in an assortment of diagrams and maps.

There is much value in having students see the literary documents for themselves. This applies to liturgical texts themselves and to passages in which Christians have described or interpreted what they experience in worship. Ever since Bard Thompson's *Liturgies of the Western Church*, published more than thirty years ago and still in print, there has been an increasing availability of basic texts. What a delight it is to have such things as volume 53 of *Luther's Works* and how useful it would be to have Irmgard Pahl's *Coena Domini I* in English translation! Now one has to be selective because so much is available; a few decades back we did not have many choices. It is wonderful for students to be able to see for themselves and not have to take our word for what is in texts. Occasionally they see things we missed and often their questions make us reexamine things familiarity has obscured for us.

Christian worship is not experienced in books but in worshiping communities. Robert Frost tells of the scientist who catches and chloroforms a butterfly to study it but then no longer has a butterfly. Worship, too, is living tissue and must be studied in the context of living communities. It is taught best in worshiping communities.

Worship as a learning experience demands careful discipline and structure. I think there are two aspects: one must experience the broadness of one's own tradition. Anglo-Catholics need to worship with Anglican evangelicals; white Roman Catholics need to worship in black parishes, not to mention in Eastern-rite parishes. But just as a philologist who knows only one language knows none, it is important to experience the worship of unfamiliar Christian traditions in order to understand one's own better.

The teacher can be of great help to students in organizing a list of the dozen or so Christian worship traditions present in most metropolitan areas in this country: Eastern Orthodox, Eastern-rite Catholic, Roman Catholic, Lutheran, Reformed, Anabaptist, Anglican, Puritan, Quaker, Methodist, Frontier, and Pentecostal. To these can be added three or four Jewish traditions and Islamic worship in many communities. The yellow pages of the telephone book will be most helpful in organizing lists and providing addresses and telephone numbers so students can check times of services. The Reformed tradition will appear under Presbyterian, Christian Reformed, or Reformed Church of

America; Puritan under United Church of Christ or Unitarian/ Universalist; Anabaptist as Mennonite; Quaker as Society of Friends; Frontier as most Baptists, Churches of Christ, and the Christian Church (Disciples of Christ); and Pentecostals as Assemblies of God, Church of God in Christ, or titles with the words Pentecostal or Apostolic in them. For those who work in churches on Sunday, Jewish services occur at other times as does Seventh-Day Adventist worship. Students can share their observations with classmates; I begin Monday classes inquiring about liturgical experiences over the weekend.

It is not enough to turn students loose; they need careful instruction on what to observe while they participate. They must look beyond the words that are said and sung. They should be instructed to note who the people are (age, race, sex), what roles each group plays (including the ordained clergy and choir), what is the architectural setting of the worship, what visual arts are present, how people arrive and leave, what actions happen (such as offering, receiving communion, baptism, etc.), what leadership roles are apparent (usher, reader, presider), who sings and how, the uses of music, the use or not of printed materials, use of the body (handclapping, hands raised), and how strangers are treated. Students will discover for themselves that much more is done in worship than is said. One of the best ways to learn this is to write a short report on the observation. Indeed, it may help to pretend to be a happy pagan who wandered in out of curiosity and does not understand Christian conventions. Above all students will learn that the clergy only do a small part of what happens in church. Eyes to observe may be opened wide in astonishment. Many self-contradictory non-verbal statements may appear. We profess inclusivity and exclude children, for example.

An important item in teaching worship today is how to make it manifest justice. If we can heighten students' awareness of worship as a forum in which power and control are important components, that will be a major benefit. Students ought to think through how worship has often been an implicit source of injustice. Who counts? How often does the minister sit down, i.e., delegate authority? Is the pulpit, as J.A.T. Robinson said, "six feet above contradiction"?

The pedagogic question is whether one does a week or so on worship and justice, making it a discrete segment in the course. Or does one make it pervade the entire semester? There are advantages to either method: intense focus versus diffuseness. It must not be assumed that justice is simply a matter of feminist issues or that it can be confined to changing the wording of prayers and hymns. Issues of roles in the community and actions in the assembly are equally important. Even courses in liturgical law can be used to see how much can be done to bend things toward justice and sometimes, we hope, to subvert the system. Teaching liturgy is a very political act, and in politics nothing happens by accident; it happens because someone planned it and made it happen.

The Teaching of Liturgical History

Most of liturgical scholarship has been of a historical nature. Of the fifty-four Ph.D.s in Liturgical Studies from Notre Dame all but five have been historical in subject matter. There is a strong case to be made that students who do not know the history of Christian worship are not well equipped for ministry; indeed they are doomed to repeat history if they do not know history. So the question is not whether to teach history or not but the most effective means for teaching it.

There are two options: a vertical or diachronic approach or a horizontal or synchronic approach. I prefer the former because it allows students the possibilities of seeing things develop over the centuries as practices and beliefs evolve. One can trace the disintegration of initiation in the West from its early unity through the Anabaptist challenge in the sixteenth century down to the R.C.I.A. in our time. Students see both continuity and change on a single topic. I admit that the horizontal method has advantages in comparing simultaneous developments, say in initiation and Eucharist, although these developments are often not intrinsically related but purely accidental.

We have a hierarchy in liturgical studies: Eucharist, initiation, and maybe ordination occupy the top rungs; the daily office, time, and the preaching service are perched on lower rungs; and healing, marriage, and burial squat at the bottom. *The Study of Liturgy* hardly mentions these last. Yet for the marginal Christian—and there are millions of alumni and alumnae of the churches—weddings and funerals may be the only link to the worshiping community. In terms of evangelization the rites of passage may be even more important than the Eucharist. How much is our teaching weighted to the interests of past scholarship and how much to the needs of real people?

We have some temporal discriminations, too. Protestants cannot understand their own worship unless they comprehend late medieval piety and practices. Not having had a baroque age of piety, or rather only a mild dose of it, many Protestants have remained the last custodians of much of late medieval piety and many practices including a penitential Eucharist or infrequent communion. Protestants have had more trouble removing medieval accretions to the ordination rite than Roman Catholics. Since everything prior to 1517 is a jointly-shared heritage Protestants need to know better these areas of their history in order to understand their worship today.

At the same time Roman Catholics need to know Protestant liturgical history because they have repeated so much of it, right down to the charismatics. By being more free in the post-Tridentine period Protestant worship was able to adapt to changing social and cultural patterns. Even the term "inculturation" was devised by a Protestant missionary and within six years was being used by Pope John Paul II.[2] The extreme example of inculturation is the Mega-Church movement of recent years that makes one wonder whether successful inculturation is all that desirable. We now may have to show its limits! Protestantism has often proved to be Catholicism fifty years ahead of itself. Since we are training people for future ministry Roman Catholic students need to know the possibilities that have been explored and, sometimes, discarded.

Both Protestants and Roman Catholics need to know far more about their own North American heritage. The Enlightenment changed worship even more than the Reformation for many Protestants and shaped social institutions for all of us. But it scarcely gets mentioned in most histories. Herman Wegman dismisses recent centuries in fourteen out of three hundred sixty pages even though this period has been the most productive in liturgical history. One cannot go to Mass and leave the Enlightenment outside the doors although the effort is certainly made. If thirty percent of the audience of television evangelism (I prefer to call it televised worship) are Roman Catholics, how can seminarians be ignorant of the American

[2]Anscar Chupungco, *Liturgical Inculturation* (Collegeville: The Liturgical Press, 1992) 25–26.

Frontier tradition in worship? The Americanization of Christian (and Jewish) worship should be a major component of historical studies.

The net result is helping students to see the diversity of Christian worship at any time and period. As Paul Bradshaw has shown so brilliantly in *The Search for the Origins of Christian Worship* (Oxford, 1992), history turns up no facile homogeneity. The first rule of history is that everything is more complicated than it seems. History is messy. Students need to sense the variety within as well as between traditions. At no time in history can one speak of "the Church" unless one means all the churches. (Titles such as *The Church at Prayer* are particularly misleading since that book treats of but one Church, "a" Church, not "the" Church.) The natural world demonstrates the Creator's love of variety; the history of liturgy simply replicates this. We need each other since we all inhabit similar social and cultural situations.

On another tack let me say that the history of time seems to work best in introducing students to liturgical history. We all have a secular contact in liturgical candy: corn candy at Halloween, ribbon candy at Christmas, and jelly beans at Easter. We share the same civil holidays. So it is an easy step into how Christians keep time. But in so doing, one is also introducing the sacramental principle of the tangible making the spiritual present. And one is also preparing the way for learning how the calendar will function in the Eucharist, in daily prayer, and in preaching services.

The Teaching of the Theology of Liturgy

I can be briefer on this topic simply because I know less about it and it is not my specialty. I am not discussing liturgical theology, which I take to mean the effort to identify theological belief on the basis of liturgical statements. By the theology of liturgy I mean the basic concept patterns of worship itself plus the more specialized areas of sacramental theology, theology of proclamation, and theology of spirituality. Since my own predisposition is historical I tend to treat these areas in terms of their historical development, but others with different gifts might treat them better in systematic terms.

It is particularly important to see the relationship of piety to liturgical practice and understanding. Removing the chalice from the laity makes sense in terms of the scrupulosity of the twelfth century and the fear of spilling the blood of Christ. The laity must have been greatly relieved. They did not worry about destroying the process of initiation that was already falling apart in the West. And so a theology of concomitance evolves hand in hand with piety.

The greatest conversion experience in my own teaching has come about in moving from a normative approach to a descriptive approach. After years of trying to reform United Methodist worship I came to feel maybe I should have spent those two decades listening to United Methodists. Instead of giving students rebuttals to the oft-heard statement: "The Lord's Supper would not be meaningful if we had it every week," I have come to ask "what are they saying?" or "what is going on here?" Perhaps the laity are telling us that special events have a power for them that we fail to recognize with our minds already made up.

There is indeed much bad news for liturgists in the forum *The Awakening Church* (The Liturgical Press, 1992) which shows how little concern Roman Catholic laity have for the type of questions that clergy are trained to answer. Nothing seems of less interest than the eucharistic prayer, the subject of the greatest amount of liturgical scholarship. Much seems to focus on the importance of being a community, of doing together whatever is done, and it may not matter greatly what that is. Some respondents even spoke of the priest doing his "magic" at the altar. But few neglected the significance of being together in church.

A frankly phenomenological approach has the advantages of recognizing the plurality of possibilities in Christian worship. The real criterion then becomes that of survival. If something survives in worship presumably the Spirit uses it and it has value. If the Willow Creek mega-church type of worship survives one must concede its value, little though I appreciate it at present. If the Frontier and Pentecostal worship traditions are the most rapidly expanding in the world at present (some scholars expect them to reach 57.4 per cent of the population of Brazil in 2010 at present rates of growth),[3] then they are worthy of our recognition. The Holy Spirit has never played in monaural. We must recognize the heterogeneous character of Christian worship and try to understand what the Spirit is saying through the churches.

[3]David Stoll, *Is Latin America Turning Protestant?* (Berkeley: University of California Press, 1990) 337.

The teaching of the practical features of liturgy has two aspects. The theoretical aspect has evolved in recent years from a subject called "pastoral liturgy" to ritual studies done with a focus on Christian worship. The specifically practical aspect teaches on the mundane but essential level of operating instructions. Both are essential for future ministers and priests.

The theoretical, still a relatively new discipline, involves some understanding of the dynamics of human societies and how they communicate ritually. The sciences of sociology, cultural anthropology, and psychology are essential here and ritology has become a science itself although often with no special interest in Christian liturgy. In recent years semiotics has become especially important. It was in this area that Mark Searle was a great pioneer; in a posthumous book he dealt with semiotics and church architecture.[4] His 1983 presidential address to the North American Academy of Liturgy stands as a monument to recent developments in the theoretical aspects of the practical side of Christian worship.

At stake here is the quality of celebration, celebration done with full awareness of the human dimension in worship. How humans signify that which is meaningful in their lives is a basic concern. How the sign value can be heightened to make what goes on more adequately expressive is likewise central. I am not sure that much has yet been written on the theoretical level that is useful to seminary students. It is still so much easier to talk about validity and legality than quality of celebration, yet the former are so much less important.

The more specifically practical often receives more attention. At its lowest level this involves crisis control. What do you do if some one alleges an objection at a wedding? Chances are if you have a plan of action it will never happen; count on it if you do not. And students need to know, in most traditions, how to hold and wash a baby if they are not already parents. It is not advisable to pick them up by the ears! No matter how good one's theology of initiation is, if one drops the baby, it is a disaster. One needs to be prepared for the best man to drop the wedding ring in a grate or the ring bearer to refuse

---

[4]Gerard Lukken and Mark Searle, *Semiotics and Church Architecture* (Kampen: Kok Pharos, 1993).

to give it up. These are tricks of the trade and need to be taught or the best knowledge of history and theology is set at naught.

The canons and rubrics of different churches will vary as well as the seriousness with which they are kept. Here teaching worship in ecumenical seminaries becomes more sporting. What may be prescribed for some churches may be proscribed for others. Recognizing the priorities of different churches may be exasperating but it is necessary for students to learn to be themselves. There is not much point in teaching United Methodists to swing a thurible but for some Episcopalians it is uplifting.

Nor can the spoken word be neglected. Here it is especially important to help students see the genre in which they are speaking, especially when praying. Different types of prayer are written and spoken differently, yet many presiders mouth them as if they all came out of the same teleprompter. Instruction in the various genres of prayer is essential for presiders.

In traditions where pastoral prayers are assumed necessary, practice must be given in writing pastoral prayers that speak *from* the congregation *by* the minister *to* God. They are not announcements. When lay people call this the "long prayer" they may reveal one common fault, for length is not as essential as depth. And preparation is a necessity. John Wesley wondered why preachers carefully prepared sermons for us worms but dared to address Almighty God in prayer with no forethought. *Ex tempore* means appropriate to the time, not merely *ad lib*.

One of my favorite one-liners is that when one can write a good eucharistic prayer for a specific congregation on a particular occasion he or she is ready to graduate from seminary. But that means a firm grasp of the biblical and theological essentials of the Christian message as well as genuine knowledge of the people. I am not advocating the use of such original prayers but it is a good test to see if students understand the forms eucharistic prayers can take thoroughly enough that they can write one within those contours. One even sees published collections by people who obviously do not know what a eucharistic prayer is meant to do. History, theology, and practice converge in this exercise.

A similar practice deals with the much simpler task of writing a collect. At least we can get students to take the verbs seriously and not spend all their time on adjectives.

Today one of the most important skills to be taught in practical liturgy is how to work well with a large assortment of people. Many people are often involved in planning, preparing for, and conducting worship. One needs to appreciate the skills, rights, and sometimes sheer stubbornness of those involved. A special sensitivity is necessary in appreciating the goals and objectives of Church musicians. Despite all the jokes liturgists make about Church musicians worship would be inestimably poorer without them. The average priest or minister is even less adept at working with visual artists. The "I know what I like and I like what I know" approach is hardly a sufficient criterion. As a result, the liturgical art one sees in churches is rarely more profound than the decorative art found in parsonages. It is a real adventure to bring seminary students to meet professional artists who know what they know. And frequently, from the catacombs to the present, competent artists outside the Christian community can depict the Christian message better than incompetent artists within the community. How to teach seminarians to see is a challenge. Visual literacy certainly does not come with ordination.

Finally, there is much to be said for videotaping students in leading various rites for a group and then playing it back for class criticism. Unfortunately the student who does it worst may help one teach the most. It is hard for a student to argue with the camera; seeing is believing. And it is good for the group to share in the criticism but dangerous if they start to enjoy it. Every student ought to be able to see himself or herself as the people will be seeing and hearing them for years to come. Then maybe they will realize what a privilege it is to lead God's people in worship.

It has been a joy to be among the first generation of full-time professors of liturgy. It is even more joyful to think of those who are gradually replacing us and to envision that they will carry the art of teaching worship beyond where we have gone. The profession has gone far; they will take it much farther. That is our greatest reward, a future with hope.